AHIDDIBAH TSINNIE

Yes, I Took My Meds

A Memoir

First published by Ahiddibah Tsinnie 2020

First edition

ISBN: 978-0-578-68119-1

This book was professionally typeset on Reedsy.
Find out more at reedsy.com

For my moms. Without your passion, sacrifice, love, education, and forgiveness I would not exist.

In beauty I walk
With beauty before me I walk
With beauty behind me I walk
With beauty above me I walk
With beauty around me I walk
It has become beauty again...

Walking in Beauty, Navajo Blessing
Way Ceremony.

Contents

Acknowledgement iii
BIPOLAR DIARY 1
Trying to Be a Kid and Growing Up Too Fast 18
Wizard of Oz, Spankings and My Heroine 22
Pine Creek Canyon 41
People Pleaser 44
Fishing and Fireworks 52
Roadside 70
It's Complicated 74
Daughter of Girlfriends 77
Survivor's Tale 84
Inciting Incidents in School Settings 92
Depression and Drinking 101
HAB 107
Revealing Secrets and Letting Go 118
Boys of European Summer 123
Teens Bring About a Child 129
Miracle Boy 133
Scholarships, School, and My Son 139
When You Think It's Love 153
Jesse 170
The Sister I Chose 175
Road to Teaching 183
Co-Teaching 190

Dichotomy of Classes 195
Food Drive 206
Losing the Best Job in the World 212
He Always Chose Me 216
Spending Time with my Brother 224
Brawl Buster Bartender 231
White Lens 235
Walking Many Roads of Religion 243
Those That Walked On 249
Endless One Night Stand 258
Dating Post Doug 271
My History with Bipolar 275
BIPOLAR DIARY 284
Shadow People 308
Bugging Out 313
Loving Me 318
About the Author 324

Acknowledgement

I want to thank my family and friends for going on this journey with me. Without them, I wouldn't have a book.

I have to thank my first readers who read my blog and encouraged me to turn this into a book. Myers, you are my everything. Lynn Parker, thanks for reading, reading and rereading every draft I put in front of you. Moss, thanks for the wonderful description and the thoughtful feedback. Roper, thanks for reading and being a great boss. Maureen, thank you for your insight. I used it. I really enjoyed the wonderful years of teaching together. Enjoy retirement. Athena, thank you for reading the blog and being my only subscriber. You are the best sister a girl could ask for. You have done so much for me. I love you. Felicity, thank you for always being there for me since I was twelve and lost. Thanks for your feedback and reading. Katrina, shideezhí, I'm so happy our bond has grown closer. Thank you for your thoughts and feedback. I love you. Margaret, thank you for being the best editor ever. I lucked out. Thanks for your support and encouragement in my passion project.

Dad, I love you so much. I learned we don't always speak the same language but we love each other very much. I love you and hope we have more time with each other. Danita, thank you for being there for me and my brother. I love you.

Pattycakes and Jessican, I love you more than life itself. You mean the world to me. Thank you for taking care of me when I couldn't always take care of me. I love our little family. Always be there for each other.

My aunties, thank you for raising me. Thank you for being surrogate mothers to me. Thank you for teaching me.

My nieces and nephews, thank you for bringing me joy. I love all of you. You are wonderful, talented people. I have loved being a part of your lives and seeing you grow.

My cousins, my brothers and sisters, thank you for being my siblings. Thank you for being my family. Sharing your art. Sharing a piece of fry bread and stew. I love you all.

Pat, thanks for the cabin and giving me a place to decompress and write. I love you, brother.

Dani, I love you.

Tom, I miss you every day. Thank you for letting me tell some of your story.

Mom and Mom2, I love you. Thank you for letting me share my story. You are the best moms anyone could ask for. Thank you for raising me in a house knowing nothing but love and generosity. Thank you for teaching me to love without conditions and to give with gratitude.

BIPOLAR DIARY

Are You Off Your Meds?

December 4, 2014

I am bipolar.

What came first? The pill or the crazies? It is an ongoing debate. A debate I have with my dragon while I am dressed as Batman. Did the meds spin me out so far as to talk to dragons, or was that always there locked deep inside my creative brain?

It's truly a challenge to look inward and see how absolutely fucked up a human being can be and then to realize that fucked-up person is you. This is said with much love to my fucked-up self.

At almost forty years old, a divorced mother of two, a schoolteacher, living in Las Vegas where I grew up, I look back on my rollercoaster life with gratitude for the abundance of joy, love and devilish fun. I am grateful for the rock-bottom destruction. I am grateful to my high-flying Batman persona that leaps out to chop down unsuspecting trees. More on that later.

My brain is rejecting the doctor's diagnosis and prescription for my bipolar state. Currently, I'm slowly titrating off Seroquel. Apparently, screaming at people to go fuck themselves and referring to others as double dumbasses or fucktards is not appropriate teacher talk. And here I thought I was doing well with the new dose of meds. I was so hopeful that I wasn't spinning out into a manic episode. I was doing everything I was supposed to do.

Create a schedule. Stick to that schedule. Be so predictable that you could be stalked and accosted. I decided to try running five miles a day, going to dance class four days a week and teaching yoga for my mom one night a week. I was also staying late at work to catch up on work or stay caught up. I was staying late at work so I wouldn't have to drive far to the dance class, but then I wasn't eating much. This late-night samba then ate into my sleeping time, which drove me to sleep in later and later. Ultimately, I started having trouble getting out of bed to run my miles, let alone meet with my trainer. Schedule ceased. Epic failure, and everyone is a fucking asshole.

I knew I was slipping. My speech was louder and faster. I had painted my monitor with tiny yellow sticky notes to keep me on task. Except, the sticky notes aren't really sticky, and they had delicately reorganized themselves on my desk like flower petals. No rhyme or reason. Just pretty. Maybe my feet and legs, shaking constantly, emitted a vibration so powerful it rattled the glue at the core of the sticky notes and released them.

Self-monitoring. Rapid speech, anger, wanting to punch people in the face, hating everyone I work with, especially that cunt cheerleader coach, dumb fuckers who can't read. Anger, anxiety, aggressive behavior. Pretty sure the meds are not working. Seroquel, you asshole! Thanks for playing the chemical balance game. You fucking suck. Back your bags, bitch, you are on a one-way trip to the toilet, but only after I have severed you into half-sized bites to slowly choke you out of my system.

My brain is foggy. My brain is fighting itself. Mild depression with a little turbocharge of mania.

Taking my mood temperature is fun. Tired. Depressed. Not suicidal. Suicidal ideations. Anxiety. Sleepy. No energy. Lack of hygiene. This is a huge one for me. When I'm at this stage, I simply don't give a shit if I have showered or brushed my teeth. I do draw the line at ass wiping, and that is only because if you don't wipe your butt well, you are asking for diaper rash and who wants to be depressed and smell like Desitin? That could be the last pin pulled.

The dragon is not here right now. I do kinda wish my crazy brain and my "normal" brain would clash, and I could meet my dragon. Unfortunately, the only thing that I'm seeing that isn't there is some creepy fucker who keeps standing on my table. It's very disconcerting.

* * *

Batman, Bonkers, Bonfires

January 2, 2015

If you have a heart condition, amusement parks remind you not to ride the roller coasters or to do so at your own risk. Unfortunately, when you are bipolar, you don't even realize you got on the ride until after it is over. It doesn't matter if you have gone through a depressive or manic episode. Both leave you with a strange awakening when the dust has settled, and the ride is over.

Sometimes, you can see this demon creeping up on you. Sometimes, you just wake up one day with it sitting on your chest, trying to smother your hopes and dreams. However, if you admit to seeing a dragon, you are probably already on your way to a manic episode.

Most of my life, I've suffered more from the depression side of bipolar illness. I've had hypomanic episodes and only recently started having longer manic episodes. Manic behavior is triggered by many things and different things for different people. I have pinpointed my behavior to emotional attachments, overextending myself, working too much, indulging in my amazing artistic talent, insomnia, and continuing this cycle until I have saved the world. Note the grandiose god-like abilities I contain in this fleshy body of awesomeness.

The night before Thanksgiving, I stayed up cleaning, rearranging the furniture, dusting, reorganizing, prepping. All the cleaning led to me noticing the patched holes in the walls, so of course, I needed to paint those. Then, the baseboards looked so dingy next to the new paint. How could I leave out the door frames? All of this was done with a one-inch brush around four in the morning. I couldn't leave the garage door looking like shit but didn't want to pour paint, so I just spray-painted it. By 6 am, I finally wound down and went to sleep, only to get up at 8:30 am to make the turkey and continue with normal turkey day festivities. That should have been a clue, the one-inch brush.

I don't remember the order of events. I can't discern between Friday, Saturday, and Sunday. I do know that during those days, I wore a Batman onesie and destroyed my backyard trimming palm trees. The poor garden didn't deserve to go like that. I tried to start a bonfire in the fire pit outside that almost made me start a fire in the kitchen because I couldn't find a lighter. I called and texted many people, inverting the subject and predicate and inventing my own spelling. My new favorite addition to this manic behavior was seeing a new friend, or creature, a four-foot-tall red dragon with black spikes that talked too much. I kept shushing her. A friend of mine suggested I name the dragon, so if I go Batman gardener again, she will know who I'm shushing. Her name is Pandora.

I unwittingly fought with myself. I bruised my arms and legs. Fell into the walls bruising my shoulders. Fell and bloodied my knees. I fell out of bed and landed on my face, giving myself a bit of a shiner. In an attempt to quell the manic behavior, I took a sedative and continued to take them until I had taken them all. I don't remember taking them and don't know if I was intentionally taking them. Drugs and alcohol are an interesting chemical cocktail in the manic mind. They don't always affect the person in the manic episode. It's the gasoline for an uncontrollable fire.

As the days unfold, I see the worry on people's faces. My boss and friends from the school where I teach show their concern. My son, Jesse, shouldn't have to take care of his mother. He is the only one who lives with me now. Everyone's eyes are sad, the corners of their mouths turned down. Worry lines crease their faces. There's no assurance from my mouth that can appease them. Their look is pure concern. Real concern that makes me concerned.

I reverted to my plan of action. All people with a mental illness should have a plan of action. I finally included my friends and family in it. I called my doctor, took someone with me, and prayed they would just adjust my meds and send me home.

Prayers answered.

The spinning wheel in my brain has subsided. The other shoe hasn't fallen. I am also concerned. The mirror image of the mother of dragons is a suicidal nutcase who gets admitted to a psych ward or hallway in nothing but a gown and net underwear. I'm waiting like a lab rat to see if the dose will allow me to stay on this universal plane.

It's hard to admit you are bipolar. It's hard to admit you need help. It's hard to take medication. I have found my way and accepted these limits.

* * *

Bipolar is known to be genetic. It is passed down through the generations, often skipping generations. It is masked in families by drug and alcohol abuse, often a form of self-medication. There is also, typically, a traumatic event that sparks the bipolar. Alcoholism runs in both sides of my family, and I believe mental illness is present there as well.

I was always a sensitive child. I would cry easily and get my feelings hurt at the drop of a hat. That intensified after I was sexually abused as a little girl. My mom does not have any of these traits. She's not an alcoholic or mentally ill. My brother, who died ten years ago, was an alcoholic and suffered from depression and extreme anxiety. His anxiety was so bad at times that he had trouble going into crowded stores. If he couldn't see the exit, he would panic.

In this book, I've gathered pieces of my life. My illness, childhood, and adult life. An invisible thread connects and binds all aspects of my life, but just because they are connected doesn't mean one can explain the other. Mostly I want to share my experiences of what I know, what I've learned from whom, and what I love. To find the connections of these invisible threads that reach from past to present, I accept that no one perspective can make sense of it all. Being bipolar is being alive, just more, living in the moment. Too much more. But all of it – the mania, the energy, the agitation, the obsession, sadness, fear and hurt – are distortions or exaggerations of normal emotions. I'm still me in the end.

* * *

Writing a book also feels impossible. I wrote this book in a manic episode. All the buzzing energy of a manic high, full of grandiose thinking. The dragon wasn't present. There wasn't psychosis, but I was pretty manic. Thoughts came through my mind like a rapid-fire machine gun. With each round, I needed to get the idea on paper or the computer. I wrote and wrote. I thought that I was writing a best seller. I wanted my ideas and life to be shared with everyone. I thought my story needed to be told. When you are manic, this over-the-top thinking is common.

Originally, this was a collection of short stories and diary entries. I have kept some of the diary entries so you can see the thought process of the bipolar mind. I'm not crazy. I'm a real person with a lot of difficult feelings to sort through. The book is as linear as it can be.

Now, while in remission of symptoms from the bipolar, I don't have that feeling of it being a bestseller. I'm constantly doubting my writing ability. I doubt my voice and experiences. My thought processes are subdued. I think what I wrote is worth telling. I think it may help someone who has bipolar share their thoughts and not be alone in their mad thinking. I hope that survivors of sexual abuse will come forward with their stories and seek help. I hope my voice allows others a voice. I hope my stories entertain and shed light on my life.

While rereading the book from a "normal" mind, I have found it to be humorous, grandiose, honest, and self-deprecating. My family and friends keep asking me if writing this book was healing or a chance at self-discovery. I have learned that I am a strong person. I have learned that I have grown through trial and error. I make mistakes like anybody. I was hurt and grew from that. I am ill and try to get through it the best I can. I don't know if I truly learned anything new about myself, but I realized my life was something I wanted to share with others. I hope you find it worth reading.

* * *

Mixed Episode. Take 1

August 9, 2018

I analyze my mood constantly. I was hospitalized for the second time for the bipolar. I had a plan of action for mania but not so much for depression. The problem was I wasn't really depressed. It was a mixed state. Fun times if you have never had one. This was a combination of highs and lows all within a 24-hour-period. I wasn't necessarily feeling low, but

I was weepy. I felt high and loud and sing-songy.

Fear ultimately led me to the hospital. A pervasive fear of hurting myself to the point of suicide flooded my brain. I felt powerless. I felt like I would burst if I didn't harm myself. I just wanted relief. I knew if I cut open my arm with a knife or razor blade, the pain and voice inside me would quiet. As the blood flowed, so would the pain that was racing through my mind.

As a child, I cut myself all the time. Didn't know I was a baby bipolar then, but I was always in a state of depression. This may stem from the sexual abuse (more on that later) and the family inheritance of the crazies, but it always felt better after the first cut.

I didn't cut myself this time. I burned myself twice with a lighter. Immediately the pain of the depression lapsed into calm. The screaming inside my brain quieted, and I felt at peace.

I woke up the next day hypomanic. I swung from one tree to the next. One mood shocked into another. This hypomanic episode felt different. I felt spacy. I felt elevated but not overtly happy. I felt if I moved, I would not be able to stop. I had no concentration. I couldn't watch TV or focus enough to read a book. Which super sucked, because I was on the last novel in a series. I could do nothing but sit and watch the birds and chipmunks.

All of this was happening while the eerie voice inside my head kept telling me to grab the fish knife and slice open my wrist. Just do it lightly. Just enough to make it bleed. The thoughts became harder to ignore, but I did ignore them. I surrounded myself with people.

I spent the first week of that episode with my friend at the cabin in Utah I share with friends. But not really there. Just existing because I was afraid I would be found out. People would learn that I was not right in the head. So, I did nothing. I sat. Drank my coffee. Smoked my cigarettes and just observed nature. Tried to channel that calm.

Elevated, the thoughts and desires became more intrusive. The fact that I had already hurt myself made me realize I didn't want to do it again. It didn't stop me from almost doing it again and again. Each time I smoked a cigarette, I considered burning myself with the hot end of the cigarette. Pushing the red cinders into the fleshy part of my arm.

I returned to the cabin to spend time with Aunt Margaret and Cousin Carrie. Carrie with her warm smile and calm demeanor. I feel closer to her than all my other cousins. She is the calm I always need. She is the voice of reason in any situation. I felt out of sorts, but I kept hiding the returning darkness. We spent three great days together. The day they left, I was to spend another two days by myself, isolated with the birds and my destructive thoughts. Within minutes of my family's departure, I gravitated to the sharpest knife in the cabin. I picked it up and started crying. I saw no other way out of the hell I'd been in for weeks. It scared the shit out of me. I cleaned up, packed up and left the cabin for the three-and-a-half-hour drive back to Vegas.

I called for help. I left messages. I cried. I listened to music. Finally, Michelle, my friend and co-worker from school, called me back. I bawled hysterically. I couldn't communicate what I was feeling. I felt scared and isolated. I wanted to hurt myself. I was driving at 80 mph. I didn't want to die. I didn't want to be hospitalized. I just wanted to be in my own bed, curled up in the dark.

But as much as I wanted to isolate, I knew what I was feeling was not normal. I needed help. Michelle was the one person who would not hold any punches and make me get help. I knew I would end up in the hospital even if I didn't want to.

I got home safely and tried to stop crying. My friend and her family took one look at me and suggested the hospital. They found an emergency room that had a psych ward at the hospital in case I needed to be admitted.

There is nothing like a psych ward to make you feel sober and normal. It's the snake pit effect. Within an hour of being admitted with blood pressure 199/111, I felt calm. The urge to hurt myself had dissipated, but I was still waiting to be assessed.

ER psych wards are greatly lacking in services. The room was set up with no bathroom, no water, no TV, no access to phones, just four gurneys and plastic pillows with nurses shouting, "Back to your bed!" if you moved to the doorway.

After several hours of feeling normal, I was assessed and deemed not a harm to myself or others. I was released back into the wild under the condition I see my doctor ASAP.

I am currently under a medication switch. Titrating down one set of meds, Geodon, the antipsychotic, and upping the new med, Latuda, which I don't think is covered by my insurance. Should be interesting to find out.

I am out of work for two weeks, pending the med change and mood stability. Today is the second day of decrease and new meds. The first day I felt hypomanic. I was busy. Couldn't focus. No books or TV. I only slept four hours. Last night I got about ten hours of sleep, and I feel less manic but no focus still.

I'm upset I do not get to start the school year with my kids.

I'm upset that I have to pay for an eight-hour hospital stay that did nothing but give me a time out and a pill for high blood pressure. Overall, I feel better, like I could work, but the unknown is the unknown. I could freak out tomorrow.

The upside... no staff development days.

* * *

Glimpse at Coming Down

New Year's Day 2019

At the heart of the matter, I am mentally ill. Today I am hypomanic, coming off a manic energy that had me buzzing so hard I thought I might drive myself to the hospital or call the doctor. Instead, I adjusted my meds and waited it out. Slowly it has simmered down to a slight shimmer instead of a loud, intense blaring and buzzing inside my head.

I have been manic since the beginning of December. This has been a strange episode. First episode on the new cocktail of medication, the Risperdal, Lamictal, temazapam, Ativan, Benadryl, and Topamax. In fairness, the Topamax and Benadryl were added once the mania started to build.

I saw the psychiatrist right before Thanksgiving. I was doing okay. Nothing really to speak of. We added a small dose of Topamax to help with the binge eating and extra mood stabilizer. It helped with those. Then, something strange started to happen.

I began to get irritable.

Out of the main four symptoms bipolars get—depression, mania, anxiety, irritability—irritability is the one I never get.

But lo and behold, I was hit with a wave of disgust and hatred of all things human. The sound of breathing bothered me. It was a chore to do my job at school and listen to children be children.

I had to closely monitor my mood because I knew it was a symptom, and I was not myself. I just felt off. It was, as I said, strange. I also just felt this anxious feeling of dread. Not quite depressed and not exactly dread. I didn't feel like something bad was going to happen; I felt weird and uncomfortable. I felt paranoid. Like people were watching me. I knew that this was a symptom, and nobody was watching me, but it was happening.

I could not recall that I had these kinds of symptoms all mixed together before.

When I drop low and get depressed, I feel like I am catching a cold. My body starts to hurt. I feel sick. My head hurts. I withdraw. I lose my appetite. I lose interest. I can't concentrate. Things become grey. My vision becomes darker and out of focus. I get tunnel vision. I can see myself moving slower and slower. Time stops, and I'm caught in a dream or a trap. I can't see myself in the mirror. It's fogged up. I feel this monster coming for me. It sneaks up on me and traps me in its claws. I'm a prisoner for an unjustified amount of time until my mind sees fit to release me. Then the fog lifts like steam after a shower. I see my reflection in the mirror.

This episode was different. I had shadows of all different feelings. Anxiety, paranoia, some depression, mania, irritability. I didn't know how to label it or how to process it. I didn't know what to expect.

I started to sleep less. I didn't know if it was a mixed episode. I didn't know if I was going to start losing my shit, hurt myself and need to be hospitalized, or if I was just going a little manic. It was a new sensation. In reflection, I think it was the start of a mixed episode that ended up being a manic episode.

The irritability and paranoia left, but the mania stuck around. Sleep lessened and became restless. I was waking up each hour or two, then sleeping an hour or two, getting a total of four or five hours of sleep a night. This has been the case for the month of December.

Mania scares me in a different way than depression. What scares me about depression is that I could be so far gone that I could want to kill myself, and what scares me about mania is that I could be so high up that I could hurt myself and not know that I had done it.

I have learned that I need to focus when I am manic. Sometimes sitting and doing nothing is the safest choice. The energy is unfocused. It's dangerous to unleash it. Once it is unleashed, it only manifests more energy. Laws of physics and all.

If I start to clean, I only find more stuff to clean, and soon I'm on my hands and knees with a toothbrush, scrubbing the grout on the floor. Or painting the wall with a one-inch brush. It all leads to another project.

I try to do small things. Things that have a beginning and an end.

Right now, writing offers that tiny bit of focus. I have a little bit of focus for that.

I am not a religious person. I am not sure what I believe in, but what I have found in this manic episode is peace in going to church. I don't know why, but I have gone to church every day for the past six days. Haven't missed a day since vacation has started. I think it's part of the mania and the compulsion to do things that I have found comfort in the church. Who knows what will happen in time?

The mania has been ongoing for a month. During this month, Aunt Tillie died, and a student died from suicide. It has been challenging. Due to the mania, I have not been quite processing the sadness of these events in the way I normally would. I feel them but not to my core. The suicide made me feel suicidal and triggered thoughts of self-harm for a short while. I worked past that, but I quickly ended up back in a manic state and stayed there.

Went back to the doctor during semester exam week, and he upped my dosage on the Topamax and wants me to take the Benadryl to sleep. I upped the Topamax: still nothing. I was zipping and buzzing like lightning. Christmas Eve, I upped to 100 mg. When I woke up, the buzz was muted but still there.

The buzz is still there. The lack of focus is still there. I'm still hypomanic. Not full-blown mania but hypo.

Oh, and during the mania, I shaved the dog. Poor thing. Better the dog than my own head like a Britney Spears moment.

* * *

Leveling Out?

January 19, 2019

I monitor my mood in eMoods. According to my chart, I'm leveling out. However, I don't feel quite normal yet. I don't know how to explain or express it. I'm getting sleep. Restful sleep without waking up several times a night. I am dreaming again. Strange things, like Clint Eastwood kidnapping John C.

Reilly and I'm in the getaway car. I am taking my meds and eating healthy. I am walking a couple of times a week. But my mood is hovering on the edge, not knowing which way to go.

It's like a scale before anything has been placed on it. It's set at zero, but the hand is hovering over it with something to put in the bin. Just waiting and looming.

I feel these bursts of energy and racing thoughts, and I think I must be going hypo today. Then, next moment, something triggers me, and I'm crying. Big tears. Glasses fogged up and all. Nothing really to speak of.

I went over this with the doctor. He thinks the mania is on the rise again. Waiting to come back. He doesn't want to increase the meds yet but wants me to take the Ativan as needed to take the edge off the mania and see if that helps lessen. He wanted to increase my number of pills, and I told him I didn't want access to that many pills. He asked me if I had made attempts. I had told him yes but not in many years. Twenty years. But still, I didn't want to tempt fate or a bad day. He didn't write the script. I told him I would make do with what I had.

I always start to get dodgy around this time of year. Coming up on my brother's birthday. It isn't for another six weeks, but it is coming up.

I will just have to see what happens. I have continued to go to church. I have listened to daily masses on YouTube. I go to church three days a week. I have started a new healthy eating plan. (I refuse to say DIET!) It is a way of life. I have introduced walking as a way of channeling some of the extra energy, but that becomes obsessive for me. I just want to walk all day long. But I'm pushing 300 pounds and have gained a hundred pounds in the last two years. Some due to med changes and some due to poor eating habits. A combination of poor self-care and depression.

It is just a new adventure. A path that needs to be taken for my health. The med change in September caused a forty-pound weight gain. Ten pounds a month. I figure it took me two years to put on this weight, it will take at least two years to take it off. So, I will be fighting the good fight.

Two fights now. Mental health and physical health. Hopefully, the two will meet in the middle.

Trying to Be a Kid and Growing Up Too Fast

My childhood, overall, was happy. I have great memories of my family, my mom and brother. My parents divorced when I was three. I saw very little of my dad, who's a full-blooded Navajo. My mom is white. My mom and dad met in Colorado. They got married a year after my mom graduated from high school. She wore the same dress to graduation as she did to her wedding. It was a simple dress. My dad was in the military. My parents' divorce was brought on by infidelity on my dad's part. Also, I don't think my dad liked that my mom had joined the women's lib movement. Shortly after the divorce, when I was about three, he was stationed in Germany. The divorce was best for all involved and eventually led to happy endings.

We were poor but never went hungry. Even on a pauper's budget, my mom made sure we had healthy food, right down to the terrible whole grain, brick-like bread we ate. We never had sugar cereal or sugary desserts. My brother and I would have killed someone for some Fruit Loops. Instead, we had Cheerios and Shredded Wheat—the biscuit kind that you had to break up. I once tricked my mom into buying a sugar cereal. It looked like a healthy cereal with a yellow box, but when we got home, she read the ingredients and I got a talking to. I played the innocent, but deep down I was deceptive about it. I knew it was sugar and I wanted it. I lied. We never had snacks lying around, except raisins. We got tangerines and nuts in our stockings at Christmas. I was always shocked at the fact Santa brought other kids' candy.

My mom worked three part-time jobs while putting herself through school at the University of Nevada, Las Vegas. In the divorce, my mom got a hundred and fifty dollars a month for each of us kids until we turned eighteen and maybe something like that in alimony for a few years. That helped while she was going to school. She spent long days working, early evenings cooking, and putting us to bed, and late nights typing at a typewriter writing papers for school. She has grit, and I'm grateful for what I learned from her about persistence and reaching goals.

And even with all she did, she still made time for us.

* * *

First Memory

I don't know how old I am precisely, but this is the first memory I have stitched together. I am small. I am wearing footie pajamas. We're living in our brown house on Chelsea Circle. I am asleep in my bedroom. Something loud is happening outside my room. The hall light is on. I can see it peeking through my closed door.

I am very tired. I get out of bed. I can feel the sock things on the bottom of my footed pajamas as I walk to the door. I have my bankie, my woven, pink security blanket with fringe on the ends, in one hand. I walk out of my room and into the hallway. As I step into the empty hallway, something flies over my head. I think it is a Frisbee.

Scene ends. Fade to black.

Next Memory.

I'm on my back in the back seat of our car, looking out the back window. I'm watching the hazy yellow streetlight blur by as we drive down the street late at night. It's so dark out the lights are almost blinding as they pass rhythmically every so often. I'm still in my pajamas. I think they are yellow.

We stop.

Next Memory.

My mom is standing on the porch of a house with a yellow bug light, holding me. The screen door is outlined in black metal adornments. My brother is next to us, also in pajamas. Aunt Cindy opens the door and brings us inside.

The adults talk about something. I put my head in my mother's lap and go to sleep.

Now, from what I was told and putting things together, these memories all happened in one night. My mom and dad had a fight. There may or may not have been drinking involved. The Frisbee that came down the hallway was not a Frisbee but a huge speaker. It missed crushing me by inches. I guess I heard the commotion and came out to see what was going on and walked into the fray. My mom, upset, went to her sister's house. Her sister lived a few blocks away.

That is my first memory. Always surviving something.

* * *

I don't remember my dad leaving. I just remember him being gone. I remember the absence of him. I wanted him to be there. I remember him coming home one time. I lay on the couch with him, on top of his belly and chest. We watched *The Lone Ranger*.

Wizard of Oz, Spankings and My Heroine

Every year CBS would play the *Wizard of Oz.* It was a big deal at the time because it was pre-VCR or DVD player. The only way you could see the movie was TV or at a special showing in theaters.

My brother and I knew all the words to the songs of the *Wizard of Oz* because we listened to the record all the time. We didn't have a TV for a very long time, so our only form of entertainment was listening to records. We had Disney stories, rock and roll, musicals and opera. When I was very small, the opening of the *Wizard of Oz* used to send me scurrying to my room and hiding under a blanket. The idea that the witch would sweep in and get me frightened me.

When I was about five, we settled in to watch the *Wizard of Oz.* It was winter. A blanket had been tucked under the large crack under the front door. Our little brown house was small. Three very small bedrooms and one bathroom. Thin brown carpet. The walls were white. There was faux wood paneling on one wall. Another wall by the hallway was actual stained wood; that was where we would hang our stockings on Christmas. A large window looked out onto the large front lawn with two trees. The front door needed to be replaced. The crack under the door was more like a gap, close to four to five inches. It was not just a small crack where air seeped in. Gusts of wind would blow in during the night if the blanket was not tucked under the door. We didn't have the money to replace the door, so the blanket did the job.

The thermostat had been turned down to save money. We were in our pajamas. The three of us, my mom, Tom and I, tucked under a thick blanket, sat in the large rocking chair together, and watched our black and white television that didn't have any sound. I don't know where my mom got the TV. We were just excited at having the opportunity to watch the *Wizard of Oz*, even if it was without sound.

My mom had popped popcorn and melted butter. She drizzled the butter on the popcorn and sprinkled it with salt. We munched our popcorn. Between snacking, we spoke the dialogue and sang the songs. We knew all the words and songs due to listening to the albums all the time.

I made it about halfway through. Not sure about Tom. I just remember waking up in my bed the next morning under several blankets warm and toasty.

For years, my mom, my brother and I reminisced about this memory fondly. We didn't have much, but we had each other. We were poor. Growing up, we knew we didn't have a lot, but we didn't realize how poor we were. My mom hid that from us. On my mom's shoestring budget, she put gifts for Christmas on layaway: Star Wars toys, tutus, mini construction tools.

Tom and I told this story to his friend at the bar while his friend was bartending, over drinks. Our friend started crying and poured us another drink. He said, "That's the saddest shit I ever heard. You guys had the saddest fucking childhood."

My brother and I laughed. It's funny. It's all in your

perspective.

* * *

I can count on one hand the number of times my mother put her hands on me as a child and not use all my fingers. All occasions, I must have been under the age of five because I was in preschool. I went to a Christian preschool. I think it had been arranged by one of my mom's friends who was helping her out. One day, I forgot to put my underwear on and only realized once I started climbing on the jungle gym and got a breeze up into my privates. I was so shocked at that cold touch of air that I halted mid-step. I cried with embarrassment and had to call my mom to bring me some underwear.

My mom once told me told me that she stopped spanking my brother—when she was pregnant with me—when she saw the terror in his eyes after she came at him with a wooden spoon for something he had done. She had chased him down the hallway in anger and into the corner of his bedroom. She saw his little form cowering in the corner in fear of getting spanked. She never spanked him again. That didn't stop her from the two times she put her hands on me.

The first occasion I recall I was in the kitchen of our little house on Chelsea. My mom was cooking dinner at the stove. I could smell chicken in the oven. The room was warm because the oven was on. It was a bit chilly outside, a small breeze in the air. Brown leaves rustled on one of the big trees in the back yard. The leaves were starting to fall and collect on at the base of the tree.

I wanted to go outside and play with my brother. I probably wanted to go into the treehouse in the other big tree in the yard. My mom simply asked me to put a sweater on. I told her no. I stamped my little foot on the linoleum tiled floor.

My mom sighed and said please. She went and got the red sweater for me and handed it to me. She again instructed me to put the sweater on. I stomped my little foot again, holding the sweater in my hand, and said no. I said I wanted to go out and play.

My mom looked at me and grabbed me. I fought her. She wrangled me into the sweater, not so gently, and went back to the stove. The sweater always reminded me of the red of Red Riding Hood's cape. It was a deep crimson. It had a design on either side of the buttons that wound its way up from the bottom hem to the collar. It was starting to get tight; I was outgrowing it. Once I was in the sweater, she told me to button it up.

Frowning, I told her no, again.

My mom had had it. She turned from the stove, bent over, took my little hand and with a slight tap, smacked the top of my hand with her hand.

I burst into tears.

My mom barely touched me. I don't think her touching me even made a smacking sound. It didn't leave a red mark. But I thought the world had come undone.

My mother had never struck me before. I was devastated.

She told me to button my sweater and I did. She told me to go outside and play. I did. I cried the whole time. But I did.

The second time my mom had to discipline me by putting her hands on me was with a spanking.

* * *

It was in the morning. We were running late. Mom was trying to get my brother, herself, and me ready to leave the house. She told me to get dressed. Seems like an easy enough task.

I had my heart set on wearing this dress. It reminded me of a *Little House on the Prairie* dress. It was brown and white, with stripes of brown and yellow flowers running up and down in rows. It was long and rested at my ankles. There was a brown ribbon high at the waist and a brown collar. The sleeves had white ruffles and poofed out a bit. I just loved it.

The problem with the dress is that I had already worn it, and it was dirty.

My mom told me to get dressed.

I left my room and went to the laundry room. I riffled through the dirty clothes and found the dress. I went back to my room and got out of my pajamas and put the brown dress on. My mom came to my room and saw me in the dirty dress. She came over to me and, not so gently, yanked it off and instructed me to get dressed again.

She left.

I proceeded to get dressed in the brown dress again. I sat on my bed waiting for my mom. Rushing around, my mom came in to check on me. She sighed and said, "You can't wear that; it's dirty. Take it off."

She yanked me out of it and threw it on the floor. She found something clean for me to wear. She put the clean clothes on the bed and left my room.

As soon as she left, I put on the brown dress again.

When my mom walked back into my room, she had had it. Swiftly, she grabbed and took me over her knee and spanked me. I had never been spanked before. I don't recall how many swats I got. Probably three.

When she was done, she took the dress with her. I got dressed in the clean clothes and finally, we left the house.

I cried all the way to school.

My mom never spanked or slapped my hand again. For the most part, I listened to my mom and was a compliant child. I almost always did what I was told except clean my room. I was a bit of slob.

* * *

I hoarded things and I hated cleaning my room. It was a chore I refused to do and often got in trouble for not doing. Sometimes, I'd make my bed, but that was where I stopped. I didn't touch the rest of the room.

My room was small. Ten feet by ten feet. The room was taken up mostly by my twin bed. It was covered in homemade, patchwork quilts and scratchy sheets. I had a pillow that had one side was day and the other side was night. I flipped it each morning and night. I thought if I didn't, the sun wouldn't rise or set. I had a wooden toy boy that was just a wood box. I had a strange dresser; I think my dad had made it. It had a top drawer and underneath two doors that opened to reveal a few shelves. It was stained a dark wood stain, almost black. It was strange because it looked like a face. The top drawer had two knobs that looked like wide-set eyes. The doors beneath opened like a mouth, and my clothes sat in rows like teeth. I always felt like it was breathing. My room was painted light pink.

I had what I like to call princess curtains. They were made by mom's friend. They were bright white linen edged with white eyelet lace. There were two panels that covered the window from top of the ceiling to the floor. There was a ballast with the eyelet lace. Two lacey pieces were used to pull back the curtains to reveal windows where you could see the trees and grass in the front yard.

Toys, Barbies, Barbie's bathtub, stuffed animals, toys made from paper, artwork I'd drawn on cardboard or construction paper littered my floor along with dirty clothes and clean clothes I tried on in a fashion show I never put away. I never threw anything away. I never put anything away. This would make my mom insane. There was no lid to my toy box.

My mom would warn me about cleaning my room. I'd go out to play and come back to find my mom cleaning my room. She cleaned my room like troops clean their bunks at bootcamp. She would throw away all my paper crafts and the toys I had made. Toys that were broken. All the junk I didn't want to get rid of, she would throw away. She did this several times while I was a child. I had been warned. I would just sit in the hallway and cry, locked out of my room, as my world was being bagged up for the trash.

I'd come back to a clean room. Bed made, with stuffed animals neatly placed on the pillow. Toys in the toy box, not overflowing.

I'd go outside to the trash and riffle through the trash cans looking for any of my lost treasures. I'd find a toy or two I couldn't live without. Most of it truly was trash. My room would stay clean for a while, but I'd fall into bad habits.

I'm still a slob and a hoarder to some extent with books. With the mania, I clean more often.

* * *

When I think about my mom when I was little, I remember her hair. It was long, dark, thick and full. It was past her waist to her butt. In the summer, she would wear a bandana in her hair while she did yard work. My mom seemed so much taller than me. When I grew up, I would be an inch taller than her at five foot nine inches. My mom is so skinny, I always thought her bones were hollow like a bird's. She is beautiful with her hazel eyes that look greener in the sun when she smiles. She has to be careful in the sun because she has porcelain skin and burns easily, something my brother and I never experienced.

When my dad left, my mom took responsibility for doing all the chores around the house. I remember her mowing the large back yard. We had an electric lawnmower. It did not have a bag to catch the grass and she would have to rake the grass after she had mowed the lawn. When my brother and I got older, that was our job.

I remember my mom mowing the grass during the summer, wearing a yellow bandana, a t-shirt and jean cutoffs. She was singing "The Bare Necessities" from *The Jungle Book.* She was bouncing around like Baloo the Bear. Every so often, she would stop the mower and run into the house, open the freezer and stick her head inside and cool off. When my mom was done, she would have a glass of sun tea.

My mom became involved with the National Organization of Women (NOW), an organization that was fighting for the Equal Rights Amendment (ERA). She said politics was one of the divides between her and my dad. She became involved before the divorce. It sparked my mom's evolution from being a docile housewife into a woman with her own mind. My mom is still very involved in politics. It makes her blood hum or boil depending on if you are talking about Democrats or Republicans.

My mom found some really great friendships in NOW and working for the ERA. These women fostered my mom and had a hand in raising us. They babysat us while my mom worked and went to school. When the ERA didn't pass, the women found a local Statue of Liberty and draped her in black cloth. They did it early in the morning because it was considered vandalism.

She pursued two degrees in criminal justice and women's studies. She was the second person to get a degree in women's studies from UNLV. It was a new program.

During that period, while my mom was working and going to school, money was tight. We learned to have fun with little to no money. We played cards and board games. At the end of our hallway, we had a game closet that was stacked high to the ceiling with treasured board games and our worn sports equipment. We went hiking on the weekends. We went to the park. My mom taught me how to catch a pop fly and to hit a baseball. My mom got down and played Barbies with me, when I could find them in the mess that was my room. Tom would sometimes join with his Stormtroopers.

In the middle of the night, my mom would wax our little kitchen floor. She would move the kitchen table into the living room. It would be late in the evening. We would always play Monopoly while the floor dried. We never made it through an entire game. We'd go to bed before the floor dried, and in the morning, the table was back in place for breakfast.

Years ago, when my mom was a kid, an aunt of hers had told her that wet wax was explosive. If you stepped on a wet waxed floor, you'd blow up. My mom believed her into adulthood. I'm not sure when she realized it wasn't true, but she told us that story. It always made me giggle.

My mom learned to change the oil in her vehicle. I remember her putting on some sort of worker clothes and changing the oil. I tried to be helpful and hand her different tools. I think I was more in the way, but I remember handing her a wrench.

We celebrated with a nice dinner when my mom graduated from college and got her first job at the jail as a class tech, processing inmates. She never walked for her degrees. She said she didn't have anyone who would be in the audience to cheer her on, and she wouldn't have the time off. My mom also cut her hair into a bob. I was sad because I loved her hair, but she was glad to see it go.

My mom loves to laugh. She introduced us to *The Three Stooges.* We had an early appreciation for Moe, Larry and Curly, but not Shemp. My mom and Aunt Cindy took my cousins and us to see a showing of *The Three Stooges* at UNLV one night at a family showing. It was late, but I remember laughing with my brother. My mom loved them so much that in our hallway, with the family portraits, there was a framed portrait of The Three Stooges right along with Tom and me.

She also instilled a love of reading. We went to the library once or twice a week and checked out the maximum number of books we could. My mom would spend nights reading to us when we weren't reading to ourselves. We would take turns being in each other's beds. Tom would be in mine or me in his. My mom read us *Call of the Wild* and *White Fang.*

I remember being snuggled down in my brother's bed, listening to my mother's voice describe the cold wilderness. I never made it very far in the stories. I only got the gist and, as an adult, had to reread them to understand them fully. While my mother read, I would fall asleep in my brother's bed, staring at the Bambi mural painted by my dad on my brother's wall.

She taught us how to fish. She would make us practice casting our fishing poles in the backyard with a clothes pin attached to the end of the line until we could do it right. She also made us practice rolling up our sleeping bags. She was very practical. When we did catch a fish, which wasn't very often, she taught me how to gut the fish and not be squeamish about it. She taught me how to build a fire and keep it going.

My mom is fascinated by bugs. She would have been a good entomologist. She would trap all kinds of bugs and have us observe them for days and then let them go. She would trap black widows and have us observe them so we would not be fearful. That didn't work so well with me; I'm still petrified of spiders. She would put spider egg sacks in jars, and we'd watch as the spiders hatched.

My mom eventually moved from being a class tech to an officer at the jail. To do that, she had to go to the police academy. She was an older recruit. She had already been doing the job for a while but had to retroactively attend the academy. It was difficult, but she managed it. This time, she cut her hair very short. By now, I was used to it being short. We celebrated her graduation from the academy with another dinner. It was the leap out of poverty.

My mom grew up very poor. She had to watch her brothers and sisters while her parents went out drinking. Sometimes they would be left in the car while her parents spent time in the bar. They would be left without food and drink for hours. My mom knew poverty. She knew what it's like to survive that.

She didn't want that for me or my brother.

My mom worked hard and persevered. She did not treat herself. She did not binge on a manicure or pedicure for herself. She ate leftovers every day. Her leftovers fit in an old, tiny, yellow margarine container because we didn't have Tupperware. My mom always gave us the largest share. She made sure we were taken care of and loved.

Most nights while I was in elementary school, my mom was home to cook dinner. Our small kitchen and dining room were one and the same. The stove had a small counter on each side. To the right of the stove, the space formed an L where the sink was. To the right of the sink was the dish drain board. Next to that was the avocado-colored refrigerator.

The floor was made up of linoleum tiles that had a brown and black flower pattern on them. They were the kind of tiles that had sticky backs and were put together by sticking them to the concrete floor. As a little kid, I would take white paper and different colored crayons and use the bumpy pattern of the tile to rub a pattern of the flower on the paper. I would do it for hours.

Originally, the main wall of the kitchen/dining room that ran into the living room was faux wood. My mom eventually removed it when she renovated the house. But when we were little it was still there.

We had an oval brown table that rocked when you sat at it and four chairs. The fourth chair was pushed against the wall with the table to make room in the small kitchen/dining room area. With the table pushed against the wall, the wobble and rocking were less. We still needed a matchbook shoved under one of the legs of the table to keep it steady.

From the kitchen table, you could look into the living room

and out the framed front window to the street. On the windows hung the ugliest drapes made from horrible fabric. It was tan with horizontal stripes of other shades of brown. It was awful. It wasn't a big house. A little over nine hundred square feet. The furniture was sparse. An old wood rocking chair and small plaid couch that my mom had reupholstered with a plaid brown and black. A TV on a wobbly stand and another for our record player completed our living room.

My mom was making spaghetti for dinner one night. The pasta was boiling on the stove. She asked Tom and me to start the salad. We had a green salad with every dinner. It was always romaine lettuce, tomatoes, cucumbers, and celery. We had Russian dressing or Italian dressing. No matter what the main meal was, there was always a salad, and Tom and I were responsible for making it.

We always made a joke about the president having salad at the White House and asking someone to pass the Russian and then correcting himself to say the Russian dressing. This was a time when the Soviets were a threat, and we made light of the situation. My brother really got a kick out of it.

My mom would usually have music playing while she cooked. The evening she cooked the spaghetti, she was listening to *The King and I.*

We had seen the movie with Yul Brenner and Debra Kerr. I was fascinated with the big, hoop-skirt dresses Debra Kerr wore as Anna. I wanted one so bad. I used to draw pictures of them. I wanted one for Christmas. I don't know where I thought I was going to wear it.

The melodies played in the background as we got plastic plates down from the brown cabinets and set the table. I almost always ate my dinner on a McDonald's collectible plate.

My mom dished out the spaghetti. My mom and brother filled their plates with salad and began to eat. I made sure that my spaghetti and salad were not touching each other and ate all my salad first. I had to eat my salad before I could begin to eat my spaghetti. I had to eat my food in a certain order, and my food could not touch each other or mix.

The song changed to "Shall We Dance?" We all looked at each other and smiled. My mom knew that was our favorite part of the movie.

My mom said, "You know it's just a polka?"

Tom asked, "Do you know how to polka?"

"A little. I danced with my mom somewhere. She taught me when I was little. Probably at a bar," she replied.

My mom grabbed Tom, who had a mouthful of spaghetti, and pulled him into the living room. On the next beat, my mom was dancing with Tom, shouting out, "One, two, three, four. One, two, three, four."

Hand in hand, arm in arm. They turned and turned around and around, dancing the polka. Spaghetti flew out of my brother's mouth as he laughed with joy. I sat smiling at them, turned around in my chair.

When the song played its last note, my mom looked to me and said, "Your turn."

She started the song over on the record player and grabbed me. Tom stood to the side. My mom and I danced all over the living room. In my mind, I could imagine I was wearing the pink hoop dress Debra Kerr was wearing, sweeping the floor and rustling as we bounced to the music. Due to the lack of furniture, we had a grand ballroom. I was breathless and giddy when the song was over.

* * *

Dance was something that made my blood hum from an early age. I loved dancing. I danced everywhere.

I only recall tidbits of my first performance as a dancer. I was a strawberry. It was a tap dance. What I do remember is Aunt Cindy liberally applying makeup to my face, which I absolutely loved. There was blue eye shadow, mascara, blush, and red lipstick involved.

I used to dance in the living room. I did this awesome dance move in my living room to some sort of music. I would run, jump to the lip of the couch, spin, turn and kick my leg high, arms high in the arm, then drop down to the ground and sashay off. I would continue to do this with a little kick ball change mixed in somewhere. I just made up dances, and this was always my power move. I did this once at my aunt's house on the rez, and my cousins just laughed, and I never did it again.

Around the age of seven or eight years old, my mom enrolled me in dance classes. I was taking a combo class of tap, jazz and ballet. It was a community class. An introductory class. I took classes with the same instructor, Yasmine, for about a year until she recruited me to take lessons at her studio. It was very far across town. I don't know how my mom was able to swing the cost of the lessons or the driving, but she did. And I loved her for it.

Yasmine was an excellent instructor. She taught a wide variety of dance. She always had fresh ideas. She was also a belly dancer, which was something I also wanted to do but was too young for at the time. Eventually, I would learn belly dancing, too. Her studio was set up like the inside of *I Dream of Jeannie's* bottle. Pillowed couches and sheer drapes. She smoked these thin, dark cigarettes. She was flamboyant and just lovely.

For years, I took a combination of dance. We would practice and practice. Then we would perform at malls, old folks' homes, convention centers and food festivals. I remember performing ballet to the Blue Danube Waltz at the mall. We performed at the University of Nevada, Las Vegas' Ham Hall. We did a jazz dance to "Hangin' Tough" in peacock-blue catsuits with fringe and sequined collars. One time we did a tap number for St. Patrick's Day at the Tropicana Casino.

I practiced all the time. I tapped my way to school. Sometimes I wore my tap shoes to school so I could hear my taps on the concrete. While working in the school cafeteria to get free lunch and handing out lunches, I practiced my shuffle ball change. I lived for my dance classes.

When I wasn't dancing, I was playing with my brother in the street or climbing the trees in the front yard. Our front yard had two huge chinaberry trees. In the spring, when they blossomed, they had tiny pinkish, purple flowers on fine stems that were very fragrant. We would pick them and place them in vases in the house. My mom had a special vase just for her flowers. It was a small crystal vase with an etched flower design, about four inches high. It had a narrow neck and was fat at the bottom.

The sad part about the tree was the blossoms only lasted a short time and then the berries came. They were ugly tannish yellow berries that fell everywhere throughout the yard and the sidewalk in front of the house and into the street. They needed to be raked up and swept up. We only did it every so often.

Every kid on our block fell victim to the chinaberry tree

berries. The berries would get locked into skates and freeze up the rollers. It would stop you dead in your tracks and send you flying face-first to the ground. It didn't matter if you were on roller skates or a skateboard; if a berry found a wheel, you were doomed. People avoided our home and skated a wide circle around.

* * *

I often wonder if my brother was born angry. Maybe it isn't accurate to say that as a baby, he was angry, but he was prone to anger from a very young age. The spirit born within my brother was always troubled.

We both faced a variety of obstacles. We grew up being one of the first kids of divorced parents in our neighborhood. We were the product of a bi-racial marriage gone wrong. We lived with our white mom and did not resemble her. We were the token Indians in school and were called out to speak on behalf of the entire indigenous world. We were also dressed up as Indians with paper feathers.

This was in the school district I now teach in. My brother struggled with other aspects of being Indian. The problem was he wasn't Indian, and he wasn't white; he was a half-breed, a mixed blood. Chief and Tonto. He was called all these things to his face and behind his back. He was teased and picked on. I don't know why, but I wasn't teased for being an Indian. I was accepted. Maybe because Tom was a bit darker skinned than me, I don't know the reason, but he was picked on and I wasn't.

The hurt from this bullying was masked by anger that turned to comedy that hid in the alcohol and drug abuse that would consume his life and steal his light. He rarely discussed these things with anyone and only did a few times with me.

I am reminded of my first meeting with my brother. As told to me by my mother. After I was given the name Ahiddibah and sent on my way to live my life, Woman Who Goes to War met Doola, the Little Bull.

My mom was expecting cooler weather for my arrival and brought a warm, neutral-colored outfit to take me home from the base hospital. She dressed me, knit cap and all. My black hair was slick with sweat. Once home, she called my brother, "Doola, I want you to meet your sister."

Cradling me in her arms, she gently sat down on the plaid couch. Curious but cautious, my brother came to my mother and looked expectantly at the bundle in her arms. A gift he assumed was for him. A gift, it had to be, since his mother had been gone. She pulled back the yellow blanket from my sweaty face. Quietly, my brother peered in at my tiny newborn face, still puckered from birth. Puckered and sour went his face when he realized it wasn't a gift.

SLAP!

That was the first greeting my brother gave me. Upset by the gift of a sister, he whacked me upside my head as the first official greeting and introduction to my brother.

Shortly after this introduction, the Little Bull tangled with War. A few weeks after my birth was my christening. My godfather wanted to buy lunch for everyone and purchased McDonald's. My brother was given a happy meal. Toy, burger and fries. The adults carried on in the kitchen, eating their lunch and talking. Soon, it was too quiet. My brother had disappeared with his happy meal. After I became a child of Christ, my brother decided to reward my newfound faith by giving me his French fries. My mother found him huddled over my cradle with an empty French fry container. All the salty fried sticks were stuffed in my mouth.

This was the first of many attempts on my life by my brother. Any chance he was given, he would smother me with blankets and hide my existence in his world. My mom would leave the room only to come back and find me gasping for air under three quilts.

How did I ever survive the first month?

Even with all these battles, my brother became my best friend.

My brother and I are mixed blood, born of two worlds. White and Navajo. Brown and white minded. We had two sides to us. I was happy for the most part and loved to dance. My feelings were easily hurt, I was sensitive, but eager to love and please. Tom enjoyed being in nature and had fun playing with his friends. He was easily prone to anger and lashed out. Mostly he lashed out at me.

Maybe that was because we each had two sides. Maybe it was because there were things we understood about each other. My brother teased me incessantly. He hurt my feelings without apology. It wasn't until I was an adult that I realized he did this to make himself feel better about himself. He was angry at the world, angry at my parents being divorced, angry at being a mixed-blood Indian. Nature is where Tom found solace. In his younger years, it was at Red Rock. In his later years, it would be in San Diego at the beach.

Pine Creek Canyon

When my brother was in elementary school, he went on a field trip to Red Rock Canyon. (Red Rock is a park on the outskirts of Las Vegas. It used to be a treasure only known to locals, but now it is as busy as the strip, known for its hiking trails and beautiful scenery.) On the trip, they hiked a trail called Pine Creek Canyon. On the trail, there is an old home site with the remains of a basement that looks out onto a grassy valley. Beyond the valley, to the north, is the pine creek.

When my brother came home from the trip, he shared his wonder with us. The next weekend we went to the park and hiked the trail. It wasn't a long hike. It starts out slim but widens out to a rocky, dry creek bed. You follow the creek bed to a dry, dusty trail. Through wandering sticky brush, sage and cacti, you see lizards darting in and out. You can hear the creek in the distance.

This trail and the abandoned home site became our getaway. We hiked here all the time, especially during the summer, to play in the creek. We would come in our swimsuits and play all day. Depending on the season, sometimes the creek would be high enough to swim in. Other seasons it was just deep enough to wade in.

Every year we spent time catching tadpoles and frogs. We would catch frogs and bring them home with us. I don't know what my mom was thinking. I swear, we must have singlehandedly decimated the frog population. Poor things. We didn't know any better. We loved the frogs. We played with them. We kept them in boxes. They would escape and end up in the neighbor's pool.

We looked forward to hiking the trail. It was our entertainment. As a family without a lot of money, Red Rock was free entertainment. We would pack a lunch and spend all day in nature. It was wonderful. We played outdoors. I don't know what my mom would do, maybe she brought a book or just basked in the sun. I was busy with my brother and the frogs.

One time, we had decided we wanted to find the source of the creek. We got up early and planned a big hike. My mom made us a basket of barbeque chicken thighs, apples, and carrots. The one thing I especially remember was the miniature Coca-Colas she found. They were half-sized cans. It was a mini six-pack. She bought them special for our special hike.

We got to the park early. We hiked past the house, further up the trail than we had ever gone before. As the sun got higher, it got hotter, and I got tired. My little legs could not keep up with my mom and my brother. I petered out.

We stopped for lunch. We made a nice picnic. Everything tasted so good. The cold chicken, veggies, and fruit were delicious. But the very best thing was the cokes. Of course, Mom only packed three. The other three were going to be for some other special occasion.

After lunch, I could not soldier on. I told my mom and brother to go on without me. I would guard our picnic area. They left me and went to find the source of water. I don't know how long they were gone. I fell asleep in the sun.

They woke me up when they got back. The sun had moved. They said they hiked as far as they could but could not see the source of the water. It was too high up. There was no trail leading up that high. Tom was disappointed.

We packed up our picnic and started to hike out. On our way out, we went down by the creek to cool off and pick up a few frogs.

For years we would hike this trail. We would bring visitors. I would bring boyfriends. I have brought my children to play in the same creek I played in as a child.

People Pleaser

I'm not blaming Tom about the incident I'm about to describe. I do wonder why he just left me. It's something that stuck with me, and I wish we had talked about it while he was alive. Now, I'll never get to ask him, "Why?" I'll always be left with lingering questions and thoughts and feelings about this incident. There's so much to being a kid that you don't get at the time it happens. One of the reasons I'm writing my memories down is to see if they make sense. I'm not sure if they do.

In the backyard of the house I grew up in, my dad had built a blue treehouse in a large tree for my brother and me. You had to climb up the tree to get into it. It would seat about six kids, three on each side of the large box of the house, and you had to slide down a metal pole on the other side to exit it. My brother and I spent a lot of time playing in there during our childhood. A lot of the neighbor kids spent time with us, too.

The kids in our neighborhood ranged in age. Across the street, there were two kids, Lacy and Bill. Lacy was a few years older than me and Bill was a few years younger than me. Lacy and I played mostly together, as we were the only girls in the neighborhood. Bill was the youngest in the neighborhood.

Tom was lucky. There were several boys in the neighborhood. Jim lived next door to us. He was a year or two older than Tom. He had a swimming pool in his backyard and a basketball hoop in his front yard. Don was the same age as Tom and had the best bicycle on the block. His parents were rich and bought all the newest toys for him. He was spoiled. There was also this teenage boy who came around and played with us. He hung around but wasn't always there. I don't remember his name.

I always wanted to be with the boys. They were always having so much fun. Sometimes they would let me be the person they would jump on the ramp with their bikes. I would lie down just after the ramp, and they would all jump their bikes over me. I only got nicked a couple of times.

Sometimes, the whole neighborhood would play games of kickball in the street. We lived on a cul-de-sac, so we didn't have a lot of traffic to interrupt our games. Lacy's dad had painted a square for kickball and four square in the street and we would have games. Nobody wanted me on their team. They would pick Bill over me.

If Lacy was busy, I always chased after the boys to play with them.

One weekend, the boys were in the treehouse. I climbed up to see what they were doing to see if I could play with them. Three of the neighbor boys, the teen, Jim and Don, were seated on the bench to one side with my brother opposite them.

I asked them if I could play with them. They said they had a special game I could play with them, but I couldn't tell anyone.

I agreed. I just wanted to be a part of something. I was bored in the house by myself. They again warned me it was a big secret, and I would get into trouble if I told anyone, even my mom.

I told them I understood.

They all took down their pants and underwear. My brother went out the door and down the fire pole.

I was confused and embarrassed. Why did they have their pants down?

They said we were going to play a grown-up game. They asked me if I wanted to be a grown-up, and I said yes.

They said I needed to put my mouth on their wieners. That's what grown-ups did to each other. I asked them if they were sure. They all agreed it was true.

I had no idea, but it seemed valid. Why would they lie to me? So, I did.

They tasted like salt. It didn't last very long. But I did it to each boy. I sucked on each boy for just a few moments.

After I had done it, they all kind of laughed and put their pants on and told me to go away. They also told me to keep the secret. They told me that I was very grown-up, and they would let me play again.

I liked the fact they thought I was a grown-up. I didn't realize anything had been wrong about what I had done.

It happened a couple of times. No more than three that I can remember. Each time my brother left.

My brother and I never discussed this situation as adults. I have never discussed this situation with anyone until now. My need to fit in and be a part of a group drove me to be with these guys and keep this secret. This was a secret I kept.

As I got older, I was embarrassed. I didn't want my brother to get into trouble. I didn't know how he would be perceived since he left me in that situation. I was unsure how it would look.

I don't know if he remembered what happened. It was so

long ago. Tom and I shared a lot together, but never this. It baffles me that in all the things that Tom and I discussed, this topic never once was broached. I don't blame my brother. I do wonder what he thought was going on or what he thought they were doing to me.

That treehouse was taken down when I was about twelve. The tree cut back, and a shed was built near it. Because of what happened later, this memory has a strange quality. I wasn't really hurt and yet I knew enough to be embarrassed. What stays with me is I just wanted to please the boys. I wanted them to like me. Even after the abuse, I sought out their attention. The abuse did not continue, but I still wanted them to like me.

* * *

I was lonely, but I wasn't friendless. I had a best friend, Dani, whom I met in second grade. Dani and I rode bikes together. We attempted to ride skateboards, but mostly we carried them and tried to look cool. We spent a lot of time in the swimming pool, even in the winter, with our lips turning blue. We were huge water babies.

Her mom, Jamie, would take us to her grandmother's senior living home and we would play in the pool all summer. We would be the only kids since it was a senior living community. We were good kids and didn't make too much noise. Dani was able to dive into the pool, and I was always in awe. I couldn't do that, so I just jumped in. She was so elegant.

At the senior center, the old men taught us how to shoot pool. They taught us how to hold the pool cues and not rough up the felt. We weren't very good, but it was the first time we got a taste of a game that we would love for a lifetime. Dani would go on to become a pool league champion as an adult.

Dani and I spent all our time together. We watched Daniel Russo fight in the *Karate Kid* and thought he was dreamy. We practiced the crane kick in one of the rooms.

Dani always wanted to see how much I loved her and tested me constantly. One night, while I was staying at her house, we were sleeping in a full-sized bed. It was kinda high up off the ground for an eight-year-old. I remember having to kind of jump to get into it. I decided to build a fort in the closet instead, a cubby to sleep in. Dani was sleeping in the bed. At some point during the night, Dani had rolled off the bed and onto the floor; she was out cold. I was either not asleep or it woke me up.

I got out of bed and lugged her back into bed. She was not light by any means. I put her back to bed; she was still asleep. I went back to my cubby. A few minutes later, she rolled out of bed again. Whap! Hit the floor. I folded my blankets back, got out of my cubby, and proceeded to put her back to bed. I got her tucked back in bed. This time I tucked the blanket under the mattress so she couldn't roll out of it. I had just got back into bed and snuggled down when Whap! Again, she hit the floor. She still appeared to be asleep. Exasperated, I got up and lifted her sleeping, deadweight body back into bed. Tucked her in and went back to my cubby.

No sooner had I tucked myself in bed, then she rolled out and fell again. This time I left her there and I went to sleep. At some point, she got up and put herself to bed. Years later, she told me that she wanted to see how many times I would put her back to bed. She was testing me to see what a good friend I was. I guess I passed.

Dani had this great black and gold furniture. We decided

we could play detectives. We smeared our fingerprints on the furniture, then made up a story about murder, then lifted our fingerprints with baby powder and tape. We listened to Fleetwood Mac as we sleuthed our way through an evening. I thought it was quite inventive. I don't remember the story going very far. We didn't play that game too often. It kind of ended once you lifted the fingerprints.

At Dani's house, I ate all kinds of new foods. At my house, we had whole wheat bread, very little sugar and sweets. At Dani's house we had sugar cereal, Kool-Aid, pudding, and a host of other things. Dani's mom was a most excellent cook. I had hominy for the first time. She made a tomato and pepper salad with garlic. My mom detested garlic and would always make a comment about my breath when I came home from Dani's house. Garlic was in most of the foods I ate at Dani's. I loved it.

Most of all I loved having a best friend.

* * *

Even at an early age, I was developing a habit of people-pleasing. I went out of my way to be the calm in the storm. I didn't like it when people were upset. It caused me great anxiety.

Pete Walker talks about trauma being in four forms fight-/fight and freeze/fawn. Most people are familiar with fight, flight, and freeze with a traumatic event. In fight, a person responds aggressively. In flight, a person responds by fleeing. In freeze, a person responds by going numb to the situation. Walker writes, "Fawn, according to Webster's, means: 'to act servilely; cringe and flatter,' and I believe it is this response that is at the core of many codependents' behavior."

Codependents struggle to assert boundaries in a relationship. Due to the trauma, they just want to make things right and be agreeable. They set about saying yes to everything and overextend themselves. People pleasing. They put everyone's needs in front of their own. They are very anxious people.

I didn't know it at the time, but I was a freeze/fawn. I froze during my abuse. My trauma created fawning behavior in me. I always associated it with the fact that I am an empath. I feel people's emotions. I am a sympathetic crier. I see tears and I cry along with whoever is crying. But it's more than that. It relates back to my trauma. It would be years before I would see that cycle.

Dani would fall out of bed, and out of concern I would put her back. Tom would yell at me, and I would run back to him and ask him to play with me. The boys would abuse me, and I would ask if I could be a part of their line up in their jumps at the ramp or play kickball and be a part of the team.

I just wanted to be included. I never wanted to be isolated. My closest friends were my stuffed animals. They were my friends. I had Dani. We were closer than sisters. We were blood sisters from poking our fingers and sharing our blood, but I still wanted the connection to people.

I always went out of my way to make sure I did the right thing. I listened to my mom. I followed directions in school. I listened to my teachers. I kept the peace.

Tom and I had a turbulent relationship. He was verbally abusive with me as a young kid. He called me names – stupid, dummy, idiot. He would rough me up sometimes, never anything too hard. He never hit me. It always made me cry.

Sometimes I would tell on him; sometimes I wouldn't. I would always forgive him and seek out his company again.

His room was forbidden. I wasn't allowed to go in there. The older he got, the more forbidden it became. The older he got, the larger his vocabulary became and the harsher the words he used with me. Fucking loser, asshole, bitch.

I found my voice and turned some words back on him. We verbally sparred and found a meeting of equal ground.

No matter how mean my brother was, I always went back to him. He was my brother. I loved him. I wanted to be with him. As a little kid, there was only one time I remember him being a protector.

We were flying home from Colorado. It was my first time flying. We were unaccompanied minors flying on Frontier. I wanted a soda. Tom bought me a soda. There was turbulence, and I got scared. Tom reached over and took my hand and said it would be okay.

It was moments like that that I knew my brother loved me. He never had to say it. Through all the idiot and dummy comments, beneath it all, I knew he loved me. In that moment, he showed it. I always felt it. That's why I always went back, even when he was mean.

Fishing and Fireworks

My mother was born in Leadville, Colorado. As kids, we would spend part of our summers in Colorado Springs with our grandparents, then camp in Leadville a few nights. Sometimes it would be a week or two vacation with our mom and sometimes we would be left longer in our grandparents' care. My mom and dad divorced when I was three, and I didn't see my dad often.

We always drove to Colorado. We took the southern route from Las Vegas through Flagstaff and Albuquerque. It was easier on our little gold 1975 Volkswagen Bug, and my mom said the drive was prettier than the northern route. We always stopped at a grocery store in Albuquerque and bought fruit. Those were our road snacks, peaches and cherries.

Once we got to the two-lane highways, my mom would roll open the sunroof of the Bug, slow down a bit, while my brother and I would take turns trying to hit the road signs with the cherry pits. I don't know that we hit anything. I know being as small as I was, I definitely didn't hit anything, but I like to think I heard a ping or two from by brother's throws.

We would arrive at our grandparents' two-story white house, trimmed in green. Bricks were at the base level, lining the basement windows. A small but very green yard surrounded by metal fencing was in front of the house. A gate led into the yard. There was an uneven footpath to the front steps of the porch. As I walked the footpath, there was some sort of bush on the left, taller than me. It had little pink flowers on it, and it smelled good.

Once I got to the porch, my grandfather would be waiting for me. He'd be wearing his sunglasses and flip-flops, smoking a cigarette. If it was hot out, he'd be shirtless. He had his throne, a metal chair with padded cushions that only he sat in. It faced the street and the footpath. Next to it was a porch swing for visitors. I loved to sit or lie down on that swing and talk to my grandpa.

Our trip to Colorado was focused around the Fourth of July annual fireworks display at Freedom Park. They hold a huge fireworks show with a live orchestra. They begin the event playing the 1812 Overture. They had the cannons and all. Once the cannons boomed, the first fireworks danced across the sky.

My mom loved this. We loved this. It was our annual tradition for as long as I could remember. We had a method to navigate the madness of the event as well. My mom and grandpa would leave early and drop one car off near the park, then return home. Near the time of the event, we would all squeeze into my grandpa's car that smelled of stale cigarette smoke and drive to the park. This way, we would be able just to walk a short distance to our car and go home. We never had to worry about parking.

This tradition carried on from the time I was a small child until I had my first child. My mom continues to go to this day. We would picnic at the park for dinner and wait for the fireworks. We always had the same blanket. My mom made this red, white and blue patchwork quilt blanket when my brother was very little. It was very heavy and durable. We took it with us everywhere, camping and to the parks. Anywhere that required sitting in the grass or snuggling up against the cold. It was a good blanket. I still have it. It needs repairs as the edges have come apart.

The week or two we spent in Colorado was split between the Fourth of July and camping. Once we had our fireworks, we would then travel to my mother's birthplace of Leadville to camp. It wasn't a great distance from Colorado Springs, just a few hours.

Before leaving for Leadville, we had to prepare for the fishing expedition. We had to catch our own bait. My mom taught us to become nightcrawler hunters. In the evenings, we would go into the lush, green grass of my grandpa's lawn, armed with a flashlight. The lawn was about ten feet by fifteen feet. He had watered the grass heavily in the late evening to push the worms to the surface. In the dark, with our lights pointed in the grass, we would look for bait.

They would be peeking out of the earth. We would have to quickly paw at them with our fingers and gently, but firmly hold them down. Slowly, we would pinch them and extract them from the ground. We would put them in our empty coffee cans that held a bit of soil. Night after night, we would continue the hunt until we deemed we had enough. Sometimes, we would feel we had fished out Grandpa's lawn and would go to the park in the center of the street. This would occupy a large part of our evenings. Soon, we would leave for Leadville.

My Great Aunt Bernie, my grandma's sister, lived in Leadville. Bernie had short graying brown hair. It was curly because she curled it. Her husband, Bone, had passed away when I was in the fourth grade. My grandparents had been in Las Vegas when he passed. They took me out of school early, and I went with them to the funeral. There was still snow on the ground when we were there for the funeral in May.

Mom, Tom and I would visit her home before and after we camped. She had a small little house. The house was taller than it was wide, even though I remember it being a single-story home. It could have had a basement. The house was a light pale color, faded probably because of all the snow. I don't remember there being a yard. There were steps leading up to the door.

We usually took a meal with her. She was a pleasant woman. I loved being around her because she was so loving. One time while we were there, Tom and I noticed that she had collected wishbones from chickens or turkeys around a glass. We asked if we could make some wishes. She said we could. There must have been about twenty or so hanging on the rim of the glass. To my mother's horror, we made wishes on all of them, breaking the bones in half. We had a pile of broken bones and an empty glass. My mother was embarrassed, thinking we were only going to take one or two. Bernie laughed and said it was fine. Bernie was like that, good-natured.

After we left Bernie, we would head to our campgrounds in Turquoise Lake, five miles from Leadville. Turquoise Lake is a 1,788 square foot reservoir shaped like a boot. It is crystal blue. Some areas you could just walk to the lake from your campsite. Other places, you had to drive to fishing sites. It was surrounded by tall pine trees. It smelled clean and crisp. You were surrounded by wilderness and cut off from civilization.

We would find a little spot and set up our camp. Tom and I

would set up chairs and pull everything out of the car, while my mom set up the tent. Once the tent was set up, we would put everything inside the tent for sleeping, and my mom would get the fire going for dinner.

The chairs were circling the fire. There was a chair Tom had claimed early in the day, which I loved. It was a beach chair. White metal with yellow mesh for the seat and back. It sat low, inches from the ground. A perfect camping chair to be close to the fire to roast hot dogs and marshmallows.

Tom had gotten in and out of the chair a couple of times. Now he was holding a roasted hot dog at the end of a stick. He got up once more to get a bun. He fixed his hot dog and returned to his chair. The chair I wanted, but he called dibs. He must have sat down with a little more force than usual or the chair was a little more worn than we thought.

With hot dog in hand, Tom proceeded to sit and fall through the chair all the way to the ground with a thud. He clutched his hot dog so tight that the dog slipped out of the bun and onto the ground next to his butt in the dirt.

I laughed out loud. My mom snickered.

Even in the darkness, I could tell my brother's face was red with embarrassment. He didn't think it was funny. He threw the bun into the dark. I just laughed some more. My mom asked if he was okay. Tom grunted and tried to get out of the broken chair.

The problem was, the more he tried to get out of the chair, the more he wedged himself in. His legs were practically stuck in the air. He couldn't get a good grip on the handles to pull himself out. The more he struggled, the farther down he went. My mom started laughing too.

Tom finally started laughing. We all laughed.

"Can someone help me?" he finally asked.

My mom went over and pulled him out of the broken chair. I told him that's what he got for calling dibs on my favorite chair. He stuck his tongue out at me and got another hot dog. My mom got a blanket for him to sit on. There were no more chairs.

We roasted more hot dogs. Then roasted marshmallows. We popped popcorn in the tin foil pan that specifically said, "Do not use over open flame." I was always worried we were going to get into trouble or trouble was going to find us, but it never did. Mom did great, and the popcorn was delicious.

Bundled up against the cold mountain air, in front of our roaring fire, we would quote lines from movies. My brother was the most talented at this, but I wasn't too bad. I had my niche, too. My brother was the master. He could hear anything once and repeat it with gusto. My mom's favorite movies to hear from us were from Mel Brooks's movies, specifically *History of the World*, *Young Frankenstein*, and of course, *Blazing Saddles.* We entertained my mother for hours with retellings of the Bullshit Artist, the Count de Money, huge knockers, bean farts, and where da white women at? I don't know if it was doubly funny listening to these lines coming out of little kids' mouths or that it was just good material, but my mom laughed and laughed. We did our bits each night we camped. My mom did not let us swear ordinarily, but when we quoted Mel Brooks, it was fair game. My mom was still lenient when it came to this since we learned most of our bad words from her when she came home from working at the jail as a corrections officer.

She tried once to institute a swearing jar. She stopped with the swear jar after she owed five dollars.

For two days, we would fish at the lake. Each morning we would have cereal. We were excited to catch some fish. We would be nagging my mom to hurry up so we could get out on the lake to catch the fish. We just knew the earlier you went, it would be easier to catch fish, so out we'd go. We'd drive around until we found a spot, hike down to the edge and fish.

We'd be out there for hours. Casting, watching our bobbers with steely stares. Sometimes they would dip. We would yank our poles and reel them in, and nothing. There'd be nothing. This went on all day. We would drive around to another spot on the lake. Cast out and wait. Watch the bobber. Fish would take the bait. Reel in and nothing. Finally, my brother and I would get bored and start throwing rocks. This would irritate my mom, who was quite enjoying her non-fish- catching day and tell us to go further away. It would further annoy us that only a few feet away, another fisherman was reeling in a very nice-looking trout.

Pretty soon, even my mom would give up hope that we would catch anything. We would drive back to camp with nothing to show for a day on the lake but fewer nightcrawlers and salmon eggs.

For some reason, we always thought we were going to catch the big one. We always prepared ourselves for the idea that we were going to have trout for dinner. We never bought dinner food. We always figured we were going to live off the land. Every year, we were sadly mistaken. Thank God there was a Pizza Hut in town. It was one of the few times we got to eat out.

We would go into town, grubby, sweaty, and smelly from the bait. We'd wash up in their restroom and order our food. Tom and I would be delighted that we could order a soda, which we never were allowed at home. We enjoyed our piping hot pizza. We enjoyed it even more so as it had started to rain, and we didn't look forward to going back to our tent where it would be cold and dripping.

It was amazing how on our trips Tom and I didn't fight like we did at home. When we were at our grandparents' house, Tom would go back to picking on me. On the road, things were peaceful.

After dinner, Mom would load us back in the Bug and drive us around the town. Leadville is a very small town. There is a main road with small shops that line the road. We never stopped or shopped in them. They were for tourist and since my mom was from there, we didn't consider ourselves tourists in that sense.

The tour did not take us very long. She would show us the places where she lived. A hole she jumped in as a kid by a telephone pole that to her seemed huge. She showed us a hill that was the hill all the kids rode their bikes down. She told us the sad story of Baby Doe Tabor. She told us how about the silver mines closed down. She told us about the Unsinkable Molly Brown and how she made it rich on her silver mines, unlike Baby Doe.

Molly Brown was a Leadville local whose husband struck it rich in a silver mine. They came into money and she became a socialite. She was new money and not really accepted in the rich society. She was a survivor of the Titanic. There was a movie made about her, *The Unsinkable Molly Brown*, with Debbie Reynolds. She was also a figure in James Cameron's *Titanic*, played by Kathy Bates. She is brash and outgoing. That's how they portray her.

Elizabeth McCourt Tabor, known as Baby Doe Tabor, met

Horace Tabor, a man twice her age. He divorced his first wife and married Baby Doe. It was a huge scandal. He was wealthy and had silver mines along with other investments. They eventually ran out of money and became poor. He had told her that the Matchless Mine would never run dry. Baby Doe died guarding that mine believing her husband that the mine still held riches.

My grandma told me a story about when she was a kid, that Baby Doe was still alive but in her older years now. Baby Doe used to visit people around Leadville and go from house to house for tea and beg for food. She had pockets in her dress and would take the cookies and cakes from the table and put them in her pockets for later. Baby Doe lived on the outskirts of town. She used to hang the *Denver Post* on the outside of the porch to keep the flies away. My grandma and her friends used to run up to the porch and tear down the papers or throw rocks until the papers fell down. My grandma would cry about that when she told me that she was now an old woman. She was sorry she did that to Baby Doe. My grandma said that her father was one of the men that carried Baby Doe out of her home when she was found dead.

I found these rags to riches stories fascinating. They were like fairy tales. They didn't seem real. But I knew they were real. Grandma had talked about Baby Doe as a real person. I'm sure the myth of the person had grown over time. I liked that someone could overcome their poverty and get rich off the land.

On one of our camping visits to Leadville, when I was eight or nine, the rain had died down a bit, and darkness was starting to settle, so we headed back to camp. As expected, everything was wet. We couldn't start a fire. We just went to bed. The three of us curled up in our sleeping blankets and fought off the cold mountain air. It rained all night. I woke up to the thunder and lightning. I could see it flash and illuminate the tent. I don't think Mom or Tom were awakened by it. I just remember watching and listening.

Then I realized that my whole side was wet. For a minute, I thought I had peed my pants, but it wasn't warm, so I ruled that out. There was a hole in the tent and a puddle of water had formed on my side of the tent. My sleeping bag was soaked. I didn't want to wake anyone up, so I just tried to scoot over out of the puddle and move away from the wet part of the bag. It didn't work too well. I got really cold.

At some point, I went back to sleep. I woke up with my mom breaking camp. Tom was still asleep. I got up, and it was freezing. You looked like a dragon breathing out icy puffs of air. The coldness showing with each breath. Everything was wet, and it looked almost icy. Mom said we were going to Aunt Bernie's for breakfast. I woke up Tom, who had slept most comfortably in between Mom and me, and helped pack up our belongings.

We rang Aunt Bernie's bell, clearly waking her up. She had on her nightgown, and her hair was in rollers. She saw we looked rough and immediately invited us in. The house was so warm. Bernie made us tea, eggs and toast. Hot drinks and hot food were most welcome to the chilled body.

Next, we were allowed to take hot showers and put on clean clothes. We stayed the night with Aunt Bernie. We played cards and watched TV.

The next morning, we packed up and made our way back to Colorado Springs. We didn't stay but a few more days before we had to go back to the heat of Las Vegas. On our way back to

Vegas, we didn't stop for fruit. It was a direct drive. If Mom got tired, sometimes we stopped at a rest stop, and she'd sleep while we played on the rocks.

I always loved our summers in Colorado. We would sit on the porch with our grandfather while he smoked a pack of Pall Malls and drank a Diet Pepsi with Jim Beam. Sometimes, we would harass our grandmother and sit with her in her bedroom and watch her watch her soap operas. My grandparents' bedroom was small and cozy. There were two twin beds. Grandpa's bed was pushed against the wall with the window. Grandma's bed was more in the middle of the room. Their beds were separated by a nightstand. Grandma's TV sat on the brown wood dresser to the right of her. Sometimes, we would just veg out and watch cable TV in the living room because Grandpa had HBO. The fishing and no fish. Aunt Bernie. Pizza Hut. The fireworks. But mostly, the time I got to spend with my mom and my brother.

The time in Colorado was not structured. My mom didn't have to go to work. We didn't have to do chores. We got to eat sweets and ice cream every night. That time was the best. It was uninterrupted golden time that I cherished and still do.

* * *

Probably because I loved him so much, I was always an easy target for my brother. He could always make me cry. My mom would ask me why I would let him rile me up like that. Why did I let him get to me? No matter what I did, he always found a way to get to me. He was unbeatable.

One time when I was about seven, he convinced me to play poker. I had no idea how to play poker. We had always just played go-fish or crazy eights. I didn't know anything about gambling. He showed me his idea of poker. He card-sharked me. He convinced me I was good at playing.

Once he was sure I had the game down, he then said we could start betting. I had all my money in a blue, rectangular, metal lockbox with a combo lock that was broken. I kept all my valuables in it. At first it was just pennies. Then, the pennies turned into nickels and dimes. Pretty soon, he had me betting and losing my life savings.

I had no idea what I was doing. I'm not even sure we were playing poker. It was just some card game he made up, but he took all my money. When I cried to my mom about it, she said we shouldn't have been gambling and said he won the money fair and square. I don't know about fair, but that was the end of it.

I had a collection of stuffed animals that I loved. Tom was upset with me because I was having a tea party with my stuffed animals and he wasn't invited. We were home alone while my mom was at work, and I guess he was lonely or bored. I posted a note on my door, "No boys allowed!"

He promptly stormed in and abducted all my stuffed animals. He held them hostage in the bathroom for hours. He made noises that he was beating them up. I became unglued. I was in hysterics. He said he was breaking, my rabbit, Bun-Bun's ears.

I was so upset I made an emergency call to my mom's work at the jail, where she was a corrections officer. If this wasn't an emergency, I didn't know what was. I was so upset, the operator at my mom's job could barely get out what was wrong and quickly found my mom at the jail. When I told my mom what was happening, stuffed animals locked in the bathroom being abused and tortured, she came unglued.

She screamed at me that this was not an emergency. She yelled at me to put Tom on the phone. I yelled at Tom that Mom was on the phone. He came to the phone but locked the stuffed animals in the bathroom and pocketed the key. He got an earful and was almost in tears. He hung up and gave me the key to the bathroom.

I freed my stuffed animals. Bun-Bun's ears had been broken. I wrapped them in an ace bandage. I just cried.

Always the victim.

His friends got in on the torture too.

I was in my room at night. I was young. I was listening to a record, minding my own business when ninjas burst through my bedroom window. Two ninjas, dressed in black, head to toe. They were rambling on about something. Then one of them side kicked me in the chest, and they went scurrying out the window just as quickly as they had burst through the window.

My chest was aching. I was frightened. I went running to my brother's room. The door was locked. We never lock our doors.

He finally opened it.

He looked so calm. I was hysterical. I was crying.

I told him ninjas attacked me.

He and his friend Shawn just looked at me and smiled. Then I saw in the corner a mass of black clothes. They were the ninjas. I was pissed. I told him I was going to tell Mom. I never did.

Another time, Dani and my brother ganged up on me. We were watching TV and all of a sudden they sat on me and pinned me down. Tom sat on my butt, and Dani sat on my shoulders.

They started popping my toes and my fingers. I hate to pop my knuckles or toes. They just sat on me until it was all done. I just cried.

My brother would go out of his way to get the tears rolling.

My mom's friend Jeannie would always stick up for me. Jeannie was wild. Even her hair was kinda wild with a reddish-brown hue. She was like a hippie chick. She smoked marijuana. I caught her doing it once and she told me I couldn't tell my mom, even though I didn't really know what it was. She worked with my mom at the jail as a nurse. She was san out lesbian. She was always fun and made me smile.

She once gave me a sticker when I was feeling down that said, "I feel like a fire hydrant and all my friends are dogs." It was a blue sticker with bold white letters. She just came in my room and stuck it on my closet door. It stayed on my closet door until we moved from that house.

I must have been around ten when she was watching us one time while my mom was out of town. Tom had been picking on me, and I was upset. Jeannie said I should get back at him.

The idea of getting back at Tom had never occurred to me. He was just so much bigger than me and stronger. It seemed forbidden.

She had an arsenal of ideas.

I went with something simple.

Tom and his friend Shawn were sleeping in the living room. Jeannie and I painted their toenails and fingernails hot pink while they slept. I didn't know what was going to happen. Jeannie just said to wait and see.

I woke up hearing, "Oh, my God! It won't come off!"

"Dude. It's on your feet, too."

"Hey, why are my toes pink?"

"How do you get this shit off?"

I came out of my room, smiling.

Tom was frantic. We were going to Wet-N-Wild, the water park, in a few hours, and he could not be seen with pink nails.

"How do you get this off?" Tom asked me.

"You don't. It just has to wear off with time," I replied with a grin.

He started to cry.

Shawn started to laugh.

"You can't do this to me. There are going to be girls at the park. They can't see this. There's got to be a way," he pleaded.

Jeannie came out of the bedroom.

"If you promise to be nice to your sister, I'll give you a solution," she said.

Tom swore on his life.

Jeannie gave him the nail polish remover. My life was very peaceful for a while until it wasn't. Tom went back to his usual bullying techniques. Shawn, however, never forgot and always made a joke about the nails.

A couple of years went by, and Tom being Tom, he was rude to me yet again. This time I had had enough.

We shared a phone line from a wall jack that was between our rooms in the hallway. A long phone cord attached to the phone could pull the phone into either of our rooms. The phone was one of those clear, see-through phones, with the colorful inside working parts.

I was already sleeping. The next day, I was doing a marathon walk for cancer or something. I needed to get up early to do the walk. I went to bed early, being responsible. Tom came in late and woke me up.

He didn't just come in and gently shake me and say, "Hey,

sister, do I have any messages?"

No. He kicked my bed until I woke up. Light was shining into my dark bedroom from the doorway. He said, "Finally! Hey, dummy. Did I get any messages?"

Ugh! I was so pissed. It was close to midnight or after midnight. I yelled at him to get out of my room.

After that, I couldn't go back to bed.

I tossed and turned.

All I could think about was what an asshole he was.

Then it dawned on me. He was an asshole. He deserved to be punished.

My brother was quite the prima donna. He was all about his hair. He had thick, black hair. It was everything to him. He was all about his looks. He was very handsome. He used only the best product. Usually Vidal Sassoon.

I went into the bathroom and dumped half of the hairspray down the drain. I promptly filled the rest of the bottle of hairspray with peroxide. I put his hairspray back on the counter.

I went back to bed and tried to get some rest.

This was a long con.

For weeks, my brother used that hairspray. Slowly his hair started to turn from black to copper.

He was working at a car wash place and thought it was changing color from working in the sun. I just let him think that.

He used half that bottle of hairspray.

At some point, I felt guilty. We were getting along so well. No fighting. No teasing. Maybe it was when his hair was orange, a month or so later, I confessed. I told him what I had done.

His jaw dropped open and closed. He was speechless. Then,

he was chasing me, and I ran. He was going to beat my ass. I ran for my life. I ran to my room and locked myself in my room until my mom came home.

He told on me. My parents laughed. I can't remember if I got in trouble. I don't think I did. He told his friends, which was a mistake because they thought that was the best prank ever pulled.

I never tried to pull anything on my brother again, and he was never really mean to me again.

That was the end of everything. Our relationship changed.

A few years after that, I was wearing this raggedy, old, faded, black, zipped-up hoodie. It was my winter jacket. Tom was in shock that was what I was wearing to school. He said, "No sister of mine is wearing that shit. Get in the car. We're going shopping."

We went to the Meadows Mall. We strolled into Dillard's Department Store. I ended up buying the same jacket he had. A black leather bomber jacket. It was $200. He had the money and just bought it for me.

That was how things went from then on. He took care of me. He was generous.

He went from torturing me to taking care of me. From being my nemesis to my best friend. I still have that jacket. I can't wear it because I think of him, but I take it out and hold it. I wrap it around me. It's like getting a hug from my brother.

Tom continued to be generous. When I graduated from college with my bachelor's degree, he bought me a beautiful necklace. It's a silver necklace with a small pendant. The pendant is about the size of a dime and shaped like a four-cornered flower. In the center of the flower is an aquamarine stone. I wear this necklace every time I want to feel close to my brother, like I wear the jacket. I always wear it on his birthday and the anniversary of his death.

As Tom and I got older, he continued to take care of me. Whenever we went somewhere, he paid for everything. He made good money as a bartender. He paid for breakfasts, movies, pedicures, dinners. He paid for it all. He would give me twenty dollars and say to spend it on something just for me and not on the kids.

He knew I didn't make a whole lot of money as a teacher and having the kids to take care of by myself. He just stepped in and helped me out. There were times when he helped me pay some of my bills if I was short. He would give me gas money. In our later years, he supported me both financially and emotionally. We had grown closer through our struggles as kids. We both knew what it was like being poor, and he didn't want me to have to go through that with the kids. As I said, he was generous.

Roadside

When I was little, my dad was my favorite person. I couldn't wait to be around him or get a letter or gift from him. The distance was so great that the gifts were very few. During my childhood, my brother and I received gifts on our birthdays, Christmas and Easter. While my dad was in Germany, the gifts always included gummi candy. I loved getting anything; it made me feel closer to my dad.

One summer—I was about ten—I was so excited. My dad was coming to pick us up and take us to the reservation.. My dad is a full-blood Navajo; I am half. It had been a while since I had seen my dad. I was super excited to spend some time with him and my aunties.

Once we got to the reservation, we stayed with my dad's sister, Margaret, who is my dad's bestie. They are thick as thieves. I love seeing the two of them together. They are always smiling together and laughing in each other's company.

My aunt taught us all how to make jewelry. We learned how to bead necklaces and bracelets for the tourist. They were definitely authentically made by Native Americans. We were cheap labor, and I loved doing it. I would work for hours following her patterns and guidelines. I would string beads and crimp wires all day in between play when it was too hot outside.

When it was time to go roadside, we would all wake up early. The smell of coffee would be lingering in the air. We would eat our breakfast and head out the door.

One morning before we left, I found my aunt's make-up. I found a red lip liner pencil. I had recently seen a magazine article about geishas. I thought it was beautiful how their eyes had been lined with red in one of the pictures. I thought it would be cool to line my eyes like the geisha girls, so I did. Nobody seemed to notice that I had these red-lined eyes.

By the time we got roadside, I had fallen asleep in the van. Everyone set up the stand, and I remained in the van asleep. It warmed quickly in the desert and even more quickly in the van in the sun. I woke up sweating.

I got out of the van. I opened the door, and a light breeze kissed my face, cooling off the sweat. I walked over to the stand to get out of the direct sunlight. My brother was the first to see me. He took one look at me and started laughing loudly. I had no idea what he was laughing at. I was constantly the cause of his laughter, but I didn't see how waking from an early nap could trigger his amusement. Maybe it was my hair. I ignored him and went off.

I found my auntie. She took one look at me and laughed. I was puzzled. Everyone was laughing at me. Taking my hand, she led me over to my dad, who also laughed at the sight of me. I was beginning to feel upset. I didn't know why they were all laughing.

Finally, my auntie grabbed one of the mirrors from the stand. She handed it to me and told me to look. I took the mirror from her and gazed at my reflection.

While I had napped in the hot van, my geisha lip liner/eyeliner had run down my face like red tears. I looked like a deranged, crying clown. It was funny, but I was embarrassed. I immediately started to cry. Crying was always, and still is, my go-to emotion. That only made everyone laugh even more. It wasn't mean laughing; they gave me a towel and some water to wash my face. Needless to say, I never tried to be a geisha again.

We continued to sell jewelry roadside the rest of the day. Nothing else happened.

At some point during that summer, I thought it would be a good thing to sell cool drinks to the tourists. I asked if I could do that. My dad said yes. He went with me to the 7 to 11 and purchased different sodas and ice. We put all those things in the cooler. I think we sold them for fifty cents a can.

It didn't go over as well as I thought it would. Only a few tourists bought them. I was making very little profit. My brother had taken to helping himself to my soda stash, without my knowledge. At the end of the day, my dad asked me for the reimbursement of his investment from my soda adventure. I broke even and barely had any soda left over. My brother had drunk most of my stock. I decided that the soda business was not for me.

Whenever we would sell roadside, my aunt would give us a percentage of what we sold. We would keep track of what we sold, and at the end of the day, she would give us our money. It was a nice way to earn some cash as kids. We didn't make big sales, but sometimes we could make some money.

Many tourists came through. Single car families stopped all the time, but the real money came from the busses that frequented our stand. Most of the busses were Asian tourists of some sort. They loved the Native American stuff. They would buy one of everything. It didn't matter what it was. They were infatuated with it.

One time, my brother was talking to a group of tourists who were looking at some pottery.

I overheard him say, "Yeah, I made that."

The tourist exclaimed, "Really, you made this?"

"Yeah, I made this one, too." And he held up another piece of pottery.

My brother has never made any pottery in his life, except maybe something with Play-Doh.

The tourist became very excited and started to speak in his native language to a couple of other people around him. There was a buzz of excitement. A few other people gathered around the tourist my brother had been talking to.

The tourist said, "I want to buy the pottery, but I want to take a picture with you."

My brother said, "Yeah, that's fine."

In the end, the tourist took a picture with my brother. The tourist left with his Indian pictures and pottery. In truth, it was authentic Native American pottery, just not by that Native American.

I remember thinking, I couldn't believe he had swindled that guy. I still can't quite believe it. My aunt had no idea. But the guy was gullible and willing to believe anything, and my brother was young and hungry for a sale. The bottom of the pottery was signed with someone else's name. The tourist had a good story to tell. He got an authentic Indian experience.

It's Complicated

While I was under the age of twelve, we visited the reservation with my dad a handful of times. I'm not sure at what point he came back stateside. I remember he was stationed in Colorado for a little bit. Tom and I visited one summer while we visited our grandparents.

While my dad was in Colorado, we took swim lessons in a very cold pool surrounded by green grass in mild weather. I was very homesick. I cried for my mom. I remember trying to crawl into bed with my dad and his wife. They wouldn't let me sleep with them. I kept having to be sent back to my bed. I don't blame them. I don't always like the kids sleeping with me. I was little, but I remember just being homesick. I had stomachaches and they gave me some sort of creamy medicine from a blue bottle to ease my stomach. It was also the first time having to eat liver. It was disgusting.

At some point, my dad moved to Maryland. My brother and I never visited my dad in Maryland as kids. My parents could never agree on who was going to pay for the flights to Maryland. My dad wanted it to come out of the child support. My mom said she couldn't afford it. My dad said he couldn't afford it. It really was a matter of money why we never visited the East Coast. Then, as we got older, we just never discussed visiting. I had the wedge between my father and me and I don't know what the relationship was with my dad and Tom. We just never visited.

When I was twelve, I was angry at the world as teenagers can be. My dad called for my birthday. My dad and I struggled with phone calls. We rarely talked throughout the year, mostly only talked on my birthday. We talked about the weather and a little about school.

As the phone call was ending, my dad said, "I love you."

I replied, "Okay. Bye."

He responded, "Aren't you going to say you love me?"

"Why should I say I love you when I hardly know you?"

My dad became upset and hung up the phone. He called right back, but I wouldn't speak to him. I could hear my mom speaking to him from the other room. I was crying.

My dad, my hero. The man, who I just wanted to love me, had said he loved me, but I was upset. It made sense to me. We hardly knew each other. We had only seen each other but a handful of times. We talked on the phone once a year for my birthday. We received presents. In my teenage mind, that wasn't love; that was obligation.

Looking back at this situation from a parent's perspective, thirty-odd years later, I have a very different view. As a parent, I would always love my child, from the moment they were born. I would care for that child, even if they were on the opposite side of the world. I would never stop loving them. I would have been devastated had my boys said what I had said to my dad. My heart would have been broken. I'm sure my dad felt that.

That phone conversation changed things between my dad and me. Our relationship became strained. We had always struggled to talk about things, but now we never talked. My dad and his family continued to send cards for my birthday and Christmas, but I had made a void in our relationship.

The next time I saw my dad was when I was sixteen. My brother and I drove to the reservation for a family gathering. My dad was visiting from the East Coast. It was a nice visit. There wasn't any hardship. I loved seeing my dad. He was great. He hugged me and kissed me. He told me he missed me. It hurt my heart that I had said those things as a kid.

* * *

My dad had two daughters with his second wife, Natalie and Katrina. For most of my life, I was the baby sister—felt like the baby sister—when in reality, I was also a big sister.

Growing up, we lived separate lives. We never saw much of each other. We rarely visited one another. We grew up on opposite ends of the country. They lived in Maryland and I lived in Nevada.

I met them as a child on a few occasions when my dad picked up my brother and me to take us to the reservation to visit family. They were kids; I was a kid, just a few years older.

I was a little jealous of them. I was jealous they got to have a real family with a mom and our dad. It seemed so perfect. I didn't want to leave my mom, but I wanted a little bit of that.

Daughter of Girlfriends

After my parents divorced, my mom went on one date with a man that I can remember, but for the most part, she was single. She went to college, took care of us, and then found her career working in the jail as a corrections officer. She went on to become the first female lieutenant at the jail.

One day, she introduced us to a woman named Regan. Regan came over to the house many times and spent a lot of time with us. Then she moved in with us as my mom's roommate. They shared a room. I didn't think anything about it. I was in the third or fourth grade.

One day, before I left for school, my mom pulled one of those, "I've got to talk to you when you get home." That shit made me crazy when I was little and gives me massive anxiety now as an adult. While walking to school, it hit me what she wanted to talk to me about. I paused in front of the green two-story house. Stopped dead in my tracks, I took a deep breath, said out loud, "My mom is gay."

Hmm, I thought.

I continued to walk to school. The thought passed through my mind as I counted the cracks in the sidewalk and looked for my friends to come out and walk with me. The thought was in my mind and out just as quickly.

I did not think about it at all that day at school. When I returned home from school, I didn't think about it.

Sometime that evening, my mom and I had a discussion about it. My mom was upset and anxious about talking about the subject. I was very accepting. It was my mom. I just loved her.

She told me it needed to be kept a secret. I couldn't tell anyone. It was a matter of safety. If anyone knew, my brother and I might be taken away from my mom. People might think she was an unfit parent. People would be prejudiced and discriminate against her. They might hurt her. There were lots of reasons to keep it a secret.

Regan was my mom's first big crush in the gay world. Regan wasn't very tall, but she was taller than me. She had light brown, curly hair. She had a swagger when she walked. Regan was sort of accepted as a part of our lives. Not everyone liked Regan, but they tolerated her because they loved my mom. My mom is a very loving person. She is kind and sweet. She has the patience of a saint. If she had become a nun, like she thought about at one time, she probably would have become a saint.

I didn't mind Regan. I thought she was fascinating. She was in an all-girl rock band named Karizma. She could sing and play instruments. I got to try out all the instruments, including a saxophone that I could squeak out "Mary Had a Little Lamb" on. Regan gave me a used red drum set. I kept it in my room. She was nice to me for the most part. Except when it came to food.

She was a stickler for eating what was put in front of you. I was not a picky eater, but we were never required to clean our plates before. I also did not like seafood. Canned tuna was the only seafood that I could handle.

My first disagreement with Regan came when she cooked scallops for dinner. Nasty little squishy, fishy-tasting things. It was disgusting. I was required to eat everything on my plate. I don't think my mom was home. Regan was in charge. I had to eat the scallops. I excused myself and went to the bathroom, where I rinsed my mouth with Anbesol. I returned with a numb mouth, chewed and swallowed the nasty scallops, possibly biting a cheek. Then I went to the bathroom and threw them up.

My brother did not get along with Regan from the get-go. They fought and fought. Tom would say the sky was blue, and Regan would say it was green. It didn't matter what it was, they fought over it.

My mom would try to be the peacekeeper. I kept my head down. It was not a peaceful time in our household, but my mom was in love. How could we fault her? She deserved happiness. She had been without companionship for so long. But did it have to be with Regan?

Things with Regan did not last long. Regan got physical with my brother. I don't know what preceded the incident, but they had been arguing. Regan grabbed Tom by the front of his shirt, twisted her hands into fists in it and slammed him against the wall. She got real close to his face and was yelling at him.

Shortly after, Regan moved out. My mom was alone again but not for long.

Soon after, my mom met my stepmom. Their friends, sort of on the sly, introduced them to each other. They started dating. They fell in love.

We loved Sara. Sara had short, dark hair and beautiful,

brown, shining eyes that lit up when she smiled. Sara's smile filled her face and everyone's with joy. It brightened up the world. She moved to Las Vegas from Illinois. She was younger than my mom. She started off working security and then became a police officer. While she was going to the police academy, we used to drill her on the codes for the calls. She would drill us on the make and model of the vehicles in front of us while driving places. She was fun. She was not mean. She didn't make us eat bad food. She had a sense of humor. She liked to go do fun things. She would do kid stuff.

When it was decided she would move in, my brother was over the moon. Sara had the nicest furniture Tom had ever seen. He was sold on Sara, just based on the furniture alone. We could get rid of our old furniture and have some nice new stuff.

Sara became an instant part of our family. She fit like a missing piece. Everyone liked her, not just for my mom's sake, but because Sara was a genuinely nice person. Plus, she had a great laugh.

At some point, Sara was no longer just my mom's girlfriend; she was my stepmom. She was my parent.

Sara co-parented my brother and me in all the necessary ways.

She taught us how to drive. She taught us how to defend ourselves. She taught us how to stand up for ourselves. She taught us to be great human beings.

When my brother was being bullied at school, she found a Kung Fu teacher and took him for lessons. She didn't just drop him off and leave him. She trained with him. In turn, sometimes, I would train with them too, if they needed an extra person.

She always took the time to be interested in our lives.

When I thought I wanted to be a marine biologist in the sixth grade, Sara took me to scuba diving lessons. I became the youngest certified diver in Las Vegas at the time. Sara and I went to diving school together at a little place on the east side of Vegas. We did our open water dives in Lake Mead on Pole Line Road. An ear infection caused Sara to miss the last open water dive with me. I was certified, and she was not.

She taught me to change out the distributor cap on my car. My white Geo Prism had malfunctioned on the way back from the rez. Tom and I barely made it back. Sara diagnosed the problem. She said the best way to learn was by doing. So, I did.

She was tough on us. She was a strict disciplinarian. She was someone I never wanted to disappoint. She abhorred liars and cheats.

One time, I was supposed to return some movies to the movie store. I had already driven all the way home. We lived on the outskirts of town. I realized as I pulled in the driveway that the movies were still in the car. I figured I would do it in the morning. What harm would it do? I'd pay the late fee.

I went inside the house. Sara asked if the movies had been returned. I lied that they had been. The phone rang. The movie store was asking if the movies had been returned. Sara said yes, they had been. The movie store said no, they hadn't been. Sara hollered at me, "Did you or did you not return the movies?"

I responded, "No, they are in the car."

She told the movie store they were on their way right now. I got right in the car and returned them.

Man, she was hot. I got a verbal beating about lying and whatnot. She was so disappointed in me. I felt it all week. It was hard letting her down. I tried not to lie again, but of course being a kid I did.

Sara is the most loving person in the world. When I was pregnant with my son, Patrick, I almost miscarried. I had moved out of the house. I was couch surfing and didn't know what my future held. When I got into trouble, I called her. She immediately picked me up and took me to the doctor. She then made a plan to let me come home. She loved me unconditionally.

Sara is not only the best thing that happened to my mom; she is the best thing that happened to my brother and me. We grew up with the best parents. I did get the family unit I was always wanting. I did not get a mom and a dad, but I got a mom and mom.

I've watched over the years as people have discriminated against my parents. When they bought their first house, they went over to insure it.

I remember walking into the insurance company office. The man was cold and unwelcoming. He was being difficult. I don't know all the grown-up logistics that were being gone over, but I saw my parents' reactions and felt the chill in the air. My mom paled and was near tears. At some point, they said something to the man about not needing his services and got up and left.

It was a strange shuffle getting into the car. It was a silent walk with heavy air around us. Immediately after getting in the car, my mom started to cry. Sara was frustrated. She reached a hand over to my mom. It was the first time I had seen blatant bigotry in refusal of services for a gay couple.

My parents solved their problem by finding new a new insurance broker who welcomed them both and did not discriminate against them. I think they are still with him to this day.

My parents have been together for over thirty years. That's longer than many straight couples. They have a healthy, loving relationship. They raised two great kids. I am lucky that my mom fell in love with such a beautiful woman. I lucked out to have mom to the power of two.I am lucky to have been raised by such powerful women. I am blessed to be the daughter of girlfriends.

Survivor's Tale

When I was eight or nine years old, my uncle, Evan, sexually abused me at my grandparents' house in Colorado. I locked it away and didn't tell anyone but my grandmother until I was fifteen years old.

My mom is one of nine siblings. My grandmother had two daughters from a previous marriage. Then she married my grandfather and had my mom and six other children. My mom is the oldest. My mom is the only one out of her siblings who does not have addiction issues with alcohol or drugs.

Two of my uncles, Evan and Kevin, were often unemployed, homeless and drunk. They often lived at home with my grandparents. When my mom came home to visit, my grandpa kicked them out of the house to live outside or in the shed. They rarely slept in the house. But when she was gone, they came back inside the house.

While we were guests at my grandparents, my brother and I slept in the living room. We took turns sleeping on the couch and on the floor in front of the TV. There was this giant velveteen pillow with fringe that we used as the main pillow. It was like a headrest when we slept on the floor. Then other pillows were propped against it in front of the coffee table.

It was my turn to sleep on the couch, but Tom had somehow

convinced me to give him my turn on the couch for TV time the next day. As I lay on the hard, thinly carpeted floor, I already regretted my deal and felt I had been swindled. My brother was a pro at getting his way and had likely persuaded me with one of my favorite things on TV. Probably another showing of *Mommy Dearest.*

It was dark. Late at night. The TV was off. The lights were off. The curtains were all closed. The front door was closed and locked.

I felt somebody lying next to me. A rough hand inside my shirt, brushing my skin. Slowly the hand started rubbing between my legs.

My eyes popped open. I thought I was dreaming. I tried to sit up, but the hand pushed me back down. A husky voice just whispered to me to lie down, so I lay down. I didn't know what to do.

I wiggled. I tried to roll over. A firm hand rolled me back.

The hand kept moving. I just stayed still hoping it would just stop. I realized it was Uncle Evan. He was telling me to be a good girl and stay where I was.

He took my hand and put it down his pants. He formed my hand around his penis and made me jack him off. Once he got hard, he took his pants all the way off. He pushed my face into his groin and made me put my mouth on him. I didn't know what to do. He just kept pushing it at me. I put it in my mouth. He thrust it back and forth.

I cried.

I choked. He pulled it out.

I lay back down. I pulled the blanket back down. I didn't know what to do. I got up and went to the bathroom. Maybe if I just went to the bathroom, he wouldn't be there when I got back.

I don't know how long I was gone, but when I went back, he was still there. I was afraid to wake anybody up. My brother was only a few feet away on the couch. My grandparents were in their room twenty feet away. I was afraid I was going to get into trouble. I tried to ignore him and lay back down. His pants were back on. It looked like he was asleep.

I lay on my side away from him. As far as I could but still in my assigned sleeping area. But he wasn't asleep. As soon as I lay down, his hands were all over me again between my legs. Fingers forced inside me under my panties. He kept asking me if I liked it. He didn't wait for an answer; he just kept doing it. I kept trying to roll away, but I kept getting rolled back.

I don't know when it stopped. I don't remember going back to sleep. It's just blank and black. Lost time.

The next thing I remember is my grandpa coming in and opening the curtains in the living room and asking how I slept. I wanted to tell him everything. I just didn't know what to say.

I waited for my grandma to get up. She was a late sleeper. She didn't get up until the afternoon soap operas started. I went in to see her, and I told her. I sat on her bed. The curtains had just been opened. She was still in her nightgown. I cried and told her everything that happened to me. I told her that Evan had done these terrible things to me.

My grandmother called my uncle into the room. He sat on grandpa's bed. The light was shining in on me through the window casting him in a shadow. She asked him if he did these things that I had accused him of.

He responded, "I did. I had a little too much to drink. I'm really sorry."

My grandmother said, "Okay. This is over. Go give your

uncle a hug. We will never talk about this again."

That was that.

I never told anyone about it again. Not a soul. I began to suffer from insomnia. I had nightmares.

* * *

It was shortly after that, back home in Vegas, that I made my first suicide attempt. I went into the bathroom and looked for anything labeled poisonous. I found some sort of cleaner. It was blueish green. There was about a quarter of it left in the bottle. I drank it. It tasted terrible. I looked for other things in the bathroom that would be unsafe to consume but couldn't find anything other than the toothpaste saying it was unsafe to eat in large quantities. I ate some of that, too.

With a minty mouth and an upset stomach, I went to my room to die. I lay down in my bed, curled up, hoping to die.

It happened quickly. I didn't make it to the bathroom. The vomit came before I could even react. All over the thin brown carpet by the doorway of my closed room. Just liquid. I don't recall anyone being home. I got to the bathroom between heaves, leaving a trail of blue mess. In front of the toilet, I mostly dry heaved and cried.

I cradled the toilet and tossed what was left in my stomach up. A bit of blue with an after-mint taste came up. I felt defeated.

I quickly got some towels and cleaned up the mess I had made. I still don't recall anyone being home. I was alone. I cleaned up. Changed my clothes and put myself to bed.

I stared at the ceiling wishing to die. Why hadn't I died? How come I failed at that? Why couldn't we have something that could actually kill me?

I felt so defeated. I felt too embarrassed that I had failed at killing myself to tell someone that I had felt like killing myself. I didn't even know how to reach out to someone. I just sat there, alone in the dark.

My first attempt. A failure and a success. I suppose after I didn't succeed, I was relieved. I didn't really want to die. I just felt like it at the time. The moment passed as they always do.

I don't know why I didn't want to tell my mom. I didn't tell anyone. I was confused. I had a calamity of emotions I didn't understand. I felt if I told on myself, I would get into trouble. I needed to keep this secret like I kept the sexual abuse a secret. Who would believe me? What was I really thinking? I didn't truly understand the emotions I was going through. I understood I was in pain, and I wanted it to stop. I understood that death was an ending that would stop the emotions that were playing havoc in my mind.

Looking back, I know my mom would have helped me. She would have gotten me the help I desperately needed, and it may have changed my whole life, but I wasn't ready to let go of my secrets. They were locked in my fortress of solitude.

It was during this time I stopped sleeping. I could only sleep if the radio or record player was playing. It would play and I would fall asleep, but around two in the morning, I would wake up and could not go back to sleep. I would get out of bed and go watch TV. When I heard my mom's alarm go off, I would go back to bed and pretend I had been in bed all night. It didn't happen every night, but many nights.

* * *

After the abuse, I was quiet. I played by myself a lot of time in my messy room. I stopped changing my clothes. I didn't care that my clothes were dirty. I only changed them because my mom expected me to change them and noticed when I didn't. After I told my grandma about the abuse; I was hurt by the way it had been handled—but it had been handled. An adult that I had trusted and loved told me that was the end of it. It couldn't go any further.

I wanted to tell my grandpa, but my grandma had said that was the end of it. I wanted to tell my mom she would do something, but grandma had said that was the end of it.

It ate away at me. I felt a light go out in me. I tried to live my life as a little kid as I had before, but things were different. I was different. I felt dirty, like I couldn't wash off my uncle's touch from me.

I was always a bit shy around people I didn't know. I never spoke to grown-ups I didn't know. I needed to be prompted to speak and introduce myself. I never ordered my own meals in a restaurant. I didn't do that until Sara came along and forced me to start speaking up for myself. I retreated further into myself.

I didn't tell anyone about the abuse. I didn't tell Dani. I just sat on that secret because it had been dealt with by a trusted adult.

I felt sad and alone. I sat with my stuffed animals in my room for hours at my little house in my little room. I was depressed. I stopped sleeping at night. I couldn't think straight. I would cry at times for reasons that I could not explain. This was the start of my serious mood swings.

It was always thought that I was just a sensitive child. I would get my feeling hurt easily. My brother teased me relentlessly. I would cry. He would get yelled at and I would cry. I would watch something on TV where someone was hurting, and I would cry. I would see someone's pain and I would cry. I couldn't control myself.

At times, I was fine. I wasn't always moody. I would play with other kids and have fun. But under the surface, while playing four square in front of the house, there was always this darkness bubbling. I would think about death. I would think about what it was like to be dead. Would others mourn me like I mourn others? What would it be like to be dead? Would there be pain? Would there be peace? Would I have these thoughts when I was dead? Would the pain end?

I had these thoughts as a young kid after the abuse. They were intrusive but did not happen all the time. They started to increase as I went through adolescence. I think the hormones rapidly changed my brain chemistry. The moodiness increased, and the intensity of the moods increased. The response to the mood became more desperate and severe.

Not too long after the abuse, Dani moved and went to a different school. That was hard for me even though we still hung out together on weekends. Dani and I were bonded. It was difficult for me to make friends. I was shy for the most part. I felt I didn't fit in. I was a loner. I was moody. Dani could see past all that and just accepted me for who I was. She knew who I was before all the moodiness had set in.

With Dani, I could be outgoing and loud. We could be outrageous together. She gave me confidence. We talked each other up. We laughed together. When we become teenagers, we started going to the mall. We would hike long distances to the mall just to hang out and walk around some more.

Dani moved to Montana as a teenager. We only saw each

other during the summers. It was hard to lose my best friend. We had been inseparable for years. Now, she was gone. I lost the person that I could laugh with, the person that made me believe in myself. That's when I made friends with Felicity and the HAB Posse. That emotional bond sealed in friendship for a lifetime helped me through the tough times of my teenage years.

Inciting Incidents in School Settings

When I was growing up in Las Vegas, all the inner-city kids were bussed out of their neighborhoods and into the white suburbs for most of their school careers, with the exception of sixth grade. This was the school district's way of ending segregation. They did not build schools in the inner city and allow these students to go to their zoned schools but gave them the privilege of attending superior schools in a white district to add color to our schools.

During sixth grade, however, all the white suburban kids were bussed to sixth-grade centers in the inner city, and the inner-city kids were allowed to walk to their zoned school for one year. This was how the Clark County School District solved segregation. This policy stayed in effect into the 1990s when schools were finally built in the inner cities.

This was my first time being around a majority of minority students. At the elementary school I went to, my brother and I were the only natives. There was one black student, Aquila. It was different to be surrounded by so many people of color. It was nice not to be the only brown person, even though I saw myself as white, mostly.

My sixth-grade center was Kermit Booker. It was a transition year. We had homeroom, and we rotated classes as a group. It was supposed to get us ready for middle school and how middle school classes transition from class to class.

My homeroom teacher was also my math teacher, Mr. Randolf. He had a glass eye. I recall he was a nice man but accused me of cheating. I swore up and down that I didn't cheat off Jamie's test. Even her mom came in and defended me. Honestly, all these years later, I can't say if I did or didn't cheat. It was a math test, so I might have. It's not my strongest subject.

One of the scariest things that happened during sixth grade was the PEPCON explosion. PEPCON was a chemical company that exploded in Henderson, Nevada. It was right next to a marshmallow factory. It caused both factories to blow up. The explosion rocked Las Vegas. It was like a bomb went off. Houses and buildings had doors and windows blown out. It killed two people, injured a few hundred, and caused over a million dollars in damages.

We were in North Las Vegas when the explosion happened. We didn't know what was going on. We went into a lockdown mode. We were told to stay in the classrooms. We didn't rotate to our next class. We just stayed in one room. No news as to what was happening in the world. We thought a bomb had gone off. It was so powerful the lights flickered, and the ceiling tiles shifted.

At the end of the day, we were allowed to go home on the busses. It just seemed like a really long day. Nobody would tell us anything. I don't know if it was because we were kids or that they didn't know anything. I didn't know the extent of what had happened until we watched the news that evening at home.

A few months later, my mom's friend Jeannie took me for a

drive out along the ridge in Henderson. We drove out by the explosion site. It was still blackened. It smelled like burnt marshmallows. There were splashes of burnt marshmallows all over the rocks.

One of the teachers at our school lived in Henderson. All the windows in her home had been blown out. The back door of her home had been blown off its hinges. She brought pictures to school at some point and showed us what had happened. Other than that, we were untouched by the disaster.

The PEPCON explosion was scary for me because there was so much unknown danger in the world. I remember being fearful of the world. I thought World War III was going to happen any time. I was scared of a nuclear war, and the bomb feeling of PEPCON really freaked me out, even though it was not a bomb.

I had joined the drill team at school. It was something akin to dance, which I loved to do. I didn't really know what a drill team was. I guess it was a cross between dance and cheerleading. I don't know what we were cheering for or leading or dancing for. We didn't have any sports teams in sixth grade, but we practiced our little hearts out. Plus, we got out of class to practice during the day, since we couldn't stay after school because most of us were bussed in.

Our school colors were black and yellow. Mustard yellow. Not sunny, dandelion yellow. Nasty yellow. You would think with those colors, our mascot would have been a hornet, but it was a cat of some sort. Our uniforms were a two-toned yellow and black skirt and a t-shirt that had the school name on it. Our drill team uniform included pompoms and white sneakers. I'm pretty sure I signed up just for the pompoms. It was kind of like cheerleading but without kicking. The white sneakers I remember because mine were knock offs.

At some point during the year, we had a performance. My mom and Sara came and watched me do my drill team thing. I want to say we had lunch and then they left. Dark clouds filled the sky, warning they would let loose their fill of water. They took my pompoms home with them so I wouldn't have to walk home in the rain with them after school.

After the performance, the day went on as usual. Went to class. Did this. Did that. Bell rang. Time to leave. We all started filing out toward the busses.

I started freaking out. My anxiety started buzzing. My heart was pounding. I couldn't find my pompoms. I had completely forgotten my parents had taken them home.

Donte, a tall black boy who incessantly teased me, started in on me.

"You gonna cry? You lost your pompoms?"

"No. I'm not gonna cry," I said through tears.

"You should be worried about those nasty shoes you got on. Are those a K-Mart special?" he goaded me.

"Leave me alone."

"Aw. Poor baby crying?" He laughed as he spoke. Several other kids surrounded us as he poked me in the shoulder to make his point.

Damn. He wouldn't stop. Full-on tears rolled down my face in anger and embarrassment.

Looking down, I saw a fresh puddle of water had pooled on the concrete. A HUGE puddle.

We were still slowly walking toward the busses. He walked right behind the puddle. I screamed something at him to get his attention. He turned toward me. I turned my foot sideways and dragged it through the puddle, creating a tower of water that seemed to be six feet tall.

It would have covered him completely. I would have been avenged.

However, at that exact second, my P.E. teacher stepped right in front of my triumphant wave and blocked the processional. She was soaked. Her face was dripping wet. I can still see her blinking the dirty water out of her eyes.

I was in shock. I had never done anything like that before to a student, let alone to a teacher.

I was quickly snatched up and taken to the administrative offices. I wasn't allowed to get on the bus. My mom was called and had to come and pick me up from school.

I cried and cried. Cried because I was caught. Cried because I didn't mean to hurt my teacher. Cried because my mom was mad. Cried because I was crying.

I got into trouble. I had to write an apology to the teacher. My parents wouldn't let me explain that I hadn't been aiming to get the teacher but another student; they said that wouldn't be an acceptable apology. So, I just wrote, "I'm sorry."

Donte didn't get into any trouble over this situation. He continued to tease me about my shoes, but less and less frequently. By the end of the year, he found a new target, and I had new shoes.

* * *

The second time I got into trouble was when I got into a fight in junior high school. It wasn't really a fight so much as a one-sided ass beating on my part.

Michelle Baxter, a girl who I had known since grade school,

a girl who I had classes with in grade school, called me a whore, and I lost my shit.

In junior high, I kept to myself. I hung out with some of the goth and stoner kids. I was friendly with everyone. For the most part, I kept to myself. I hung out with a girl named Felicity, but that was about it. I didn't seek out attention. I was a good kid. I didn't get into fights. I didn't cause trouble. I had good grades, except PE, because I refused to dress out, and the teacher hated me. I wasn't a bad kid.

As I recall, it was just a regular day. We were in Mr. Rolfe's math class. He was passing out papers. He had passed out papers to the front of the row, and we were to take one and hand the rest back. I took mine and passed the stack back to Michelle. She took the stack and looked me dead in the face and said, "You're a whore."

I was stunned and instantly infuriated. I held onto the papers. I stared back at her and told her, "You're fucking dead." And I meant it. I wanted to fucking kill her. Who the fuck did she think she was? How did I offend her? So what if I wore a short skirt? So what if I wore dark make-up? Why the fuck did that make me a whore?

Sure, I wasn't a virgin, but nobody knew that. Only the boyfriend I had been seeing during the summer knew that. Nobody knew him. He went to a different school. I had told no one. I had sex with one boy. I wasn't ashamed, and that didn't make me a whore.

Mr. Rolfe went on about math something or other as I seethed in anger for the next hour in class. Michelle must have realized that I was pissed because when the bell rang, she darted for the door. She was fast, but I was quick on her tail.

Right outside the door, I grabbed the back of her sweater

and yanked her toward me. I screamed at her, "Why am I a fucking whore?"

She stammered, "You're just a whore."

A crowd had started to gather around us. I said, "Oh yeah? Well, this whore is going to kick your ass!"

Let me say at this point, Michelle was all of five feet tall, maybe. That's being generous. She was also very petite. Junior. She may have been in seventh grade but easily could have been in fourth grade.

I, on the other hand, was five foot seven inches. Size 9 shoe women's. I looked like I should be playing varsity basketball.

Back to the ass kicking.

I still had hold of her sweater from behind. I hurled her into the locker. She slammed face first with a thud. She dropped all her school supplies; mine had been thrown to the ground. She looked stunned.

I stalked toward her. I grabbed her again and threw her to the ground. She hit the ground and rolled over. I kicked her, and she rolled over. Somehow her ass was in the air, so I kicked that too.

At that point, the crowd started gathering attention. I came out of my bloodlust and realized, holy shit, I was going to get in trouble. I picked up my binder and ran away. I ran not only down the hallway but off campus and across the street to Felicity's house. Her mom let me in and let me stay there the rest of the day.

I told Maggie, her mom, what happened, and she said, "Good. Sounds like she deserved it. Good for you."

I went home at the time I was supposed to go home. Except when I got home, my mom had gotten a call from the school. I had two infractions, the fight and ditching. I was being RPC'd.

A Required Parent Conference.

I explained to my mom what had happened. My mom yelled a little at me about how we don't hit people. My mom was very much a pacifist. She did not condone the violence and did not approve of my methods. I was grounded. She also did not like that I had been bullied by this girl and did like that I stood up for myself. My mom was upset that she had to take time off from work. She thought I was starting to hang out with the wrong crowd of people.

At the RPC meeting, the dean went on to say that I had really done a number on the other student. Michelle had been so scared that she refused to say who had beat her up, and it was only through other student interviews that they figured out it was me. It was also hard for the faculty to believe it was me because I was so quiet, good, and docile. They wanted to hear my side of the story.

I gave my side of the events and told them that I just snapped. I didn't mean to hurt Michelle and that I felt bad that I had done it. Honestly, I felt really bad. I had never hurt someone before in my life. I'm not a violent person.

At the RPC, the dean said being violent was unacceptable, and I needed to channel my energy into doing something creative. She had seen my art, and Mrs. Treat, the art teacher, spoke highly of me. My English teacher mentioned that my writing was also coming along nicely, and that I should consider writing for the school paper. That was where she left it.

I had a day off school for kicking the ass of a girl who called me a whore. Michelle got her ass beat for being a loudmouth bitch and a bully. I got advice to be creative instead of being violent, and I was allowed back in school.

I never got into any real trouble again. I never got violent with anyone at school again.

Note: The day after my RPC, I saw Michelle walking home alone. We walked the same route to school daily. I ran after her trying to apologize. I'd never seen anyone run so fast in all my life. I did truly feel remorseful. I learned that you can't always apologize for things you do wrong, and you don't always get forgiven for the bad things you do.

Depression and Drinking

That was the year I started drinking alcohol, lost my virginity and made my second suicide attempt. It doesn't always seem obvious to me that these things were related. I know I was uncomfortable in my skin. I thought I was ugly. I was drawn to people who said I was pretty, but I never really believed them. I had poor self-esteem. I was always looking for someone to make me feel better about myself, though I didn't like compliments too much; they made me uncomfortable because I didn't believe people thought I was pretty. I did dress in short mini-skirts, but it was the 80s.

There was no fanfare when I lost my virginity. I thought I was in love with my high school summer love boyfriend, Bryce. He was my first big love. We had hung out all summer. We had made out all summer.

He was older than me by a few years. I was just going into middle school. He was either in high school or going into high school. He was not a virgin. Our make-out sessions kept getting hot and heavy, and the pressure to do the next thing was building and building. I gave in to that pressure.

There was a buildup to it. It would always start with the making out and heavy petting. Bryce would usually start grinding on me and make a play to try to have sex. I would say

I wasn't ready, and he would back off. But he was persistent. It was always the same. Making out, groping, grinding, pressure. I wanted to please him since I'm a people-pleaser. I gave in.

I don't know how we ended up in the bathroom. Maybe it was because it was the only room in the house that had a door that locked, but we ended up having sex in his downstairs bathroom. It was dirty, and it was quick.

It wasn't romantic. No sweeping song. No basking in the afterglow. Our clothes didn't even come all the way off, just our pants.

We only had sex a couple of times, and then our fling was over. I'm sure that's all he was in it for. It was convenient. My best friend lived on the street over from him, and I spent most of the summer at her house. So, in turn, we spent a lot of time together at his house. My friend was also hooking up with his friend, so we were a duo all summer. We went our separate ways once school started. He was in high school; I was in junior high.

Losing my virginity didn't seem like anything special. I didn't understand what was so special about saving it for someone. We weren't religious people, so saving it until marriage didn't make sense. That was never a virtue that had been instilled in me. I'm sure having sex as a twelve-year-old wasn't something that was ideal either.

I didn't see what the big deal was. It wasn't all that fun. It didn't feel good; there was no real excitement except for my boyfriend, and it was messy.

My mom told me about sex but never anything in detail. My dad gave me a crude lesson about sex using a bolt and a nut to show me the details of how sex worked. I knew the mechanics. I didn't understand the big deal. I knew you could get pregnant with sex. I knew you had sex with people you loved. And at the time, I thought I loved Bryce. So, I thought I was following my heart.

Twelve years old is way too young to be experimenting with sex. I know my mom thought so. I don't recall how my mom found out that I was having sex. It was a big thing, as it should have been. She was very disappointed in me. She took me to the doctor to get a pregnancy test. It came back negative. We had a sit-down, and I promised not to have sex anymore. However, there was no putting that genie back in that bottle.

* * *

My second suicide attempt was more of a self-harm episode, though I thought I was attempting suicide. I was twelve years old. I remember being thoroughly upset. Depression was a common occurrence for me. I was easily triggered. It didn't take much.

I went to the pharmacy and bought a package of razor blades. I drew a warm bath. Got into the bath fully clothed. Pulled up my sleeves and began to cut. I sliced several deep cuts across my arms. Deep cuts but not enough to cut the veins.

It was painful. The pain triggered me. The blood dribbled into the warm water and dissipated. More water than blood. I tried to make another cut and just cried. I couldn't get the blade to cut deeper. I tried but I couldn't get it to dig deeper. I don't know if I wasn't physically strong enough or mentally strong enough, but I couldn't do it.

I stood up in the tub. Drained the water, stripped out of the wet clothes and took a shower. When I got out of the shower,

I bandaged my arms. For weeks, I wore long-sleeved shirts. I also wore lots of bracelets. Nobody noticed. I still carry the scars.

I think that's what I took away from both of these moments. Nobody noticed. I wanted to die both of these times, and nobody noticed. Both times, I took my life into my hands and I could have died, and nobody would have prevented it. It was only prevented by my own bumbling.

My mom took me to a counselor. I don't recall what the counselor was for, perhaps my moodiness. Maybe the sex. Her name was Michelle Michele. I was never open with her about my suicide attempts. I was never honest with her about my true feelings. Trust was never established, though I liked her, and we talked. We talked about boys and how I trusted them too much. We never talked about the sexual abuse.

My third attempt was shortly after the razor blades. I decided that bleeding to death was not the way for me. I was either twelve or thirteen. Again, I was depressed, seeking to silence the pain I was feeling. I didn't feel comfortable in my own skin. I didn't like who I was. I didn't want to exist anymore. I didn't think I deserved to be alive. I was not worthy of life. I swallowed a bottle of Tylenol. I thought it was dangerous in large quantities. It just gave me an upset stomach. Made me a little sensitive to the light. Mom wondered where all the Tylenol went.

I was mad because my brother and I had to paint the house the next day. We were in trouble for some reason, and we were scraping paint on the trim of the house. He was cussing and bitching, and I was miserable and sick. Legit sick from the Tylenol, but I couldn't say why I was sick for fear of getting into trouble. For fear of someone finding out my secret of wanting to die. I didn't want anyone to know. I wanted to die. If someone knew that, they would be able to prevent that from happening. If I kept it a secret, I could keep planning until I had the courage or knowhow of how to carry out my plan.

I don't know what I thought they would think if they actually found my body. I just thought I had this secret I needed to keep with my attempts and suicidal ideations.

* * *

The drinking just felt like fun, like something kids do. My mom wasn't a big drinker. She didn't keep a lot of liquor in the house. One of the things she had was a bottle of Kalua. She never drank it. The cap was hard to get off. It was sticky and crusty with age. I loved me some Kalua.

For several days, I started packing a container of Kalua and milk to take to school with me. I would sip it on my way to school. I would sip it during class. My teachers all thought I was drinking chocolate milk. One teacher even commented on how much I loved chocolate milk because she had seen me drinking it each morning. I just smiled and drank some more.

I was never caught. I would just rinse out the bottle when I was done and put it in my backpack. I don't recall how I explained to my mom that the bottle of Kalua was emptied. Maybe it was just one of those unexplained things. But once the bottle was gone, so were my morning cocktails until Felicity's mom interceded.

One weekend, I hung out with my friend Felicity. Felicity and I had become friends at Garside Jr. High during my seventh-grade year. It was a new school. I was an outcast, and Felicity was her own woman. I loved being at Felicity's house. It was wild and crazy. We danced in the kitchen. There was loud music. Everyone was always in a good mood and there was lots of drinking. We could drink, too.

That weekend, Felicity's mom bought us all a couple of bottles of schnapps. I had a bottle of peach schnapps and a bottle of peppermint schnapps.

I knew that my chocolate milk bottle would not do the trick this time, so I had to get creative. I thought and thought. Finally, I decided that an empty hairspray bottle would do the trick. Schnapps was fruity-smelling like hairspray, so nobody would know the difference.

I went to work on thoroughly cleaning the bottle. I didn't want to be drinking hairspray mixed with schnapps, although that's exactly what I got the first couple of sprays.

Now, you have to remember, this was the 80s. Everyone carried hairspray to keep their hair teased high to the sky.

Brazenly, I went to school with my schnapps hairspray. I was a little worried at first. Whenever I wanted a drink, I just went to the bathroom and took a swig. I became bolder and, in the hallways, just sprayed mouthfuls as I walked to class. Nobody gave me a second look.

It took some time to get through two bottles of schnapps that way. I shared with my friends. Pretty soon, there were a couple of us drinking our hairspray and spraying it in our mouths. It truly is a wonder that none of us were ever caught. As I grew up, I partied on and off. I never had a great dependence on alcohol. It was just fun.

HAB

Definition of Gangs: (1) an association of three or more individuals; (2) whose members collectively /identify themselves by adopting a group identity which they use to create an atmosphere of fear or intimidation frequently by employing one or more of the following: a common name, slogan, identifying sign, symbol, tattoo or other physical marking, style or color of clothing, hairstyle, hand sign or graffiti; (3) the association's purpose, in part, is to engage in criminal activity and the association uses violence or intimidation to further its criminal objectives; (4) its members engage in criminal activity, or acts of juvenile delinquency that if committed by an adult would be crimes; (5) with the intent to enhance or preserve the association's power, reputation, or economic resources; (6) the association may also possess some of the following characteristics: (a) the members employ rules for joining and operating within the association; (b) the members meet on a recurring basis; (c) the association provides physical protection of its members from other criminals and gangs; (d) the association seeks to exercise control over a particular location or region, or it may simply defend its perceived interests against rivals; or (e) the association has an identifiable structure. (7) this definition is not intended to include traditional organized crime groups such as La Cosa Nostra, groups that fall within the Department's definition of "international organized crime," drug trafficking organizations or terrorist organizations. https://www.justice.gov/criminal-ocgs/about-violent-gangs

When I was twelve years old, I belonged to a "gang" by the above definition. We were a group of three or more. We had a common name and colors. Some of us did engage in criminal activity. We definitely engaged in juvenile delinquency. "Provides physical protection from others"—yeah, we did. That's about where the overlap with the definition of gang ends. However, my stepmom told me that you only needed a few of these traits to be considered a gang. So, I guess we were a gang.

Our gang was the Hella Bad Posse, HAB. Our colors were neon pink and black. We congregated in two places, Bobby's house and Crystal Palace Skating Rink.

I met this "gang" of people on December 3, 1988. I went with my friend Felicity to the skating rink.. She was fun, loud, and unpopular. She was crude and always said what was on her mind. With that, she was kind and generous. She always gave you what she had; she would share and would literally give you the shirt off her back if you needed it. I fit in with the band of misfits. I met this gang who were also a gang of misfits. It was like the island of misfit toys; together, they were no longer misfits; they were a band of brothers bonded by their outcast status.

We started the evening by being dropped off at someone's house, then walking to someone else's house, then walking to the skating rink. My mom, had she known, would have flipped her lid. I knew I was out of bounds and doing something she didn't approve of. She didn't approve of Felicity and knew she would get me into trouble. I followed her anyway, and we roamed the streets, making our way to the skating rink. Along the way, we met Atom and picked up Dina.

At the skating rink, I met Bobby, Mitch, Ren, and Dirk. They were all accomplished skaters. I recall Mitch having a fishing knife in his boot. That should have been a warning that this was maybe a dangerous area, but no red flags or bells went off.

Everyone was kind, fun and funny. Everyone wanted to talk to me and get to know me. They were all older than me. They were all in high school, while I was in middle school. Immediately, I fell in love with Mitch. I couldn't tell you why. Maybe it was the grey fishing hat. Maybe it was the way he held my hand and kissed it in an old, charming way. But dang, I was lost. We started dating soon after.

We all skated round and round. Loud pop music was booming. Lights were flashing in the dark. The slide of skates on the slick surface of the rink could be heard echoing throughout the room. When we weren't in our claimed dark corner of the rink, we were taking turns skating with each other or skating in packs. All the boys were very proficient skaters and could turn, loop and trick skate. It was wondrous to see. I was in awe. Maybe I was easy to awe, but I loved it.

Mitch was a few years older than me. Light brown hair, almost blond, and light eyes. He had a charming smile that made me smile. He was in high school. We would talk on the phone for hours at a time. We would also write letters to each other even though we lived in the same city but across town. I would send long sappy love letters. He would send me short letters, but they were full of love as well.

Our relationship moved at a quick pace. I'm not sure how long we waited, but it became a sexual relationship. Now that I had had sex, I didn't see what the big deal was to have sex again. My parents both worked late or very early. Mitch would "borrow" his mom's car and drive over. He would park across the street in the parking lot. I would get up and see my parents off. He would be watching from his car. Once my parents were gone, he'd come over, and we'd get it on.

This happened around Christmas time. Mitch brought me mistletoe so we could kiss under it. He also brought me a Santa hat. Sometimes he would bring me a few flowers. It was all very romantic in the eyes of a teenager who was in love.

We went on like that for a while. We were hot and heavy with each other. We continued to see each other at the skating rink on the weekends as well.

Mitch was my first real love. Bryce was my first real boyfriend, but Mitch was my first real love. I loved him with every inch of my being. I wanted to be with him all hours of the day. I couldn't wait to talk on the phone with him. I was lovesick. It was the first time that I had truly felt loved. I felt grownup. I was very naive and honestly thought we were going to be together forever. Our bond was very deep. It was a friendship that would last a lifetime, but the relationship only lasted a couple of months.

My friend Laura, who went to his school, told me he had been flirting with other girls and giving out his number in their band class. He had put it on the board. When I asked him about it, he said it was for help with band. He was a band geek and a good one.

At some point, I was being pursued by another one of the people in our posse, Ren. I really did like all the attention. I liked that someone was paying attention to me. My low self-esteem ate it up. Ren called me when Mitch wasn't paying attention to me as much. Ren, I think, knew that. At some point, I kissed Ren, and that broke up my relationship with Mitch. That was the end of that for now. I went out with Ren.

Ren was tall. He had a mullet. Blond hair and green eyes. He was very sweet but could have a temper. He was also prone to juvenile delinquency.

My parents never really knew about Mitch. It was all very quiet. They didn't understand my heartbreak. But it was lessened by my new boyfriend, Ren, who my parents greatly disliked. That didn't last very long.

Felicity and I skipped school one time to visit Ren in the hospital when he had nose surgery to fix his broken nose. We rode the bus all day to get there. I was scared, but Felicity seemed to know what she was doing. This was one of the reasons my mom didn't like Felicity's influence or Ren's.

By summer, I was back with Mitch. We were on and off. Serious, not serious. My heart broke and healed. School started, and we were broken up again. It was a while before we reunited.

Around this time, I met Jeff. Jeff was several years older than me. Jeff was tall, well built, strong, blue eyes. Jeff smoked. I could always smell a faint smell of cigarette smoke on him when he hugged me. He fell in love with me first. I was just fascinated with him. He was a Canadian. Cute. Devilishly charming. Always said the right things. Romantic. He got his feelings hurt very easily. Jeff and I would go on to love each other on and off for decades. I still love him, just not romantically.

Jeff once brought flowers to my house and got mad that I wasn't there and ripped them up and left them all torn and wilting in my driveway. He was very passionate.

Jeff was always there if I needed a friend, always ready to

help.

Jeff and I kissed in Felicity's house one day, and it was great. I swooned. I got lost in those blue eyes and never wanted the moment to end. Jeff was a great kisser, and his lips were soft. It was a gentle kiss.

At the end of my eighth-grade year, we sold our little house on Chelsea and moved across town to Nellis and Charleston in East Las Vegas. Which happened to be down the street from Mitch's house. We were waiting for our house to be built in Northwest Las Vegas.

Mitch and I began to meet up again. We went back to early morning meetings having sex and sneaking around. We made all these goofy promises of loving each other. We exchanged rings of promise to marry each other. It went on all summer. Then, we moved back to the northwest side of town to an apartment near the school I would be attending for ninth grade, even though our new house wasn't done. That put the kibosh on my meetings with Mitch. Our promises left broken in the summer air.

At the start of ninth grade, I didn't know anyone. I kept to myself. I met a couple of people. I met Jim. Jim offered me a ride home with his friend Charles. When I got out of the car, I slammed the door. Charles yelled at me to be kinder to the car. Little did I know that I had just pissed off my future husband. I didn't really think much of the dude, just that he was a bit of a whiner about his car.

During ninth grade, I started dating a guy named David, and we hit it off. But there was no love there. It was dating and sex.

I didn't see a lot of my friends because we had moved far out to the northwest side of town. They all joked that they needed to pay a long-distance fee to call me out there. It was a good forty-five minutes to an hour drive to get to my house from the city or their side of town.

* * *

My parents went away for a week or maybe two. It might have been one of their trips to Greece or to Colorado. My brother and I were left alone. We were supposed to be responsible.

For the most part, we were responsible. We went to school. We fixed our breakfast and dinner. We did what we were supposed to do. We also did what most teenagers do when parents are away; we threw a series of parties.

I don't recall how many parties we threw. It was several in the course of a couple of nights. They started out as small get-togethers. They grew into large parties. I'm surprised the cops weren't called. Cars were parked around the block into the late hours of the night. We were loud. Nobody was in the front yard. We hung out in the back yard. Loud music poured from the house.

Tom had his group of friends, and I had my group of friends. We didn't really mingle. My friends set up camp in the living room, and his friends set up camp in the kitchen playing quarters on the wood table. That table forever had dings and dents from the quarters nicking it. I had that table all through college and would sometimes run my hand across it and smile at the memory.

One night, my boyfriend David came over and we went to my room. We were drunk and had unprotected sex. I had been casual about sex. Most of the time it was protected sex, but some of the time it wasn't. I wasn't really thinking about the consequences of my actions. I was just having fun. I was living the dream of house partying and playing grown-up. Drinking and smoking, having sex. Doing what I wanted, when I wanted, on my own terms, it was great.

The next night, my boyfriend couldn't come over. Jeff and my other set of friends came over. We partied and got drunk. Jeff and I ended up in my bedroom, and flirting moved to kissing to more. We had unprotected sex.

Writing this now, I cringe at my fifteen-year-old self. Of course, a month later, I received the consequences of my actions. I was pregnant, and worse yet, due to my drunken delinquency, I had no idea who the father was.

At first, I just kind of ignored the fact that I was pregnant. I denied the whole thing. I did tell David, and I told him the truth about Jeff. He dropped me like a hot potato. He wanted nothing to do with me. I didn't blame him.

I told Jeff. Jeff told me to let him know whatever I wanted or needed he would do.

I didn't know what I wanted to do. I was scared. I felt stupid. Time was marching on. I got a phone call from my friend Bobby at 3 am. Bobby was spontaneous. Bobby was like a big brother. Bobby was kind and generous. He had a heart of gold. He always looked out for me. He always checked on me. He wanted to go watch the sun rise. He loaded a bunch of people into his truck, and we took off for the mountains. We watched the sun rise. I didn't know what I was going to do about the pregnancy—keep the baby or have an abortion. I didn't know who the father was. I was really confused. He told me he would go with if I wanted and just hugged me. I was scared, and Bobby just hugged me like a big brother and told me it would be alright.

I went with my mom to Colorado. I was having morning sickness. I tried to hide it from her, saying I was sick from traveling. I had motion sickness, or the food made me sick. She bought it.

When we got back from Colorado, I couldn't hide it any longer. I told her the truth. We went to Planned Parenthood.

My mom gave me the choice: keep it or have an abortion. My mom was upset, but not as angry as I thought she would be. She was more concerned about what we were going to do. She told me I had to make a decision and that the decision was mine to make. I weighed the decision. I was not ready to be a mother. I wasn't sure I was able to go through an abortion, either. I had to make a decision, and time was not on my side. I opted for an abortion.

The clinic gave us the name of a doctor. The procedure was complicated and painful. I took two days to complete. I don't recommend it unless absolutely necessary.

I had been making bad decision after bad decision. This was a decision to get me to zero again.

The procedure and the days after are all a haze. I remember being emotional. I remember the woman at the clinic holding my hand and whispering to me in Spanish. It was a somber occasion. It was the death of my childhood. I had killed the innocence of childhood. I had lost it. I had made the first adult decision of my life, which would guide another decision in only a few more years.

I recovered from the procedure and thought I would be more careful. I thought I had learned my lesson. And I had—for about two years. I was careful. I did not want to go through that procedure again. I couldn't do that to myself or the idea that it could have been a baby. I believe in a woman's right to choose. I believe abortion should be an option. I just would not choose that option for myself again.

In tenth grade, I saw Mitch some and Jeff some. Jeff had been in a relationship with another girl and had gotten her pregnant. I had been writing Jeff all these sappy love letters. I found out that at my expense, this girl had found all my letters and read them all. They all laughed at my stupidity and foolishness. I felt quite stupid. She called me and told me to stay away from her man, so I did. I didn't send any more letters or call. I dated Mitch on and off again while dating a boy in Boulder City. In fact, when the boy in Boulder City broke up with me, I cried on Mitch's shoulder. He just laughed at me. I continued to hang out with this group of friends. Once I had my driver's license and car, I was able to drive over and hang out with them more. I had freedom and mobility to go where I wanted, even if my parents didn't really want me there. They still opposed my friendships with this group.

We hung out mostly at Bobby's house. Laura would sometimes go with me. We didn't do much but listen to music and watch movies and talk. There were dares to do stupid things but nothing too crazy while I was around. All the stupid shit always happened when I was gone. It was always, "Did you hear what the guys did?" I was never there.

Bobby moved from his house on La Bonita to another house on the East Side of town. Everyone continued to congregate there too. I remember cooking fry bread for them and other meals. I enjoyed cooking for them. They liked it too. We would all just eat, watch TV and listen to music. We would still go to the skating rink sometimes, too.

This group had their share of run-ins with the cops and had their share of misses with them, too. I remember once coming into the house and they had stolen a truck for parts. They had never done anything like that before. They weren't big-time thieves, but they just did it. That truck sat there for a long time. I don't even know if they actually got the parts off the truck. It never looked like it had anything taken off of it. Eventually, they did get rid of it, and nobody went to jail. A few of my friends did go to jail for stealing and robbery. But that's not my story to tell.

Everyone grew up to have their own stories and grew out of our gang. Several years ago, I ran into Mitch at a country bar. I literally bumped into him and then looked him in the face. I pulled back and shouted his full name at him. Then he did the same to me. We pulled each other into a huge hug. He was leaving, and I was going in. He later came back and we went off to grab a 2 am breakfast at a casino to catch up.

With the invention of Facebook, we have all reconnected. It is interesting to see where everyone has landed. We even have a chat group labeled HAB. It's funny because not everyone knows everyone in there. I was yelled at by someone in the group as not having the "cred" of a real HABer. Everyone came to my defense and shooed him away.

Revealing Secrets and Letting Go

I finally told my mom about the sexual abuse.

I was fifteen, dating a boy, and we were getting frisky. We were kissing, and he slid his hand down my pants and touched me in a certain way and BAM! I felt like I was a kid again and had just been assaulted. I freaked out. Had a world-class panic attack. Freaked this kid out. But I relived that moment and felt like I had been cut open. The wound was raw and fresh.

I told my mom. Even though I was almost as tall as she was, I sat in her lap in a chair in the kitchen. I cried as I told her my story. She cried with me. She was supportive and enraged. Shortly after I revealed the truth, she returned to Colorado to visit her folks. My uncle was hanging around. She cornered him. Actually, she tackled him in the backyard and started beating the shit out of him. He had no idea what was going on, why my mom had attacked him. My grandma was crying about her baby getting beat up, and my mom looked crazy. She told them my story. Nobody believed me except my moms, my brother, Aunt Cindy and Uncle Dave.

When it happened, everyone said, she must be mistaken. It was Uncle Kevin. Kevin did weird shit with girls. She must be thinking it was Kevin. Hell, they had me almost convinced I had been wrong. But I go back to the next day after the assault. The conversation with my grandma. The bastard admitted it. I might be foggy with the details, I might have lost time, but I was clear the next day, and he admitted it.

Over the years, I have had to interact with my uncle. Both my grandparents have died. Other family members have died. We had to go to funerals in Colorado to mourn. I've had to sit in a car with him. Sit in services with him. Have dinners with him. I have had to interact with him during those times.

I have cousins who love him. They think the world of him. They think I'm fucking insane. They think I have accused the wrong man. They think it was Uncle Kevin.

Evan has even convinced himself it wasn't him. He has even tried to friend me on Facebook. He truly has no idea that he is the abuser.

This trauma left me damaged for many years. It took a long time to be able to talk about it. Now, I can share my story.

Although there was never any legal justice served in this case, there was a bit of karma served. Several years ago, Evan fell asleep, drunk in the cold of winter. He got frostbite on both feet. They had to amputate part of one foot and all of his other foot. He can no longer walk independently. I probably shouldn't have, but I had to laugh when I heard that. So drunk that you froze your feet off. Well deserved. Could have wished it to be other body parts, but I'll take the feet.

Too bad he's not a registered sex offender.

* * *

My fourth suicide attempt was after that. I'm not sure how

related it was. It's hard to remember and to tease out all the contributing feelings. I remember feeling down and isolated from my friends. I felt alone. I felt like no one cared about me. I felt like no one would miss me.

I know we had just recently moved into a new house. I don't know how long we had been in the house, but I know we hadn't been there very long. I remember the refrigerator was new. I say this because I damaged it.

In this attempt, I decided it would be a good idea to swallow a couple of boxes of Benadryl. I took it thinking this stuff makes you go to sleep. I will just go to sleep and never wake up. Goodbye, cruel world. It's done. Not the case.

I took a very long nap and woke up extremely disoriented. I was disappointed that I was alive. I tried to walk only to find that I had no equilibrium. I could barely walk a straight line. I recall going into the kitchen for some water. I had severe dry mouth. I walked through the doorway, and everything went sideways. The floor was suddenly the ceiling, and I heard this echoing pinging sound. I blacked out.

When I woke up, I was next to the refrigerator. I had walked into the kitchen for the water toward the fridge but passed out. Somehow, I had knocked my head into the fridge. The brand-new fridge had a dent in the door and I had a goose egg on my head. Plus, my elbow was throbbing from hitting the floor.

I forgot about the water and crawled on all fours down through the living room, down the hall to my room and passed out in my bedroom.

I don't know how much time passed, but I heard my mom come home. I tried to put on my "I didn't try to kill myself face on." I attempted to walk and could a bit. I was able to walk but was a bit wobbly. I came out and greeted my mom as if nothing had happened.

The sexual abuse was out in the open, but the suicide attempts and self-harm were not. I'm not sure if the discussion of the sexual abuse had triggered the depression or the suicide attempt, but I wasn't coping well with life.

At school, I had gotten a bad grade on a test. I don't know why I was so upset. I asked the teacher to go to the bathroom. I had taken a paperclip with me. I was wearing sweatpants. I went into a stall. I unwound the paperclip and pulled my pants down. I took the pointy end of the paperclip and raked it up my leg starting at my ankle on the outside of my leg up to my thigh. Droplets of blood began to form, and I sighed with relief. I used a bit of toilet paper to dab up the blood. I flushed the toilet paper and paperclip down the toilet, pulled up my pants, and went back to class.

I didn't want to discuss the sexual abuse with anyone. I think my mom asked me if I wanted to see a counselor and I said no. I didn't have a great experience with Michelle Michele, so I didn't want to do that again.

Eventually, I just pushed the abuse to the back burner and let it go. I didn't deal with it again until college. I was having a manic episode. I wasn't thinking very clearly, but the sexual abuse popped up in my mind again and I was having trouble sleeping.

I decided I would deal with it.

I wrote my uncle a letter. I wrote to him about what had happened that night and the next morning in my grandmother's bedroom. I told him that he had confessed to the crime. I told him that I was no longer going to carry this burden with me. It was his cross to carry. I was no longer going to be a victim. I was done with having this heaviness and shame in my life. He did this to me; he should have to live with it.

I sent the letter. I never heard anything back. I felt like a weight had been lifted. I never looked back on it again.

Boys of European Summer

The next year, my mom sent me to Europe. She worked all the overtime she could get for months to pay for my twenty-one-day trip. My English teacher, Mrs. Eaton, told me about the trip. She was going to be one of the chaperones. It was twenty-one days and seven countries. Mrs. Eaton gave me a journal to write down my experiences. She inscribed the journal, "Record your memories, write now! May 1992."

It was a very thoughtful gift. I looked forward to writing down my thoughts of Germany, Austria, Switzerland, Belgium, Italy, France, and England. However, after finding my journal thirty-odd years later, I discovered that is not exactly what I wrote about.

I did write about some of my travel experiences. I wrote about seeing the Berlin Wall. A frieze of Greek gods in Berlin at a museum. I wrote about a little town, Rothenburg, with a castle in it like in the movie *Robin Hood*, where I bought a beer stein. I wrote about the concentration camps and meeting a former prisoner. He told us about his time at the camps in French.

That was the background noise to the journal. Most of my journal focused on my relationship with boys in twenty-one days in Europe.

My first entry, June 10, 1992, talked about me missing the boy I leave behind at home, Eric. At the moment, I can barely recall Eric. I think he was a friend of a friend. I don't think it was that serious. Immediately I'm writing about how I made friends with a boy named Adam. We bought pizza at O'Hare Airport in Chicago and almost missed our connecting flight. We brought the pizza with us on to the flight.

Over the next couple of days, Adam and I hung out in Berlin together. I was still thinking about this Eric dude and wanted to pay international phone costs to call him. I must have really had a thing for him.

At some point that evening, a party broke out in our room. A bunch of kids had gotten their hands on booze. My roomie, Justina, and I were not drinking, just hanging out. This is where the scene is set for the first romance. I meet Chad.

June 13, 1992, my sixteen-year-old self wrote: *Chad and I are kind of an item. He's funny but too much of a child. He confuses me. I like him. He's too skinny.*

What in the actual fuck? Oh, I cringe at my younger self. If he was so skinny and childish, why would I want to be an item with him? What happened to Eric back stateside? Did I ever make that expensive international call?

We went to the concentration camps. Chad comforted me by holding my hand as I cried. We had become such an item that the chaperones had been keeping their eyes on us.

June 16, 1992, I wrote: *Chad and I are not allowed to be with each other anymore. I fell asleep with my head on his lap. Ms. Minez, his advisor, didn't take to kindly to that and doesn't want him around me or me around him. She has been keeping such a close eye on him she followed us around St. Marcus Square.*

As a teacher, I would have done all the above actions and have with a couple of kids who were caught kissing each other on the school bus on the way to California for a band performance.

During this entry, I also note that I want to buy my ex-boyfriend's mother some lace as a present. It's beyond me why I would be buying presents for Shawn's mother. I go on to document that only a few days into the trip, there are factions forming, and they are fighting. My friend Adam is fighting with a family called the Washingtons.

Apparently, I was not impressed with Rome. I didn't spend any money in Rome. I was proud of that fact. Also, Chad broke things off with me.

June 18, 1992: *Chad informed me that he didn't want to "lead me on." Too late for that asshole. I knew last night that he liked Jen. Christ, he made the rounds with the girls...Chad and Jen got caught kissing on the bus. It was announced. I'm hurt more than mad.*

Five days of being an item and my poor tender heart couldn't take it. Ugh. But alas, my poor little heart did not linger lonely long.

June 25, 1992: *Last night, Fernando kissed me...He kisses better than Chad if that's anything. He's better than Chad. Chad is cool now. His new nickname is Clover.*

Things didn't work out with Fernando either. He only kissed me because he thought I had a boyfriend, which I did back home, and he had a girlfriend, also back home. That canceled out any wrongdoing. There wasn't much to the kissing with Fernando.

I wrote about cool stuff we saw in Paris. What I didn't write was that we went to the Louvre, Versailles, and Jim Morrison's grave. I got to see the Mona Lisa and the Pieta. I don't know why I didn't write any of that. But on with the boys.

June 27, 1992: *Yesterday I met three incredible guys. Nick, Brian, and Josh. Nick is a waiter at the Hard Rock Café "London." Brian and Josh are seniors in college in California.*

Who the hell was watching us? Jen and I were just out wandering around meeting random men in London, men who had no business with teenagers. I don't remember meeting Brian and Josh. I do remember meeting Nick at the Hard Rock. He was our waiter. I was with the Washingtons. There was a bomb scare. We were one of the few who went back to pay our bill.

Nick stared at me the whole time throughout the lunch. He dutifully filled my water. He continued to ask if I needed something. I went to buy souvenirs, and we ended up chatting. I gave him my address, and he said he would write to me.

According to my diary, this same night, Jen and I went out to meet Josh and Brian for drinks in London. I have no recollection of that. We told them where we were staying, and they came back to our hotel, but we missed them because we had gone to a show. We never saw them again.

The next day, I went back to the Hard Rock to speak to Nick. There were some kids from my group having lunch there, so I joined them. I found Nick and gave him my hotel number. He said he would call. I told him he would have to call late because we were going to see *Les Miserables.* At 1:00 am, he called. We made a date to get together my last night in London.

June 27, 1992: *He called me pretty and I knew for sure he likes me! I'm so fucking stoked. I hope this works out. I can't wait!*

Angels bless me, but I went out with a total stranger who was six years older than me. He had spiky, jet-black hair, piercing blue eyes that looked right into your soul. He smelled good. I don't know what kind of cologne, but it was delicious. I met him at his work, then rode the Underground with him to his flat. While he showered, I looked through his music. We then walked around London. Went to Piccadilly Circus and continued talking and talking. We found a pub and had a few drinks. He bought me a rose.

It was getting close to bed check. We took the Underground, and he walked me back close to the hotel. Some of my friends were running as bed check had passed, and we had all missed curfew. What were a few more minutes?

I was wearing Nick's leather jacket. There was a slight chill in the air. Nick held me and gently kissed me. He let me go. I gave him back his jacket. Then he grabbed my hand in a courtly manner and kissed the top of it, saying, "Ciao, bella." He promised he would write.

I truly did see remarkable things in Europe. I remember the cow in the window of my room waking us up. I remember the solemn concentration camps. I remember the art. The majesty of the Sistine Chapel. Not until I unearthed this dusty journal did I realize I didn't write about any of those memories, only the boys I carried on with. None of those boys mattered except Nick.

Nick and I did form a friendship. We became pen pals. He did write to me about a month later. We wrote each other frequently for about three years. We would send a letter every few weeks and call once a month. Once I had Patrick, the letters came fewer and fewer.

The last letter I got from Nick was on the back of a shoebox, very Nick. He said he didn't want me to worry. He was living with his sister in Ireland but would be moving shortly. He would send his new address in the next letter. The letter never came.

Teens Bring About a Child

I was constantly trying to find a man to fill a void in my life. I liked to use sex as power. I felt like I had control in a situation when I could offer sex. In the sexual abuse, it had been stolen from me. As a teen and adult, I could freely give sex when I wanted. It was power. I didn't always use that power appropriately, but I thought it was a situation I could control.

In eleventh grade, I met Cesar, Patrick's dad. He was not a great love of my life. But he deserves mentioning. He gave me one of my treasures. Cesar was about as tall as I am. He was proudly of Irish descent with light skin, tanned from playing football. He had dark hair. It was long on the top and would flop over into his eyes if he didn't brush it back. He had beautiful brown eyes. I did think I was in love with him, but I was not the same love I felt for Mitch or Jeff.

Cesar was originally dating my friend Laura, who was my best friend throughout high school. Laura was beautiful, with light brown hair and the most stunning green eyes. I kinda stole him from her. It did make me a bad friend. I don't recall the circumstances behind it, but I did an underhanded thing because I wanted him. I felt bad about it. She was forgiving.

Cesar and I were a brief couple who brought about a child.

He had addiction issues throughout his family. He fell victim to drugs and alcohol. I was always worried something was going to happen to Patrick in his care.

Once, when Patrick was in the care of Cesar's mother, when Patrick was about two, Patrick put on his shoes and a t-shirt. He went for a walk. He left the house where Cesar's mom was staying, near the residential downtown area. Patrick was wandering around downtown Las Vegas until a lady saw him and coaxed him inside her office motel room. She called the police.

Sara, my stepmom, got the call and picked him up. It didn't blow up too much. I got a visit from Child Services, but they didn't investigate me. They didn't even come inside the house. They just talked to me at the door,

After that, things between Cesar's family and me disintegrated. Things between Cesar and me followed shortly after. He saw less and less of Patrick. I saw it wasn't good for Patrick.

At some point, he sued me for custody. He lost. He left me a message that he was going to kill me and dump me in a desert and take Patrick anyway. I became afraid of him. I lived in fear for Patrick.

Sara had me file a restraining order.

My apartment was broken into one night while I was gone. A message was left, "I see you." I went to stay with my moms for a few days.

There were no more break-ins.

* * *

Winding up pregnant again as a teenager with Cesar's kid,

I thought maybe Michelle Baxter was right. Maybe I was a whore. Sex was a tool I was used to. I was comfortable with it.

I grew up in a strong feminist household. I was not afraid to be strong and bold. I don't think my mom had the idea of me throwing around my sexuality as part of my feminist power, but it was a part of it. It was how I thought about it.

With all that, I was still a lonely little girl seeking attention from any boy I could find. Even though I was bold at times and flirty, I could also be very shy and introverted, depending on the situation. I didn't know what I was doing with my life. I knew that with sex, I could get love and attention. I didn't care if that made me a whore.

My emotions were always with me. They were my constant companion, inescapable. I had Patrick, but I felt isolated from the world. There weren't a lot of single moms going to high school. I had swings of emotions, happiness and despair, hope and hopelessness. It was hard to handle like carrying a double load of wet laundry in your arms on a windy day. I was dealing with Cesar and his ups and downs. His cheating and saying he did and didn't want to be a dad. I didn't have a choice. I didn't really want his kind of choice, but I wanted him to carry his share. I was trying to be a mom. I was dealing with my depression. Everyone kept saying it was just the baby blues, postpartum depression—maybe that's what they wanted to think—but it continued long after that.

I was drowning, but it was all passed off as having a hard time as a single mom and going to school. I had a lot on my plate. I worked, went to school and was taking care of a kid. Who wouldn't be emotionally drained?

I would turn the shower on and cry. I would ball up a towel and wail into it. I would let out my emotions, then dry my face and turn off the water and take care of Patrick. Deep down there would be the ache of dread and knowing I was nothing and deserved nothing good in life. Some days I would want to die, but I had Patrick, and that would keep me going.

Miracle Boy

Patrick was born October 13, 1993, at 10:54 at night. Fifty-four was his dad's football jersey number. He was the only boy born on the floor that night, or I would have thought they gave me the wrong baby.

He was blond, tow-headed, with green eyes. I had dreamed I was going to have a baby with green eyes, but I truly thought I was having a girl. But there he was, 9 pounds, 8 ounces, 21 inches long and pale. I really thought I had the wrong baby. Me, with my dark hair, eyes and skin. Cesar with his dark hair and eyes. How did I wind up with a white and blond baby?

But he was the only boy born that night on the floor at Nellis Air Force Base. All the costs were covered because I was still a minor, covered under my dad's insurance through the Air Force. Patrick was born at the same hospital as me.

I turned eighteen two and a half hours after Patrick was born. It was also the weekend of homecoming. I was glad I didn't have to share my birthday with him. I liked having my day to myself. I didn't know that in years to come, we would still share our birthdays together, and mine would become secondary.

The birth was ordinary, nothing remarkable. My water broke while in line at Subway, where I worked, and we drove right over to the hospital. I was in labor and was unable to get an epidural. They only gave those to the officers. They did give me pain meds.

I remember after one of the contractions, Cesar, Patrick's dad, saying, "Is it too late to just get a puppy?" That should have been a clue as to what I was in for.

I was in the hospital for a few days and came home to my mom's house. I spent about a week at home with Patrick, finding a routine of sleeping, nursing and changing cloth diapers. I had another two weeks off school before I had to go back.

My mom gave me a baby shower, but it was mostly a gathering of all her friends. My only girlfriends who came were my friend Laura and a new high school friend, Hiesen. Felicity no longer lived in Las Vegas or she would have been there. My mom had about twenty friends, mostly from work, come to the shower. They were all very nice and gave us great presents, many of which I greatly needed as I was poor.

During the shower, Patrick started running a fever. As an inexperienced, young, single mother, the worst place to be is in the middle of twenty older mothers with decades of experience. They all had remedies and wives' tales and their own methodology on how to get a fever down.

One lady said a cold bath. Another said rubbing alcohol. Someone else said bundle him up. This went on and on. Tylenol. No Motrin. No nothing. He's too young. It's probably nothing. It could be really bad. You need to see a doctor.

My head was spinning. Finally, they all left. Patrick still had a fever. He was about two weeks old. My mom and I weren't sure if it was all the people that had tired him out, or he had caught a cold from one of his visitors. No clue. We bathed him and put him to bed.

The next morning, he was still running a fever. It was 103 degrees. We took him to a Quick Care Center. They immediately assessed him and told us to get to an emergency room. That an infant with a temperature that high was serious and they couldn't treat him at a clinic.

I had no insurance. I had attempted to get insurance for Patrick but was rejected. They would not cover him until he was a month old. No insurance meant we had to go to University Medical Center (UMC) Emergency.

They took us right in. They ran test after test. They didn't know what was wrong with him. I held my little baby while they did a spinal tap. They took him for tests. We were in the emergency room for several hours before they decided he needed to be in the intensive care unit. He was hooked up to machines and IVs so they, on the down low, transferred him from the emergency room building to the intensive care building in an ambulance.

He spent the night in the Intensive Care Kids Unit, and they still didn't know what was wrong with him. They told us to go home. We came home for a little sleep but went back early the next day. I didn't know if he was going to live or die. I felt like I was in a dream. It seemed so unreal.

We spent another day with Patrick as his temperature climbed to 105 degrees. They couldn't find a reason for the increase of temperature or where the infection was coming from.

Finally, after a couple of days, a doctor discovered Patrick had a kidney infection. He had ureteral reflux. The flappers at the end of his ureters were deformed, and urine was flowing back into his kidneys instead of staying in his bladder.

There are five grades of reflux. Grade 1 reflux means 20 percent chance of surgery and 80 percent chance of recovery without surgery. Grade 5 reflux means 80 percent chance of surgery and 20 percent chance of recovery without surgery. Patrick was diagnosed with grade 5 ureteral reflux. It was very treatable. Antibiotics daily for as long as needed. Ultrasounds of the kidney areas to see if the flappers have grown back.

After a week in ICU, Patrick was released to come back home. I was relieved. He had survived.

For years, Patrick took antibiotics twice a day daily. He saw a urologist twice a year who looked at his scans. When Patrick was five, the doctor told me that the reflux had not corrected itself and to prepare myself for the fact that he would most likely have to have surgery. In six months, he would check again and make the call.

Six months later, we did our normal scan and visit. The doctor smiled and said, "It's a miracle. It's gone. It corrected itself. No surgery."

Patrick had fallen into the 20 percent chance of recovery. In six months, his body recovered. It was a miracle. He was my little miracle boy.

The only side effect of the treatment for the ureteral reflux was the dosing of the antibiotics. The continual usage of antibiotics for the five years left white spots on Patrick's adult front teeth when they grew in. He was very self-conscious about it. It was an easy fix with caps. That also closed the tiny gap he had. Once it was done, he smiled all the time. The miracle boy.

* * *

I love my firstborn son, but I didn't always know how to love him. We grew up together. We raised each other. Patrick was born the day before my eighteenth birthday, and we would forever be linked by our births. He loved that. I hated that. I didn't want to have to share my birthday with him. I almost begrudged him that, and he was just a baby. I was a kid, too. Now, I love it, but then, I was selfish.

Patrick was a tough baby. He was a sick baby. I didn't know if he was going to live, the first month of his life. He was diagnosed with grade 5 ureteral reflux. I was a senior in high school. I was just trying to figure it all out.

I was living at home. I had the help of my parents. It was made very clear that Patrick was my responsibility. I was the one who got up with him, fed him, and changed him. And I did. I did need some guidance from my mom, and she gave it willingly. I took any direction freely.

As time went on, we started to grow on each other. We fell into a rhythm. When Patrick turned three months, he was able to go to school with me and attend the daycare center at the school. We spent more time together at that point. I was required to spend one period a day in the daycare center with him to take care of him and the other babies in the daycare.

Even though Patrick was my responsibility, raising Patrick was still a group effort. My parents couldn't resist him. He was quite irresistible. They did pick up the slack.

Patrick's dad did not play a heavy role in this. We did spend time together during the first year of his life. He did do diaper duty but not a lot of weekend or evening shifts. That was mostly by my design, not his.

After I graduated high school and started college at UNLV, we celebrated Patrick's first birthday. It was a huge celebration.

Patrick's dad and I were struggling with our relationship, so it was tense. I'm not sure we were even dating. His whole family was there, which made my mom tense. All our friends were there. It was a great party for a one-year-old who wouldn't remember a thing. The icing was blue on a half-moon cake.

Scholarships, School, and My Son

Once I was pregnant with my son, I knew the only future for me was to get higher education. I knew I wanted to be a teacher. It would take me years to reach that goal, but I knew I needed to go to college.

Since I had Patrick, going out of state was not an option for me. I knew I would attend the community college or the University of Nevada, Las Vegas. I don't know why, but I really wanted to start my college career at UNLV.

I was super excited and surprised when I got in. I had good grades for most of my schooling, with the exception of the one semester that I was fooling around when I got pregnant and stopped going to school. I had turned myself around and took my education seriously.

The next step in my plan was to get my college paid for. With the help of my guidance counselor, I applied for all types of scholarships. I applied for at least fifty scholarships. I know I wrote more than thirty essays explaining why I was the most qualified to receive financial help. I applied for single mother scholarships, Native American scholarships, Navajo scholarships, Finnish scholarships, Wal-Mart scholarships, bank scholarships. Anyone who had a scholarship, I entered my name and applied. My counselor was very resourceful. She learned everything about me and applied for everything with me. Mrs. Bliss was amazing.

In the end, I received three scholarships. I received the Martin Luther King, Jr., Single Parent Scholarship of $500, a one-time payment. I received a scholarship from the Las Vegas Indian Center for $1500 a semester for the entire time I went to school, as long as my grades were good, and I carried a full load. With the help of Mrs. Bliss, I was awarded the Marvin Lee Scholarship, which paid for books and tuition for the duration of my studies. These scholarships, along with Pell Grants, got me through the first year of schooling. Down the road, I needed to get loans to help pay for housing and living expenses.

It was great to be recognized by these agencies for my achievements. Toward the end of my senior year of high school, each of these organizations held an awards ceremony.

The Martin Luther King, Jr., Committee held their ceremony at the old Moulin Rouge Hotel. It was a historic black hotel. It was an interesting place. Martin Luther King III was the guest speaker. He told us to be proud of our achievements and to make the committee proud by going out into the world and doing good things.

The Las Vegas Indian Center held their ceremony at UNLV. It was a huge banquet. There were about ten recipients being awarded scholarships. We were all from various tribes. It was nice to see so many other Indians in the room. We were all from around the valley. I was used to being the only Indian in the room. It was nice to see so many other brown faces and to see that they were also so accomplished. Not all of them were going to UNLV; some were going to community college. There was an invocation of prayer by a medicine man at the beginning of the meal. A storyteller told us a story during the meal, and a drum group played for us before we left. There was also a silent auction going on. My mom bought me a silver bracelet to mark the occasion.

The Marvin Lee Scholarship was a very different scholarship. Mrs. Bliss had been tasked by Mr. Lee to choose kids whom she thought would do great things. She chose a few kids. She did this every year until she retired. Our gathering was less formal. We gathered for a dinner at the Bliss residence for a barbeque. We got to meet Mr. Lee. He told us that his father set up the foundation to help kids have a better future. Mrs. Bliss would oversee the funds. This group of kids would meet up once a year throughout our time in college. Our group got smaller and smaller, as kids would drop out of college and not return. I soldiered on.

Without these financial endorsements, I would not have been able to afford the university the first year. I was still figuring out how to maneuver my way around school. The scholarships paid for that year of figuring it out. The renewing scholarships kept the financial burden to a minimum. Pell Grants helped even out some of that payment as well.

All in all, school was being paid for.

Patrick went to daycare, stayed with his dad or grandparents while I went to school during my first year of college. However, my second year of college, my mom wanted me to move out and be on my own. Patrick and I moved out and lived across the street from the university in an apartment complex. Patrick called it the Blue House. The doors on the apartments were blue. He went to the daycare center across the street, which was called Cinderella.

When I had to move out of my mom's house, I had to take

out student loans to help cover the cost of rent and other living expenses. For six and a half years, Patrick and I lived off my student loans. I did have the odd job here and there, but the loans and grants paid for our cost of living. We did okay, but I owed a lot on loans.

* * *

When I got to college, I was diagnosed as bipolar. I had always suspected but had always been told that I was just sensitive and overly dramatic. Finally, something that made sense. I was mostly having trouble with depression. I went to the student clinic and met with Jamie, my new psychiatrist. He diagnosed me as bipolar type II. Bipolar type II is more depressive episodes with hypomanic episodes and not full-blown mania.

He put me on lithium. I took it for a few months. I started to get worse. I felt severely depressed. I had suicidal ideations. It was getting bad. He took me off of it.

I told my mom that the doctor had diagnosed me a being bipolar. She told me that was wrong. I was wrong. There was no way I was bipolar. She wanted me to see her doctor.

I went to her doctor and filled out the paperwork. I listed my symptoms and he said, "Yeah, it sounds like you have bipolar disorder."

My mom still disagreed. She was in denial.

I worked with Jamie for the next year or so to try to come up with a medication cocktail that would work to help keep the depressive episodes at bay. I tried countless combinations of drugs. I have lost count of the number of drugs I have trialed out of. We found a combination of Depakote and something else that worked. I had a very productive year at school.

At one point, I caught a bad cold and went to the student clinic for some cold medicine. I had a bad chest cold and couldn't breathe. They put me on a steroid pack.

Within days of taking the steroids, I went into a manic episode. I was spinning and zipping from class to class. The cold was forgotten.

I crashed from the mania and reeled into a massive depression. Jamie adjusted my meds, and I got back on track. I began to find a way to go to school, be a mom, and live life as a person with bipolar. It was a juggling act, but I was figuring it out.

Patrick and I lived in our little apartment. Again, it was a group effort raising Patrick. He was entering his terrible twos. I remember him entering the age when he no longer slept in a crib and could no longer die from SIDS. I was relieved that he would not die from something terrible. I also came to understand how parents snapped and killed their children through shaken baby syndrome or somehow fatally injured their child.

Patrick was a terror. He would run away from me every chance he got. He refused to listen to me. I would try to be calm with him. He would tell me no. I would ask nicely. He would refuse.

One night, after I tucked Patrick into bed, he began to scream and cry. I don't know what the matter was, but he did it for two hours. I didn't know what to do. I couldn't take it. I was going to murder him. I called my moms. They came and picked him up. As soon as they got there, he quietly got his wannie, his security blanket, shut his pie hole, and went with them. I was told he fell asleep in the car and slept the whole night through.

They dropped him off at daycare the next day. No problems with me the next day.

One time, we were in a department store, and he was holding my hand. I had an armful of clothes. He looked up at me. I saw the glint in his eye.

I said, "Don't do it."

He took off running. Full tilt. I, of course, stupidly ran after him, dropping the clothes. As I reached for him, he threw himself on the ground, shouting and pointing at me.

"Bad momma!" he cried with tears.

To all the shoppers, it looked like I had chased an innocent child and shoved him down to the ground. To me, he was a demon child.

We left the store without our purchases and walked home.

Raising Patrick was a group effort. A couple who lived next door, Darla and Choya, came into our lives. They took care of us. They fed us on a regular basis. We were given all types of foods to eat. Choya was a cook by trade, and a most excellent one. They also supplied us with pirated movies. On occasion, they would also babysit for me. Patrick was always well behaved for them, never a problem.

The college girls who lived upstairs loved Patrick. They would take him upstairs and brush his hair and let him play video games on their console so I could get some reading done. They did this for years.

The old man, Herbert, who sat in his chair and observed the comings and goings of everyone in the courtyard, would give him a dollar every now and again if he promised to be a good boy. He rarely was.

One time, I decided to get a pet rabbit. I named him Kalua. It was a chocolate color. I put a lock on its cage. One morning,

I got up to see that Patrick had found the key to the lock. He had Of Mice and Menned that bunny. He Lennyed the rabbit to death. Kalua was dead. Just a soft little thing of fur and bones. We didn't have it more than three days.

I had been very clear.

"Don't touch the rabbit," I firmly stated.

"Okay, I won't," he said.

But he did, and he killed it. The cage and setup cost me half my pay for the week. I was very upset. I threw the whole thing in the trash, including Kalua.

Rabbit killer. He was just a kid. He didn't mean to do it.

We used to keep Patrick's hair buzzed short. It was quick and easy. It had grown out considerably, and he was in between buzzes. I finally had buzzed down his hair.

When we walked into daycare, the lady behind the counter asked me, "Did you shave his head looking for three sixes?"

I didn't know whether to laugh or be pissed. It was rather funny, but she was talking shit about my kid. I'm the only one that gets to be annoyed and talk shit about my kid.

Another time, I was up late studying and writing papers. I went to bed very late. I was sleeping hard. A loud noise woke me up. That was never a good sign. I went out to inspect.

Patrick had somehow pulled almost everything out of the refrigerator. Milk, eggs, bread, lettuce. He had also managed to get the coffee, dry coffee creamer, oatmeal, cereal, sugar, and an assortment of pots and pans. He had poured most of the contents out of the containers onto the carpet, where he had put the pots and pans. Hardly any of it made it into the pots and pans.

I was horrified. Our food for at least the next two weeks was destroyed. We were on public assistance, and it was gone. Gone. Not only that, it was all over the carpet. The combination of oatmeal, coffee creamer, and milk in the carpet was like cement. I tried not to get mad. I just breathed and got the camera. I took pictures and decided it was my next art project. Then, I went about cleaning it up. I didn't even yell at him. Just sent him to watch TV in the living room. He happily went on his way with a stirring spoon laced with oatmeal flakes to watch a cartoon.

This mishap became one of my art project installments. I was required to do three panels of pastel drawing on large three feet by four feet drawings. I did a panel of Patrick in footie pajamas opening the refrigerator. Another panel was of Patrick sitting with all the ingredients to his breakfast soup. The last panel was of my footed feet standing over him with him looking up at me, caught in the act. I got an A on the assignment.

In this destruction of the kitchen and dining room area, I realized he was only a child, perhaps a small demon child, but my demon child. He honestly was just playing. My reaction to the situation, or non-reaction to the situation, kept us both calm. I didn't yell; he didn't cry. I didn't shout at him or put him in a time out where he wailed and wanted grandma and ninny. It was my first moment where we meshed.

I took advantage of this little light moment we had together. I took Patrick to the mall. I opened up a credit card at Sears. I bought him a new outfit with suspenders, including shiny black shoes, and had pictures taken. He looked like a little old man. He was too cute. When we got on the bus to go home, he told me he loved me and snuggled me.

Some days, Patrick was a fixture at the university with me. Sometimes, for some reason, he couldn't go to daycare. Maybe he had a bad day there and couldn't go, or I didn't have the money that week, but he would go with me to class. Patrick was known on campus. He had a big personality.

Patrick would ride his Big Wheel on campus to my classes and park it outside the door. At one end of UNLV, by the concert halls, there is a series of wide steps. Patrick liked to ride his Big Wheel down the steps. This thoroughly amused him. He would do it for hours. It amused me too. The problem was, I had to carry the Big Wheel back up the stairs for him to ride it down, and so it got old very quickly.

You had to give Patrick a countdown as to when things would end. You could not abruptly stop something. He did not transition well from one thing to another. It had to be just right. It was a little OCD. I always tried to give him a countdown, but I would sometimes forget and there would be a complete meltdown.

I took him to my history class. I'd taken him to this class many times. He was usually pretty good about coloring and keeping to himself, which is why my professors didn't mind that he attended. One day, however, he lost his shit and started talking. He didn't whisper. He started talking to me about something. I asked him if he could whisper. He got louder and louder. I had to leave. The problem was, he didn't want to leave. He liked being in the grown-up class and dug his boots in and gripped the desk. I had to drag him out of there, making a scene. He was not invited back again.

He fought me the whole way home. I had to carry him, the Big Wheel, and my backpack. It was quite the walk.

Somewhere in this timeline, we met Zaaida. Zaaida was dating Patrick's dad. Zaaida had a son, Derreck, who was a year older than Patrick. I wanted nothing to do with her. Why would I? She was my ex's girlfriend. One day, this feisty girl pinned me down and said we needed to talk. I know I was rude, and she was nothing but pleasant.

"You know I watch Patrick all the time while Cesar goes out, don't you?" she asked.

"I had no idea," I replied.

"Yeah, he plays with my son. I don't mind. He's a good boy," she stated.

"Well, thank you for taking care of him," I stammered.

"I'm not staying with Cesar for long, but I'd like our boys to stay friends. Here's my number. I'm moving in with my mom, not far from here. Keep in touch. We'll have a playdate." She gave me her number on a scrap of paper.

This moment changed our lives. This was another person who helped raise Patrick. Zaaida and her family raised Patrick too.

Patrick spent a lot of time with Derreck. They were the best of buds. Zaaida and I became very good friends. She watched Patrick a lot for me for free so I could go to school, go out on a weekend. She did so much for me. We would hang out at her house. Her mom would feed us. It was great. Not soon after, Zaaida went on a blind date and ended up married to her husband, Eric. He also took Patrick on as another son.

My parents were really the ones who had the most influence on Patrick's life. They took the brunt of raising him. Even though they set these very clear boundaries that he was my responsibility, they saw that I was floundering. They did show me how to set limits and do time outs.

We were not a spanking family. We rarely used that type of punishment, but we did use time outs. My problem was he wouldn't stay in the time out. He would just walk away from it.

I'd put him in the time out chair, and he'd stand up and kick it. Or look at me and laugh and run away to his room and slam the door. He'd do what he wanted.

My parents took Patrick many, many nights while I was in school. He had his own bedroom at their house. When they took vacations, they often took him with them. They often went to Colorado to check on my grandmother, and they took him with them. He was a well-traveled little boy.

Zaaida and Eric often took Patrick with them when they traveled, too. He got to experience camping and theme parks, something I did not have the money or means to give him. I am forever grateful to them for doing that for him.

Once Patrick turned four and a half, it was like a switch had flipped in him. He stopped fighting me on everything, and I stopped fighting him and arguing with him at every turn. We started enjoying each other. There were more please and thank yous. We got along with each other. We had entered a new stage of our relationship. I wanted to be around him, and he wanted to be around me. It pained us to be apart from each other.

That turning point made me reflect on the past four years of being a parent. I was ashamed of myself. I had been a terrible parent. Yes, I made sure Patrick was taken care of. I showed him affection. I genuinely loved him, but at the same time, I was resentful. I wanted to be able to go out with my college friends and go to parties. I wanted to be able to do college things. I wanted to do so much but was bound by this kid. I was ashamed. All this time, Patrick only wanted my love, and I fought him on it.

I didn't realize it at the time, but I was only doing what I had to to survive. I worked, went to school, took care of him. I found ways to pay for housing and food. I made us a home and did all that without a whole lot of help from anyone financially. I had a lot of emotional help from friends and family. Without their support, Patrick wouldn't have become the strong, beautiful man he is today.

I don't know how much credit I get for his younger years. I was in survival mode. I don't think I was a very good mom. I was just an okay mom. I didn't know how to be a mom. I was just figuring it out. I once had a hollering match at him whether he wanted tea or coffee at 2 am. Who does that?

* * *

When I decided to go back to school and get my master's degree in teaching, I contacted Mrs. Bliss and asked if Mr. Lee would consider sponsoring me for school. She said she didn't know, considering he had paid for my undergraduate degree.

Mr. Lee thought it was a great idea. He was closing the scholarship fund and had decided that I would be the last candidate. He thought it a great way to use the last of the money in the fund. He also liked that I was continuing with my education.

I would never have been able to afford my master's degree without Mr. Lee's help. I was in debt from the student loans I took out for my bachelor's degree. I didn't want to incur any more debt. I was able to earn my master's degree without any cost. It helped that I did it all in less than a year.

Mrs. Bliss was my guardian angel through it all. She helped me when I didn't know how I was going to pay for my dream of higher education and then even higher higher education.

She just said she would handle it. She is an amazing woman, and I wouldn't be where I'm at without her.

I recently sent her a message and thanked her for all she did. She sent me a message back:

You are an inspiration to the tenacity of the human spirit. I watched your struggles and prayed that you would make it. Not only did you make it, you excelled in a world that desperately needs your skills. I have always been so proud of you and tell so many people about your successes! I appreciate your kind words, but I think I was just a tag along, investing my time in the wonderful person, Ahiddibah.

I am very grateful to all the people that took the time to get me to where I am today. I am grateful to the community who thought I was worthy to give money to, who took a risk on a single mother with a dream. I think I did them proud. I have the degrees to prove it.

* * *

As Patrick grew up, I grew up. We grew up together. We grew closer. Our bond grew closer. He is my heart. I love him dearly. I wouldn't trade anything for the struggle we endured together because it taught me not to be a selfish person. I learned to be a giving person through him.

I have a theory. If a toddler is a terrible toddler, they get it out of their system at a young age. Then, once they are teenagers, they are great teenagers. Patrick was a great teenager.

It took a village to raise him. I'm sure he has traits from everyone. He wouldn't be here without all that help. Now, in his twenties, he is still my heart. I love talking to him. He is smart, empathetic, kind, geeky, and all-around wonderful.

When You Think It's Love

I got together with my husband, Charles, in college. My friend Jim from junior high was getting married. I had been invited to his bachelor party at Charles's house. After drinking a bunch of Goldschlager, I don't recall what exactly happened.

I'm pretty sure I made out with Jim and ended up in bed with Charles. At least I woke up in bed with Charles the next morning. That began our love affair. I was in love, love, love. I didn't remember the sex the night before, so we did it again in the morning and it was great.

I went home with the feel of new love in the air, but it didn't last. That began our on-again-off-again torrid romance until we got married and after our divorce.

Throughout college, Charles and I would go on dates, hook up and have sex and then go through dry spells of never talking. I dated guys and even lived with one whom I didn't deserve. I broke up with him, cheated on him with Charles. Poor guy left me and went back to Phoenix. I came home, and the apartment was empty. He even took my art off the walls.

In 1998, Charles and I were dating again after my boyfriend, the art thief, left. Charles had a key to my apartment. Things were going great until they weren't. He had pissed me off for some reason. He didn't call. So, I didn't call. We didn't call each other for a whole week. Then it was two weeks. Next thing I know, there's someone knocking on my door to the apartment. I opened the door. It was Jeff. He asked if he could stay for a few nights.

I was ecstatic to see him. He said he been up in northern Nevada hunting. He was heading back that way but needed to stop in Vegas and wanted to see me. He had some business here as well. We chatted late into the night.

When it was time for bed, we both got into bed. We just snuggled. I tried to make a play for something more, but he wouldn't have it. I was a bit pissed off, but he said no. So, I just let him hold me, and it was enough.

He stayed for a few nights.

The last night, I got off late from work. I came home, and he was already in bed asleep. I asked if he wanted to go out. He said no; he was leaving in the morning. I said I was going to go out but would be back before he left. I came back at 3 am, and he was gone. He left his fishing pole, flies and cologne. Baffling.

Charles called not too long after that. We got back together.

* * *

Charles and I had a lot of fun together. We drank together. We went out dancing together. We drove around town together. We rented rooms on The Strip for fun. We just had a good time together. Wherever we went, we had a good time together. There was usually drinking involved.

We would go to the drive-in a lot. We would take bottles of

booze with us and mix drinks while we watched the movies. It was nice going to the drive-ins because we could take Patrick with us. We would watch a couple of movies, eat take out, and have some drinks.

In my last year of college, I got pregnant with Jesse. Charles and I decided to move in together officially. We had our struggles. But dang, did I just love him so much. I loved him so much, I could not see the damage or the flaws.

I loved everything about Charles. I loved his dark hair and the way it turned wavy when it grew out. I loved his light brown eyes. I loved the way his voice was husky in the morning. I loved that he thought it was funny when we both read books in bed together like an old married couple before we were married. I loved that he thought I was beautiful. I thought he was beautiful.

Charles had a fish that ate other fish. Little goldfish. We drove to the pet store to get feeder fish to feed the evil monster that lived in this five-foot aquarium. At the pet store, I watched as the worker caught the unsuspecting meal and put them in a large plastic bag.

We got back into the truck and headed home. I was holding the fish against my pregnant belly. They beat their fins against me as Jesse pushed outward from inside me. Silently communicating with each other. Life to life. I started to cry. We were making a fishy sacrifice to this evil giant fish that did nothing but swim around all day. It was mean and had no purpose.

Charles looked at me like I was crazy. I tried to explain to him that these fish were alive, and we were just going to kill them. He said, "These fish are feeder fish. That's their whole purpose in life. To feed other animals and fish."

"It's not right for us to decide who to kill and not to kill," I wept.

He kept driving us home and the fish toward their death.

We got home and he took the fish from me. He took them to the tank and dumped them in. Furiously, the beast began to snatch them up whole. He chased them around. There was nowhere for them to hide. There were no plants in the aquarium. Just water. They were all going to die.

I couldn't watch. I was getting sick. It hurt my heart. The evil monster had goldfish tails hanging out of its hideous lips.

Since I was pregnant, I went off all my medication. I seemed to do pretty well. I had a few mood swings. I had a few hypomanic episodes but nothing too crazy. All my mood swings were attributed to pregnancy hormones. Nobody thought too much about it being bipolar issues.

I continued to take one class at UNLV while I was pregnant with Jesse. He was a high-risk pregnancy. I almost miscarried with him. I was closely monitored throughout. I was supposed to be on bedrest, but I didn't want to be away from school. I was afraid I'd never go back.

When I had Jesse, Charles and I moved in with his grandmother. She was an awful person. She was mean and spiteful. She had rules that didn't make sense. You had to load the dishwasher a certain way or you'd be yelled at. You couldn't do more than three loads of laundry a day or it would wear out the washer. With two young kids, it was a challenge not to do lots of laundry.

Charles had just been laid off of his job as a sheet metal worker. I was determined to finish school. I had one semester left. He told me I had to quit school and get a job, or else. I left him, moved out, and found an apartment by the school. I started my last semester. I took Patrick and Jesse with me.

I was struggling in school. I got back on my meds. I was having a hard time. I was depressed, even with the medication. I was suicidal.

My next and last suicide attempt, I know the trigger. I had a fight with Charles. He was threatening to take my son away from me. He had taken him that night. I was upset. I had just filled my meds. Some sort of anti-seizure med as a mood stabilizer and Valium. Full scripts. Full doses.

I just went into the kitchen and opened the bottles. I took all the pills. Sixty pills in sixty seconds. I drank them with milk. I hate milk. I'm allergic. I like to think it's the milk that saved me.

Shortly after taking the pills, my friend Shelly and her daughter just showed up at my door to say hi and watch TV with me. I told her about the baby being away. I didn't tell her about the pills.

I got sleepy. She said she was going to leave. Then it hit me.

I was going to die.

I told her.

I went into the bathroom and forced myself to throw up.

I threw up twice.

She said we should go to the hospital. I refused to go. I didn't want to be locked up. I was scared. I was worried Charles would keep the baby away from me.

She stayed with me until I woke up the next morning.

She watched me call and make an emergency appointment with my psychiatrist on campus, then left. She didn't talk to me for a week. She was seriously pissed off at me for what I put her through. I don't blame her. I can't imagine. I don't know what I would have done in her place.

I went to my appointment. My doctor, Jamie, did not believe me when I told him what I had done. I told him I had just filled my script. I took everything. He told me that there was no way I could have survived that amount of drugs in my system.

I again told him what I took. I told him that I threw up a couple of times, hours after I had taken it. He did some lab work and confirmed I had a whole lot of meds in my system. He confirmed with me that I was a miracle. It was a miracle that I was alive. I should not be alive. I think it was the milk.

I was closely monitored on my medication for a few months.

I started to do better.

My parents were in the dark about all of this. They did not know about the suicide attempt. They knew I had left Charles and was living at my new apartment. They had helped me move in. They had recently just finished building their straw bale house. When I lived with Charles' grandmother, I was just down the street from my parents. Now, I was across town again. We were separated and distant.

Eventually, Charles came to live with me. We couldn't be parted for long.

I should have seen the pattern. We were together, then apart, then together, then apart. This had been the way it was for our entire relationship. I was so in love that I never noticed. I also didn't notice that he was a shitheel to Patrick or that he was an alcoholic or a gambler. I didn't notice that I could have a drink and be okay, but he could not handle his alcohol. I was just in love.

We got married in 2002 and divorced in 2004.

When I got married, I asked Uncle Dave to walk me down the aisle. At first, I didn't even invite my dad to the wedding. Our relationship hadn't improved since I was sixteen. I never reached out and neither did he. We became comfortable in our pattern of not communicating with each other. The older I got, the more bitter I became. I saw him as holding a grudge about something stupid a kid had done.

Once in college, I was running out of money. I was tapped out. My last resort was to call my dad. He said, "You only call when you need something."

That upset me even though it was the truth. I had not reached out to see how my East Coast family was doing. I didn't know how my sisters were doing. I didn't know how my stepmom was doing. I didn't know anyone's health status. He called me out on the truth, and I was upset.

They sent me a check for ten dollars. I cashed it, and when I had the money, I sent it back to them. My dad did not come out for any of my graduations. He did not come out for my high school graduation, my graduation for my bachelor's degree or, later, my master's degree. In fairness, I don't think I invited him. I only informed him that I was going to walk for my degrees. I just figured he wouldn't be able to come because he was so far away, or maybe he wasn't interested in going. I had no idea what he thought because I never asked him what he thought.

Others in my family suggested that I ask my dad to walk me down the aisle, saying it was the right thing to do. I told this to my uncle, tearfully. He understood. Just gave me a big hug. He would still be there with me at the wedding and dance with me.

Our wedding was a great affair. It was low key and cost under a thousand dollars due to many people making their contributions at cost.

My parents had just built a straw bale adobe-style home. The back courtyard to their home is beautiful. It has red flagstone and pebble rock. The courtyard is enclosed with straw bale walls covered in plaster with two large rugged, antique doors that open to the south and one to the west. There is a waterfall close to the house with a pond of water that runs alongside the house. One of the bedrooms opens up to the courtyard. There are flagstone steps that you have to walk over the pond to get to the courtyard.

My dad walked me down the aisle of flagstone steps. Bubbling water churned from the pond that Charles and I got married over. A trellis of bright flowers decorated the doorway of the bedroom walkway. Tiny floating candles glittered on water as we said our vows in from of about fifty people.

A friend of my mother's played, "Can't Help Falling in Love with You" on his guitar.

We chose that night because it was a full moon of the fall equinox. As we finished our vows and proceeded to leave the courtyard, a full moon was rising in the west, full and yellowish-orange.

My dad and I danced together joyously at my wedding. I remember being very happy that he was there. I didn't know why I had felt uneasy about inviting him. When I was around him, the tension disappeared.

It was a great party.

* * *

As a newly married couple, our lives were pretty joyful. We never took a honeymoon. Instead we took my winter break from school and went to visit Charles' parents at their home in Montana for Christmas.

Traveling up there during the snow caused me great anxiety. I have a phobia of driving in inclement weather. I don't like driving on steep, mountain roads. This drive included all of the above.

Charles distracted me with talk. We had lots of fun talks. I was the navigator. We drank lots of coffee. The kids traveled well. I read a *Harry Potter* book to the kids.

Charles' parents were excited to see Jesse but less so Patrick. They treated him like a red-headed stepchild and me like a terrible in-law. I felt unwelcome. My mother-in-law referred to me as a blanket ass. I had never heard that term for Indians before, but it was obviously insulting. She didn't seem disturbed by saying it.

The kids played in the snow and built a snowman. We spent Christmas there and then I was ready to go. So was Charles. He could only take a few days of his mother, and I had had enough insults to last me a while.

We claimed there was a break in the weather, and we had to head out early to avoid the snowstorm that was coming. Charles' mother said she understood, and we left the day after Christmas.

We were planning on driving all the way through back to Vegas but got caught in a snowstorm in Idaho. They closed the road, and we had to stay in a little town that had hot springs. We were low on money but found a room.

The kids were tired and went right to sleep with the TV on. I figured Charles and I could snuggle in and watch something with the snow falling outside. That was not what he had in mind.

He informed me that he was going for a drink. He bundled

up and left. He just left the kids and me. He didn't say when he would be back. I was much in shock to be mad. I made excuses. He'd had a rough day driving. He was upset with his mom. This trip has been tough on him; he deserved a drink.

I went to bed. I didn't hear him come in. When I woke up, he was passed out with his clothes on. Boots were kicked off next to the door.

Careful not to disturb Charles, I quietly got out of bed and got the boys up and dressed. Once we were ready, I woke him up. He got up easily and was all smiles. We went out for breakfast and left the sleepy little town. It looked like a fun place and promised ourselves we would come back. Now, I can't even remember its name.

Charles drinking became a regular occurrence. We held our one-year-anniversary dinner with everyone who helped us with our wedding. I had planned it and scheduled it for over a month. At the last minute, Charles was invited by his boss to the racetrack so they could watch cars zoom around and drink. He told me he would not be coming to the dinner and left before the guests arrived.

All our friends showed up to an anniversary dinner minus the groom. I had to make excuses . That he had a last-minute opportunity at work he couldn't pass up on, and I didn't want to cancel dinner.

My guests were very kind, but they were all suspicious of the circumstances.

Once we were married, the shine faded quickly. I had one very bad depressive episode. I remember wanting to kill myself. Charles just ignored me. I cried and cried. I was on the floor of the bathroom next to the tub wanting to hurt myself. I cried myself to sleep. He just left me there and went to the bar.

We were saving for a house, the money in a joint bank account. I took the kids to Montana to visit his parents for the summer. While I was gone, he emptied the account to gamble. Upon my return, he told me it was my fault and also that I was fat. That was a problem. Hence, the divorce.

* * *

I graduated college and was left without health insurance. I went through the state on a sliding scale to get my meds. I did this while I pursued my master's degree. I stayed on my meds throughout school.

My first year of teaching, I continued to take medication. I remember one of the meds caused me to have a sensitivity to the sun, and I could not do duty outside without an umbrella.

At some point during the summer and transitioning to my new middle school, I stopped taking my meds. There is no clear reason why. I just felt like I didn't need them anymore.

When my husband and I divorced, we continued to date one another for several months after our divorce. He even joined my bowling team at work. It was like we were slowly getting used to the idea of being apart from one another.

We no longer lived together. I lived with my parents with my kids. He lived in his own apartment not too far away. We would sleep together and spend time with the kids together. I'm sure this was very confusing to the kids. I didn't think about that at the time. Honestly, I thought we were going to get back together.

The reason we had gotten divorced was his extreme drinking

and gambling. He was no longer doing that. He was attentive, loving and caring. Not just to me but to the kids as well. The divorce just seemed like paperwork.

This was just our habit. We had always broken up and gotten back together. That was our way of doing things for as long as we had known each other, for as long as we had dated each other. It was habit.

When I was in college, drinking was just an ordinary pastime. I didn't go to a lot of college parties because I had Patrick. When I turned twenty-one years old, I did go to the bars. I had a few binge nights but never ones where I couldn't remember things or wound up somewhere I didn't know how I got there. My friends told me stories about their drunken encounters. That never happened to me. For me, drinking became a social thing. You go out and have a drink to unwind. I could have a drink or two; it wasn't a big thing.

I have a thing for addicts. I wound up in relationships with alcoholics, Cesar, Charles and Doug. I'm not an alcoholic. I can take or leave drinking. I'm an emotional drinker at times. There is one drunken night I won't forget.

During the Christmas season, my parents had gone to California for day. It was a Sunday. I had decided to decorate the house. My ex-husband was supposed to come over and help me with the decorations and spend time with the kids and me. I called him and left a message. I called again, and he didn't answer. I called and called, and he refused to pick up. Finally, he did answer, and he was drunk. He said he was with "someone," meaning a woman, and would not be coming over.

I was pissed. I was hurt. I wasn't going to let him ruin my Christmas spirit. I had a house to decorate, but I was going to do it with cocktails.

I went to the store and bought a bottle of vanilla vodka and a bottle of Starbucks coffee liqueur. I had recently been to a party where a friend had made this yummy drink for me. It seemed like a festive drink to hang the holly with. I drove back home with my goods and a few other trinkets to begin the festivities.

My parents have a treasure trove of holiday decorations they have collected many over the years.

Before I dived into the decorating, I poured my first drink, half vodka, half coffee liqueur over ice in a large tumbler. I pulled out every box they had from the closet under the stairs. There must have been over ten boxes. The kids joined in unpacking the mystery boxes. They quickly got bored and went to their room to play video games.

The drink was strong but smooth. It went down very fast. I poured another after going through a couple of boxes. I was putting down the fake snow and setting up the Christmas village. I fumbled with the electric cords. I could tell I was getting a buzz, but it was a fun buzz.

I turned on Christmas music and really went to work.

I continued to drink and decorate. Pretty soon, every surface in the living room and dining room had been decorated. Everything was white, red and green. There were candles, candy canes, fake snow, fur, lights, garlands and stockings.

At some point during this frenzy, I had put the kids to bed. I had been decorating for hours, continuing to drink. I was now no longer buzzed but quite drunk.

With the decorating done, I decided I would go out for a smoke. My parents hated that I smoked. Typically, I smoked in the courtyard. I had an ashtray out there, but the front door seemed closer. In my drunken state, it seemed the best call.

I went out, without my jacket, into the freezing winter night. I sat on the bench near the front door. The front porch is not enclosed. It is open to the elements. There is a wooden bench in front of my bedroom window to the right of the door. Reddish, stamped, molded concrete fixes a square ten-foot by ten-foot pad. There are large wooden poles on each corner that go up twelve feet. They meet the cross beams. It's a very southwestern look. While smoking the cigarette, I threw up. Projectile vomit spewed forward onto the stamped concrete. I sat in a drunken stupor, vomit on my shirt and dripping from my mouth. I wiped it off with the back of my hand.

I continued to smoke my cigarette almost down to the butt. Without my ashtray, I was unsure about what to do with the butt. I considered throwing it to the wind but knew my parents would discover it by the horses, and I would get yelled at. I opted to snuff it out on the ground and throw it away in the trash.

In all my drunken glory, I walked over to the edge of the stamped concrete and onto the dirt to snuff out the butt. I bent over. The world started to spin, and I slammed into the ground face first, knocking myself unconscious.

I don't know how long I was out, but when I came to, I was cold and y face was streaked with blood and dirt. I managed to stand up. In a drunken wobble, I made my way to the door. I tried to get in, but the door was locked.

Funny, I don't remember locking the door. How could I have locked myself out? As I rattled the doorknob, I could hear the cheerful jingle of the bells I had hung on the handle.

A moment later, my mom flung the door open.

"Oh, my God! What did you do to yourself?" my mom

exclaimed.

"Nothing. I was outside smoking a cigarette. You locked me out," I responded in a slur.

My parents had come in the house from the back driveway and had freaked out. They thought I was asleep after having decorated the house. Apparently, I looked fucked up. My lip was cut open. There was dirt and vomit smeared over my face and in my hair. They went into parent mode.

Clothes and all they threw me into the shower. They just kept asking me what I had done. I kept telling them I had a few drinks and was decorating. I was smoking and fell over.

They weren't buying it.

I had drunk both bottles of alcohol. They kept asking me if I had drunk both bottles. I don't remember drinking both bottles, but I told them if they were empty, then I had drunk them.

They were in between mad and concerned.

Around 3 am they put me to bed.

At 7 am, I got up for work. I was severely hungover and smelled like booze. Every inch of me smelled like vodka. I took another shower.

It wasn't so much the alcohol smell that was troublesome; it was my face. It looked like I had gotten into a fistfight. My upper lip was split open and bruised. I had also slightly chipped my front tooth, very slightly. Enough so that I could feel the roughness of it. When I ran my tongue across it, it felt like it would cut it.

I didn't know how I would explain this.

My mom told me I should call in sick at work. I told her it would be fine. I would just say I had an accident. People have accidents all the time. My mom told me I smelled. She was still very upset with me and said we would be having a talk later that evening. I went to work.

Of course, everyone stared at me. Since I had just gone through the divorce, everyone thought I had gotten into a fight with my ex. They had all assumed he had put a beating on me. I told everyone I had fallen. Which was true. I just left out the drunken part. Everyone had a look of concern, knowing there was more to the story.

The only person that called me on my bullshit was my friend Rick. Rick was a teacher and friend I co-taught with and partied with on occasion. He took one look at me and said, "You got drunk and fell on your face. Didn't you?"

Oh my God! It hurt to laugh, but I did. He knew me so well. He was the only one who guessed it. I did tell a couple of people what had happened. They all laughed and cautioned me about drinking too much or told me not to smoke.

The tooth really bothered me. Like I said, it was just a small chip. I took a nail file and filed down the front of my tooth. It smoothed it out. I have never had a problem with it. There is a slight nick in the tooth, but it is no longer rough.

My parents had a long parent conversation with me. They threw out all my booze. They said I couldn't drink at the house anymore since I couldn't be responsible. They were very concerned about my behavior. I told them it wouldn't happen again. I was just upset, and I let it get out of hand. They made me hose down the front of the house where I had vomited on the porch. I had to take a scrub brush to it because the vomit had baked onto the concrete during the day.

On another note, they told me the house looked very nice with all the decorations. Even in a boozy state of mind, I am quite the decorator.

My drunken decorating spurred by Charles ditching me was the push I needed to close that chapter for good. I stopped going back to him. I realized I needed to move on. I didn't want to end up a drunk like him and on my face in the dirt. I needed to get my shit together. I needed to take care of myself so I could take care of my kids.

Jesse

Jesse was a dream baby. He was a perfect ten! He was exactly ten pounds when he was born. He hardly fit in the bassinet.

In the nursery at the hospital, there were all these cute, tiny little babies all swaddled up; then there was my behemoth of a baby. He was a gentle giant.

He was a great baby. Of course, he cried when he was hungry and needed to be changed. He sounded like a little pterodactyl, or what I imagine one sounds like from the movies. He was perfect. He slept through the nights and had to be woken up to be fed.

Jesse was a snuggler and a gentle soul. He never wanted to be too far away from me. We were attached at the hip. It was different than Patrick. Patrick would run away from me; Jesse would run to me.

Patrick was so hard and difficult. Everything had been such a challenge. Patrick had been a sick baby. He cried all the time. He grew into a terrible toddler. He was obstinate.

Jesse was the exact opposite. He never cried. He was never sick except a few ear infections. He was a sweet toddler and young kid. He was introverted, where his brother was extroverted.

This last point made Patrick crazy. Patrick was so excited to have a little brother and have someone to play with, though they were separated by five years. Jesse wanted nothing to do with him and was happy to be by himself. They figured it out eventually.

My theory is that if you have a rotten baby, they turn into good teens; if you have a good baby, they turn into terrible teens. This has been my experience.

My wonderful, loving, cuddling, sweet, baby boy Jesse turned into an asshole during middle school. I don't know what happened. He just flipped. There was nothing I could do to make him like me.

He hated me. He hated my school.

The kids had gone to the school I teach at for middle school. We are not zoned for the school, but it's the best middle school in the valley, and it's the school I teach at so, of course, they are coming to my school.

Patrick had no issues with coming to school with me. He liked the perks of using my classroom as his personal locker room. He enjoyed going into the teacher's lounge when others couldn't. He liked that I would bring him burgers and fries on my break sometimes. He liked that he had full use of the school.

Jesse liked these things for a little bit as a sixth-grader. He did well as a sixth-grader. Made friends and joined student council with me. He is still friends with one of those kids from student council. Jesse fit right in.

Summer came and darkness fell.

The start of seventh grade, Jesse asked to go to his zoned school. I told him no. He said it was bullshit. I told him no. There was no reason for it. It would be more difficult, and it wasn't a good school.

He started acting out with me at home. Refusing to do chores. He did okay in school; in fact, he performed excellently in some of his classes. His teachers told me that they wanted him to work ahead in his classes. At home, he was just being an asshole.

He stopped coming to student council. He ignored me in the hallways. He barely tolerated me.

One night, my boyfriend Doug took my phone by accident. Jesse was asleep. I went in his room to use his phone to call my phone to tell Doug he had my phone. When I called my phone, my name was listed as "Cuntbag."

At least he was creative. I laughed. The little shit.

I took his phone. The next morning, he asked for it.

"The Cuntbag took your phone," I told him.

He shrugged and went back to his room.

I kept his phone for a while.

The school year passed in much the same fashion. Him ignoring me. Attitude and tempers rising. Doug was the intermediary.

I don't know what happened to my sweet little boy, but he was gone and replaced by an asshole teenager.

When eighth grade rolled around, the attitude got worse. Teachers noticed how Jesse treated me. He didn't want anyone to know he was related to me. He ditched me as much as possible. He refused to help me with anything. He still made a plea to go to his zoned school. I told him to wait out the year, and I would let him go to his zoned high school if he chose that.

Halfway through the school year, I was in the middle of co-teaching a class. The custodian came in and pulled me out.

"I think I saw your son and a couple of girls walking over the overpass by the casino. If you leave now, you might catch them," he said.

Ooh, I was livid! Oh, hell yeah, I was gonna catch 'em all! Pokemon style.

I told my principal what was happening, and he told me to go after them.

I hopped in my van and drove down the road. When I got to the overpass, they weren't there, but I thought I saw them going into an apartment complex. I turned in and started circling like a shark.

I know they could see me. If they could see me, they could hear me.

I started shouting out the window, "Come on out! I'm gonna catch you. Better come on out now. It'll be better than if I find you later. I will find you!"

I circled around a couple more times to no avail. I left the apartments and went to the corner store. I checked in with my boss and gave him the report. I told him that I was going to wait them out and see what happened. He said to hurry up and get back.

I waited at the store for fifteen to twenty minutes. I got back in the van and started circling around the street and I saw them. I caught all three of the little shits. Two of them were my former students and one was my son. Pissed wasn't enough to describe how I felt.

I rounded them up and called the school police. They said they had too many calls and would not be coming by to pick them up to transport them to campus. I called my boss. He said walk them back to school. I threw Jesse in the van and made the girls walk back. I yelled at Jesse, then realized he was getting it easy riding back. I then kicked him out of the van and made him walk back to school.

At the school, I marched them up to the dean's office. They all got marked truant.

Apparently, they wanted to go have breakfast and see a movie, but the movies didn't start until later in the day.

What killed me is that I had brought Jesse to school, drove him, and he ditched and went off campus.

My boss pulled Jesse aside and gave him a talking to. He tried to find out what made him tick. Jesse was just as cold with him as he was with me. There was no getting through to him.

At some point, he started to soften. He started coming back to student council. When we started the Alice in Wonderland Dance, he pitched in. Not great work, but he worked.

Once Jesse went to high school, our relationship changed. Our relationship really changed, once Doug left our lives. It was just Jesse and me living in the house. We are good roommates.

I am no longer the evil Cuntbag. I'm pretty sure I'm "Mom" in his phone. He is, again, sweet and gives hugs. He even brings me home food from work.

With the theory that bad baby equals good teen and good baby equals bad teen, both equal good adults.

Both my boys are wonderful adults. They are good human beings. If you have to be an asshole at some point in your life, childhood is the best time. You just don't grow out of being an asshole as an adult.

The Sister I Chose

My dad and his wife have visited Las Vegas a couple of times since I've grown up. Once while my brother was alive, we took them to dinner at a Thai restaurant. Another time they visited, I took them to see *Phantom of the Opera* at one of the casinos. We had a great time. My dad and I got along, but there was still some distance. I never went to his house in Maryland.

As a result, I grew up apart from my sisters. I didn't know what it was like to have a sister.

Athena became my sister. She chose to be my sister.

We became friends when our parents worked together for the police department. Sara and her father, Frank, were partners. We got to know each other through family dinners our parents had at the Geisha House, a hibachi dinner spot. Our parents would argue over who would pay the bill first, and one of them would secretly pay the bill without the other one knowing. Athena and I would just roll our eyes at their antics.

Athena and I were in college in different states at the time, each pursuing different degrees. We saw each other when she was home for these dinners.

Athena is shorter than me. She has dark curly hair that now has streaks of gray running through it. She has bright brown eyes. Light skin. She is Taos Pueblo. She is fierce but kind and generous. She will tell you the truth, no matter what. This serves her well in her profession as an attorney in family court.

Athena and I are similar in many ways. That's what bonded us. Our parents' connection started our bond. Sara and Frank were both amazing police detectives and had a way of looking at you that made you confess your sins even if you didn't have any. They looked at you like they were going to interrogate you. Our mothers were the exact opposite. They were the nurturers, kind and patient. Our parents were similar in that way.

Our sisterhood blossomed when I was struggling out of college.

Athena gave me a job as her secretary. I had no idea what I was really doing. She just told me to do things, and I did them. She was a fairly new attorney, and I was fresh out of school with a degree in English. I needed some money and she paid me out of her pocket to get me some cash while I went to school for my master's degree.

When I was getting married, Athena came over to help me set up for my bridal shower. When people started showing up, I just introduced her as my sister. People gave my mom a strange glance but didn't ask any questions. Athena had gifted me dishes from my bridal registry that I loved, and she hated. According to Athena, that was the first time I had called her my sister.

Whenever Athena and I were together, people had always just assumed we were sisters. We only slightly resemble each other with the dark hair and eyes. We both have the native background. Our mannerisms are similar. Our loud voices and direct speaking are very much the same. So much so that when my mom went to Athena to get legal help to start her yoga business, she spoke to Athena on the phone and said it was hard to know if she was talking to me or Athena. My own mother struggled to tell us apart. It was just easier to say we were sisters.

We bonded more over the fact that we were urban Indians. We were cut off from our culture. We knew very little about our culture and our language. We were both raised in a non-native way and yearned to know more.

Another thing that bonded us was that we are both victims of sexual abuse. We have shared our stories with each other. Cried with each other and healed with each other.

Athena saw me through my divorce. She handled my divorce to Jesse's dad. She even bought me the clothes I needed to wear to the hearing. She did it all pro-bono with the help of a program. She helped me pack up my house when I had to move back in with my moms after the divorce.

When Athena was pregnant with her first child, I went to the hospital to be with her. They were playing music. The room was dark. I rubbed her feet. I kept telling her to breathe. She kicked me out of the room. I wasn't helping.

I was so excited to become an auntie when Athena had kids. It was amazing. When Mateo was born, I brought over my Navajo cradleboard. They used it to bundle him up. There are a few pictures of him in it.

I helped make a Boots costumes from Dora the Explorer for him for Halloween one year. With the leftover material, I made a blanket for him.

Athena and I sewed many receiving blankets together. Mostly it was me watching her. I just kept her company. She loves giving receiving blankets as gifts. They are easy to make. You can make a lot of them, and they are very useful and practical.

After my divorce, I spent a lot of time at Athena's house. My boys and I often spent the night at her house on the weekends. If we weren't sleeping at the house, we came over on the weekends to eat breakfast and stayed for dinners. My kid crashed on Athena's couch. Several times, my youngest son, Jesse, peed on her couch. I now have that couch. Athena loves that I have the pee couch.

Athena attempted to get married to Albert at what we call "the almost second wedding" on Thanksgiving. It was a surprise wedding under the guise of a Thanksgiving feast. It was beautiful. We decorated with fall flowers and white linen. The house was amazing.

After dinner, Athena and Albert changed into wedding clothes and came out and surprised their guests. Athena was wearing my wedding dress. The real surprise was that the officiant had not shown up. She had gotten lost. By the time she had arrived, Athena was done and decided not to get married.

The next day I watched Mateo so she and Albert could go see *The Goblet of Fire.* Athena loves Harry Potter. She told me when Cedric Diggory died the tears started flowing. She was overwhelmed by the almost wedding and the onscreen death of Cedric.

Eventually, they did get married when Maria found out she was pregnant with Eva. They did not have an extravagant wedding. We went downtown to a wedding chapel. I was wearing a Broncos sweatshirt. It was a small affair. Just a few friends and family.

Athena's husband at the time, Albert, was an excellent cook. He was always making something delicious to eat. He made the most delicious turkey dinner. His gravy was amazing. I'm glad I learned how to make it.

We spent many holidays together at each other's houses. No matter whose house it was, we arrived early to clean, then cooked, then cleaned again. I noticed whenever we cooked a large feast, Athena always made a small offering to her gods as a gift of thanks.

* * *

As I got older, I got to know my blood sisters. We began communicating with each other. Natalie was the first to reach out to me.

She came to Vegas during my birthday weekend. It was a little awkward. She was severely allergic to cats, and we had a cat. I felt bad. When I picked her up from the airport, I was on my cell phone looking for her. I kept asking, "I don't see you. Where are you?"

"Look down," she said.

She was right in front of me. Natalie is very cute, petite and short. Carmel skin. Brown eyes. Brown hair. I was so tall in comparison. I was also wearing three-inch clogs. I was taller than a tall person needed to be. We hadn't seen each other since we were kids. I didn't know what to expect.

We took an overnight trip to the reservation and visited some family. It was a quick trip with my boys. We collected red sand in bottles as we left to take a piece of home with us. I still have my sand in a glass jar sitting on my bookcase.

Natalie visited another time, and Tom and I took her to the Shark Reef Aquarium. We had a big dinner at a hibachi place.

It was a nice visit. A Facebook memory recently popped up of that night. It was a picture of my sister, my son Patrick, my brother and I sitting on my old maroon couch. All of us smiling, frozen in time.

One of the first times I got to meet my sister Katrina as an adult was when my dad and both sisters came to visit for a few days or a week during the summer. It was nice to get to know her. She seemed a bit shy but fun.

Katrina is beautiful. Movie star beautiful. Dark hair and eyes. Full lips and smile that lights up a room.

The visit is a blur. My memory is fuzzy. I remember we went to the drive-in and my dad took my boys to another movie, but that's about it.

When my brother died, both my sisters came to Las Vegas to be with me and mourn the loss of our brother. Tom had lived with them in Maryland for a year. He knew them as kids.

We were all just getting to know each other as adults when he died.

Once, I was watching *Flashdance* on cable TV. I texted Katrina, who used to be a dancer. She happened to be watching it at the same time. For that one moment, we were connected. We texted throughout the movie. It was a nice moment. I think of her whenever the movie is on.

Natalie has reached out to me on Facebook one time about diving. She messaged me that she had water stuck in her ear from diving. She asked me what to do because she knows I'm a diver. I told her to put rubbing alcohol in her ears and equalize the pressure. She was having trouble making sure it was rubbing alcohol because the label wasn't in English. I thought it was nice that she reached out to me, sister to sister.

The last time I saw my sisters was at Katrina's wedding. It

was the first time I had ever been to my dad's house.

The house was a two-story house that sat back from the road on a nice plot of land. There were lots of trees in the front yard, blocking the street. Green grass was all around. It was a great-looking house.

It was strange to be included in the family that I always wanted to be a part of. I always felt like an outsider. I still felt a bit of an outsider. The wedding was the focus of the visit. Everything needed to be done. Flowers ordered. Candy filled. Nails done.

I wasn't sure where I fit in. I tried to help out where I could. I was supposed to be the big sister. I had never really been the big sister. I was always the little sister. Tom was the big brother. I had not had a sibling dynamic with my sisters.

During the visit, Natalie taught me how to knit. She is a skilled knitter. She knits hats, scarves and sweaters. She is amazing. She taught me the basics. She sent me home with a ball of green yarn and knitting needles. I promptly forgot by the time I was on the plane. I still have the pink needles, green yarn and patch of knitting I started.

With the invention of technology, I get to be a part of my sisters' lives, even if it from a distance. Through Facebook, I get to see birthdays, dance recitals, Christmas and Halloween. I get to see my nieces and nephew grow up. I get to see my sisters' lives lived as they post. I feel I am a part of it, just a little bit. We are able to express our love and joy for each other. I get to live in a virtual world with them.

I don't know if this is just the hazard of having families that grow up on opposite sides of the country or if this is just the world we live in now where families live virtual lives, and it's as good as it gets.

I wish my sisters and I lived closer together. I only know glimpses of their personalities. I'm sure there is much more to discover about them. They are both moms now, and with that comes a lot of change and a whole new world of opportunities. They are both great moms with happy beautiful children. I hope they know I'm happy for them. I love them, even if it is from a distance.

The distance isn't a great as it used to be, the divide not as wide.

Road to Teaching

When I graduated high school, I had decided I wanted to become a teacher. I was pretty sure I wanted to be a high school teacher. When I enrolled at the University of Nevada, Las Vegas, I entered the College of Education.

During my first year in school, I took only core classes and one class for the College of Ed. I took a class in Nevada School Law. It was very boring and taught by the teacher who wrote the book. I barely passed the class. I think I passed with a C or maybe a D.

At that point, I was second-guessing my decision to become a teacher.

My second year at UNLV, I took an actual class in my field. A class about teaching. I can't recall what it was called, but it had to do with being a teacher. I was very excited about it. The professor seemed very nice.

The first day of class, he said, "I'm here to help you. If you ever need anything, my number is in the syllabus, and my office hours are listed. Please call if you need anything! I'm here to guide you on your way to becoming teachers." I was really impressed.

I bought my books and attended classes for a few weeks.

It totaled a couple of classes. Suddenly, Patrick became very ill. He had caught chickenpox. My classes came to a screeching halt. I called all my professors and explained what had happened. Most gave me the assignments over the phone and what I could do at home for the next week.

I called my teaching professor. I explained my son had chickenpox, and I would not be in class for the week. I asked what I could work on from home. He responded, "Why are you calling me? Didn't you get one of your classmate's numbers? That's what they are there for. If you can't be here, why are you even in college? When you are a teacher, you can't just call into work whenever you want. You should just probably drop my class. You'll never catch up."

I was stunned. Here was a guy who at first meeting was open and ready to help. He made sure we had his number, office hours, and knew where his office was located. The flip in his behavior was so Jekyll and Hyde that I was beside myself. I had not gotten anyone else's number. It had not occurred to me. We were still getting to know one another in class. There hadn't been any group assignments or study groups. I hadn't talked to anyone outside of class.

This was only my second year in college, and I didn't really know how to handle the situation. I hung up the phone. I had a sick toddler who required my attention and four classes that needed attending to as well.

I dropped his class and then quickly dropped out of the College of Education. My dreams of becoming a teacher died due to the one asshole.

Instead, I focused on my English classes and art. I ended up with a degree in English and credits away from a minor in art.

After college, there wasn't much I could do with a degree in

English. Who'd a thunk? I started substituting for the school district. I took about four sub jobs before I landed a long-term sub job in high school, teaching a special education math position.

Math is not my specialty. I can do basic math, fractions, some equations, but explaining math is very difficult. Explaining it to kids with learning disabilities turned out to be even more challenging. I'm pretty sure I fucked them up, but what I got out of it was a decision for a career path. I wanted to be a teacher.

Somehow, I found out about a fast-track teacher program for special education. You had to have a bachelor's degree in any subject other than education to qualify for the program. The end result would be a master's degree in special education. I enrolled.

The program consisted of nightly meetings at a middle school for four hours and then nine weeks of graduate class-work at UNLV. We did nine graduate credit hours in nine weeks. All of this was done in the course of a couple of months.

There were about forty of us in this cohort program. All from different backgrounds. Some you could tell were going to do well. Some were going to wash out. For some, this was just another job until the next thing.

After the course work and nightly meetings were completed, we were deemed ready for mass interview by the district. I barely passed my interview. I don't know why, but I came up blank on most of my interview questions. The lady interviewing me was patient and prompted most of my responses. Whatever score they gave me, they don't share, but I know I got a low score because I didn't get any calls for interviews.

Our group, now slimmed down to about thirty, was now

taking evening classes at UNLV. It was the spring semester in January. Some of my cohorts had been hired and were teaching in the classroom. There were about ten of us who had not been hired, including me.

We continued going to class, and each class, someone would come in and share the news they had been picked up for hire. By February, everyone but another guy and me had been hired. Pretty soon, even he had been picked up. I was a lone wolf.

In March, I got a call from an elementary school requesting an interview. The principal was very persistent that I come over immediately. I explained that I had been out with the horses all day and was covered in hay, muck, and manure. She said, "I have five horses; I don't mind. I need you here now. Hiring freeze starts in two hours."

I got in my car, with my shitty, muddy boots, and drove over. I interviewed in a plaid shirt and jeans with straw in my pocket. I'm sure my hair was in a mess too. The principal showed me around and then asked if I would like to join her staff. We were told never to refuse when a first job was offered. Since I had never been offered a job, I said yes.

Elementary school was not my first choice. The principal knew that it was not my first choice and maybe not my fit. She also knew I was very green and needed a lot of help. She let me observe other teachers for the first two weeks. Then I got my own classroom and an aide.

I was to teach English, reading, and math. The other teachers gave me an outline of what to do. I thought I had a grasp on it. I had all of a few months from my couple of classes in education and a few months of long-term subbing in the classroom. I was totally unprepared.

The kids were manageable. The content was challenging. I

misspelled words on the board. I taught things incorrectly. I gave wrong information. I just plugged along. Even the kids corrected me. Fourth graders knew I didn't know what I was doing, but they let me go on about it.

When I was observed, I had misspelled "elementary" wrong on the board. This was an elementary school. UGH. The baby teacher is quite a thing to behold.

The paperwork was also quite overwhelming. Writing lesson plans each week, doing the lessons and writing IEPs (Individualized Education Plans). The first one I wrote was so lengthy, my colleague just shook her head and laughed. I had done everything by the book, as I had been taught. The student had fourteen goals to address every deficit. You just don't do that. You probably should, but you just don't. But they signed it.

During that year, a student pelted me in the eye with a tack that made eye swell up. Directly after it happened, my principal walked in. I had lost all control over my classroom. I couldn't see what was happening. I was crying and covering my face. She didn't know what was happening. I was trying to explain. She just told me to go to the nurse's office. I had to teach for the next couple of days with a patch on my eye.

Another time, I muttered to myself (but a little too loudly), "What the hell is that for?" I got called into the principal's office. She sat me down and asked why I was swearing in front of the students. I assured her I had not done so. Then she told me what had been reported. I told her yes, I had said that, but not to the kids, more to myself and under my breath. She informed me that a student heard and was offended as he was a Jehovah's Witness. I didn't see how "hell" was a swear word, but okay, it wouldn't happen again.

I was frustrated that my students weren't making progress. They struggled with spelling. They couldn't remember vocabulary. They didn't know their basic math facts. I expressed my concerns to a seasoned teacher, and she told me, "Sometimes, they are just a box of rocks and dumb as them. You can't save them all, honey." I was floored. I was so doe-eyed and new to education. Every student could be saved. Every student could learn. I didn't know what to say.

In my evaluation, the principal called me in to give her news. As a new teacher, your evaluation was the be-all and end-all. A good evaluation meant you could go on as a teacher; a bad evaluation gave them reason to dismiss you. My principal said, "It took me three days to write this evaluation. It took me three different computers. Your evaluation crashed three different computers. Your evaluation is the longest one I have ever written. I wanted to give you a positive evaluation, but to give you a positive evaluation, I have to give you a lot of directives." The evaluation was several pages long. Most are about two to three pages.

In the end, my time at the elementary school came to a halt. I was surplussed. This means the school no longer has space for you at their school. There are not enough students to need the teacher. You go into a pot of teachers that then are raffled off to other schools that need teachers.

My principal went to the surplus meeting with me. I really thought after my year in elementary school, I wanted to stay with younger kids. Then a middle school opening appeared on the board. I put my name into it. I was a new hire. I didn't think I would get it. My number was 25,000 something. Nobody else put in for it. I got the job.

The next week, I went over to meet Pat, my new principal at

my new middle school.

It was a long journey, but being a teacher was my calling. I took a roundabout road to get there, but if I hadn't dropped the college of ed course, I wouldn't have gotten the bachelor's in English, which led to getting the master's in special education. Which led to teaching at the best middle school in the country.

Co-Teaching

Co-teaching is a model of teaching when two teachers are in the room. One is a general education teacher and one is a special education teacher. The room is made up of general education students and special education students. The model is supposed to work so that special education students have gen ed peers that can model for them and they get extra support from having two teachers in the classroom.

This is not how a co-taught classroom actually looks. By law, you cannot have more special education students than general education students. The classroom is usually fifteen gen ed kids and fourteen sped kids, or higher, as long as the ratio is one gen ed kid higher than the sped kiddos. There is always a sped teacher in the classroom. The admin typically throws in the English language learners (ELL) into this classroom too because, hey, why not? There are two teachers in there.

These fourteen-plus sped kids come in all varieties and levels of needs. Some are low key and diet IEP, kids with very few accommodations. Others need lots of attention or are behavior problems and have behavior intervention plans (BIPs) that require daily documentation. Almost none of these kids can read or write at grade level and most of these kids require a lot of teacher interventions. That's why there are two teachers in the room. The special ed teacher is usually running around fulfilling these requirements instead of doing any real teaching.

An ideal co-taught class is one where both teachers fluidly get to teach. Both teachers are masters in the subject area and can model and instruct students. Unfortunately, this is not what happens. Sped teachers become glorified assistants and are seen as such by the students sometimes. I have felt that way in some classes.

I learned how to teach physical science, world geography, history, reading and English at a gen ed level. All this helped me when I finally was able to teach again in my own special ed classroom.

The benefits of a being a sped teacher in a gen ed class is you learn different teaching styles. You get to learn from master teachers and baby teachers. You get to see how you would run a classroom and how you would never run a classroom. You get to develop relationships and friendships that last a lifetime.

I taught co-taught with over twenty teachers who made an impact in my teaching and I learned teaching tools from them. I had fun in their classrooms. Sedlak, Rick, Bishop, and Schmidt. I learned from them all. I developed friendships with them all. The deepest friendship I developed was with Myers.

Myers and I taught eighth-grade science together. Our classes were about the sixteen to seventeen ratio. All our desks were full. We instantly had an ease with one another. She was easy to talk to.

In another life, Myers was a chemist. She came to teaching through an alternative route to licensure, like me. It was something she was passionate about. She came with great ideas and always wanted to improve and do better. She was a magical teacher.

We both had a love of science fiction. We had a gift for finding the funny in our students. We helped each other. Myers taught me the curriculum, so I didn't seem like a glorified aide in the class. I could actually teach Newton's Laws of Motion and know what I was talking about.

We took turns teaching in front of the classroom or taught at the same time. She would teach at the board, and I would walk the room making sure the kids were on task taking notes. We were always circulating, walking the room, making rounds in case the kids had a question. I could answer because Myers had taught me the material.

We built bridges made from toothpicks and tested them with weights. We made inertia cars and tested them with eggs in them. We made roller coasters to test Newton's Laws of motion.

We had one class project that was an alphabet book. The students were supposed to come up with a physics word for each letter of the alphabet and a definition with a picture. Grant it, some of them were tricky. We looked forward to the creativity of seeing what the kids came up with. In grading the projects, it was the gen ed kids that gave up the giggles more than the sped kids. One of the kids, Tommy, had written for his "Z" ZigZags and had a picture of the rolling papers for marijuana or tobacco. He had no clue. We laughed over it and deducted points.

We just had fun together. We shared videos with each other. Our favorite was the Saturday Night Live sketch "Dick in a Box." We would play it over and over before class. While kids would be presenting in class at the front for some project, I would be sitting at the computer in the front of the room marking down grades, and Myers sitting in the back of the class. I would catch her eye and make the motion of the "Step one. Cut a hole in the box," from the video. She would start to snicker. Then I would start to laugh. Then she would start to laugh. Then we were both laughing out loud and tears were rolling down our faces. Kids were just staring at us. Finally, we would get hold of ourselves and continue with the presentations.

We would just look at each other sometimes and just start laughing for no reason. Just knowing something was funny.

Myers and I co-taught for four or five years. I learned a lot from her. I learned a lot about science. I learned about grading fairly. I learned a lot about classroom management. I taught her about managing special education students and how to accommodate them in a gen ed setting.

I learned more outside of the classroom. Myers and I built a friendship. We began spending our time together on weekends getting our toes done together every few months. Then we'd go for coffee. We spent a lot of time together.

We spent time together at the yoga studio. Myers loved the class I taught and when she had time, she always made a Friday class.

When my boyfriend Doug and I were planning on getting married, Myers was going to be my maid of honor. I asked her on bended knee with a ring pop to be my maid of honor.

Whenever I got drunk after Doug and I broke up, she would pick me up and drive me home. She only lived around the corner from me. She would take me to get my car in the morning. I would usually have to get coffee or breakfast in return.

Myers has been with me through it all. She had to move away with her husband to another state when he got a job. That hasn't stopped us from being close. We talk almost weekly on the phone. She's always there to listen to my manic ramblings and there to check on me when I'm down. I don't think I'm an easy friend, especially when I'm manic. She always answers the phone, "Hey, how's it going?"

She still has family in Vegas and comes to town during the winter break. We get together every winter to get our toes done and to see a Star Wars movie if it is out. I look forward to my winter break with my bestie. I wait all year for it. It's better than Christmas.

Co-teaching brings together two teachers of two different backgrounds and fields. It started out as a job, but it has brought together Myers and me into a friendship that will last a lifetime.

Dichotomy of Classes

This past school year I had an interesting dichotomy of classes. I teach special education English and reading for middle school. Due to the bipolar, I had an episode that prevented me from starting the year with my students.

I got a note from the sub that said my period 1 were angels and I was going to love them. My period 2 was a bit talkative, and he had some trouble with them. He was sure that they would come around once I was in the classroom.

When you are given a description of a class before you meet them, you form an opinion about them. You also think, maybe the person in the room before you did something not great, and you could fix whatever was wrong in the classroom because you are a master teacher.

The sub had an excellent feel for the students in the classes and for what the year would look like. My period 1 was filled with eager learners. A joy to teach. They asked questions. They took their notes. They worked well with each other. They were kind and helped each other. If someone didn't have a pencil, they shared their supplies. They raised their hands to ask questions. They were a truly great group of kids. I couldn't have asked for a better, more loving and caring group of students.

Period 2 was the complete opposite. They were loud and rambunctious. In the beginning, they were not all naughty. I have to say that, individually, all these kids were great kids; as a group, they were a nightmare. Together they created a domino effect of terror. One disaster after another occurred. They were rude to each other. They constantly told each other to shut up. They threw things across the room. They stole from each other. They stole from me. They made fun of each other, and not in a fun way, in a mean way. They cussed at each other. They were a tough group.

I have a reward system in my class. For answering questions, turning in homework, scoring well on tests, helping someone out, being a good citizen, you get a ticket. That ticket goes into a bucket. At the end of the week, we do a drawing for a pencil, a student store pass, and a box of candy. At the end of the quarter, I do the same drawing, only I add a gift card to the raffle. Sometimes, depending on how much money I have, the gift card is $10 to $20.

I have had this system in place for several years. It has worked effectively. Kids want to earn tickets. They want to earn the chance at a gift card. It was a hard sell for my period 2.

Throughout the year, I teach short stories. The kids love *Riki Tiki Tavi* and *The Most Dangerous Game.* Mostly they love these stories because there are movies that go along with them. They love having a movie day. I always try to teach books that have movies. They love that. But you can't always do that.

I teach a wide variety of literature to my kids. I follow a higher-grade level curriculum and break it down for my special education students. I teach them *Beowulf*, *The Outsiders*, and *The Lightning Thief*. They love getting grade-level books.

This year we added *Wonder* and for period 1, they read *Enclave*.

The months went by and we read our books. Period 1 took their notes to the novels diligently. Period 2 fought me on taking notes. They barely followed along, and there were hardly any classroom discussions, unlike the lively debates I had with my other class. It was painful.

For the first time in years, I had to develop a seating chart. My general policy was that a student could sit anywhere in the class for one week but had to choose a new seat the following week. They could never sit in the same seat each week. They had to find new tablemates. This helped them make new friends and see who they could work with. By the end of the year, they knew who they worked well with and who they should be sitting with.

My period 1 class had no trouble with this arrangement. They fluidly found their seats and made their choices. My period 2 class fought each other on where to sit. They sat next to a bad choice or complained they couldn't sit next to so and so because they hated each other. I had to carefully make a seating chart based on who could sit next to who. A few of the kids had been in fights with each other and had signed contracts with each other that they couldn't be next to each other. I had to keep them apart. It was challenging.

During the second quarter, after the seating chart had been made, we were doing biographical research. The biography project was predominantly about people of color or women who have made changes in history. There were several African American students in my period 2. The kids were having trouble choosing who they wanted to research. I gave them a list of over 100 subjects to choose from. Nobel Prize winners to athletes to congresspeople. All they had to do was Google search a few and figure out who was interesting.

I mentioned Malcolm X to a kid who was having trouble finding someone. I said, "He was a black activist. He's very interesting."

One of the other students shouted at me, "She said black. She's a racist."

A girl shouted out, "Shut up! He is black. That's not racist."

Another piped in, "How is she racist?"

First kid said again, "Because she called him black."

"Shut up! You're black! Do your work," the girl yelled at him.

It wasn't the first time I had been called a racist, but it made me uncomfortable. I usually have the talk with my students as to what they prefer to be called, black or African American. Because I was out of school for two weeks, a lot had been trimmed out of my get-to-know-you speech. It was clear that some of the kids saw me as not on their side.

During that second quarter, period 2 started to get loud. They would talk over me when giving instructions. During quiet working time, they were not quiet. I had slowly taken away their Friday fun giveaways one at a time. First, it was the candy, then the student store pass, then the pencil. They had the opportunity to earn these back, but they never did. They just continued to be bad.

I finally bargained with them. Started from zero. I told them if they had a good week, we would not only have the raffle on Friday, but we would watch a movie. They got one movie in before the end of the quarter. They just couldn't contain themselves.

Winter break was much needed by all.

After winter break, we moved on with mythology. I taught

Norse mythology with *Beowulf*. My period 1 loved the mythology. They had lively discussions on how mythology and Christianity influenced each other. They wrote great essays about epic heroism for *Beowulf*. There were breakthroughs for some of my struggling writers who were finally able to find textual evidence and support their claims of why Beowulf was an epic hero. It was the best kind of teaching experience.

My period 2 did not find interesting parallels in the mythology. They did like that Beowulf fought monsters. They did write good essays with one-on-one help. The blood and gore in *Beowulf* held their attention. The notes we took did not hold their attention. Out of the fifteen kids in the class, only three took notes. The rest did nothing the entire time we read the book.

When we got to Greek mythology and *The Lightning Thief*, I encountered the same problems. My period 1 kids were engaged with the lessons. They took their notes. They answered the questions. We had discussions. My period 2 refused to engage. They rarely took notes and talked while I read the book to them.

Instead of writing an essay for the novel, we did a one-pager. It's a one-page assessment. It's less writing and gives the kids a way to be creative. They have a large construction sheet of paper and need to fill it. They need some letters from the characters, a book rating, character list, favorite quotes from the book, and a couple of drawings. The kids like to do this. It gives them a chance to work at their own pace and give their own responses to literature.

Of course, period 1 worked diligently. They paired off and shared supplies. They helped each other find quotes. They helped each other about characters and descriptions. They helped each other draw or suggested drawings.

On Monday, period 2 started out on the right path. They had their paper and pencils. They had all week to work on the project. They were loud as usual. Throughout the week, I had students at my desk that I worked one on one with to help with ideas of what to put on their papers. It was coming along.

In period 2 on Thursday, it was super loud. As always, they were all out of their seats. My supplies were not on the back table, where they were supposed to be. One of the students had taken them back to his seat. One of the girls got up to get a colored pencil from him. She smacked the box, and the entire box of pencils exploded over the room. They all laughed. She exclaimed, "It was an accident. He hit my hand."

Exasperated, I said, "Please, pick it up and return to your seats. If you need a pencil, come get one at the back of the room. Leave the box in the back so everyone has access."

The pencils came back in disarray. The class quieted down. Students were in their seats. I sat back down at my desk.

I look up and see two objects being thrown across the classroom. PING! PING! Markers were being chucked from two different locations in the classroom.

The kids were laughing. Ice went through me. I got scary calm.

It must have shown on my face. The kids got quiet. I stood up. I didn't say a word. I just started collecting papers. I then started collecting markers. Still without saying a word.

They asked if I was going to count the coloring against them if they hadn't finished. I just looked at them. There were ten minutes left of class. I just raised my finger to my lips. I stood in front of the class. Calm. Scary calm. They were quiet.

The bell rang. They left.

I assessed the damage. They had opened every box of crayons and markers and dumped the contents all over the place. They had ripped the packages so that some of the markers and crayons couldn't go back into the boxes. Everything was scattered.

I was furious. Something had to be done. They needed to be on lockdown.

I moved my classroom around. I moved all the tables to line the walls of the classroom. I left two tables in the center of the room facing me. I made a seating chart.

I went to the administration and explained what had happened. They knew all the problems that I had been having with that class that year. They said to start sending them to the dean's office.

Now, I don't send kids to the dean's office. I firmly believe in handling your own discipline problems. It's better that way. In eighteen years of teaching, I have written a handful of dean's referrals.

My period 1 was shocked at the new seating arrangement but just shuffled chairs around to where they liked and moved them back when they were done. We were moving on with *The Outsiders*. My period 2 was moving on with writing a persuasive essay on vaccinations independently.

When the period 2 came in, I assigned their seats. One boy I had sitting right next to me.

He said, "Oh, hell no. I'm not sitting there."

"Go to the dean's office," I calmly said.

"Fine," he firmly stated.

"Just go," I said exhaustedly.

"I'm going!" he shouted.

"Then go!" I shouted back.

A girl laughed.

I looked at her. "You want to go too?"

She stopped laughing.

New rules of the class for period 2: No talking. No devices. (I used to allow the kids to listen to music). No getting out of your seat without raising your hand. If you do not follow these rules, it will be a dean's referral.

I had printed their assignments and put them in folders with their names on them. I read them the instructions. I told them if they wanted one-on-one help to come see me, and I would help them. A few of the kids raised their hands and came over for the one-on-one help. Those kids got right to work. The other kids just put their heads down on the desk and went to sleep.

This went on for the first two weeks. About four of the kids in the class worked on the assignment. The others refused to work. Seven were written up for throwing things, fighting, cussing and being disrespectful. They went to the dean's office. The class was quiet. Those that worked, worked. Those that didn't, didn't, but it was quiet.

My period 1 were angels. We read a new book, *Enclave*. They loved it. Post-apocalyptic novel with zombie-like creatures out to get you. They couldn't get enough.

Around week three, most of period 2 started working. Some of them actually finished the vaccine essay and went on to the next assignment of writing a short story.

All the assignments were independent work with me as a reference and guide. I worked one-on-one with most of the kids. There were two students who refused to work at all and did nothing for the remaining of the year.

The last assignment I gave period 2 was to read *The Count of*

Monte Cristo. It was an abridged version with a picture on the opposite side of the text to show what was happening. I think the book was a total of 200 pages including pictures. They had to read and answer comprehension questions independently. If they could not read it, they could come to me, and I would read it with them and help them answer the questions.

At different times, I would have small groups working with me. The class was finally starting to work and get on track. They were working quietly. They were working at their own pace, some were further ahead, and some were behind, but they were working and engaged.

The boy who refused to sit by me was now actively seeking out my assistance to work with him on the chapter questions and the readings. He needed some guidance on finding the right passages to answer the questions. He had actually apologized to me about his behavior. Things were beginning to get better.

The final writing assignment for this class was to write about whether they felt the Count was justified in his revenge and about a time they had sought revenge. All of them believed he was justified in seeking revenge. The kids all had a story about a time they had been done wrong. It varied from having their favorite cereal eaten by a sibling, so they did something to them, to a girl who wrote that a friend stole her boyfriend, so she cut off that girl's hair.

I asked if any of them felt remorse for their revenge. None of them felt bad about their choices. It was interesting to see.

Period 1 finished their novel and had to do their book assignment. It was a choice board. They could do pretty much anything they wanted to do to present the novel. They worked like they always did. They were able to listen to music. They had shared art supplies. They really got to play around the last two weeks of school. The last day before finals, we had a party to celebrate their hard work. I bought them doughnuts and juice.

Period 2 came in after the party and saw the remains of the party and the credits rolling from the movie. They asked if the other class had a party. I told them that period 1 had a party. They wanted to know if they were getting a party. I told them they had not earned one, but I would let them listen to music today.

They seemed a little bitter but happy with the music. They wanted to know why they didn't get a party. I explained to them that the other class had never thrown anything, never been written up, never yelled at me or at each other. They were civil to one another. They did their assignments. They were being rewarded. I told them they had the same opportunity, but they chose not to take it when they destroyed my classroom supplies and disrespected me.

One of the kids said, "You're right, Ms. T. We don't deserve a party. But we will be better."

They were good for the next two days, which was the remainder of the year.

It was interesting to have such a diverse group of kids. I have a ton of teaching experience under my belt. I used all the tools in my toolbox. None of it worked.

I had one group that was great. It was a great mix of kids. They had grit and intrinsic motivation. I didn't have to dangle a carrot. They wanted to learn.

My other group was just difficult from the start. They fed off each other's energy. They fought for attention in negative ways. It bred more destructive tendencies. I know they were good kids. One on one, they were amazing kids. Together they were a violent storm that would level a city. I moved their seats. I offered rewards. I changed rewards. I changed the point system. I adjusted the curriculum. I worked one on one. Nothing seemed to work until they were isolated.

It just goes to show, no matter how much experience you have, sometimes it doesn't matter. You just gotta push on and keep teaching; eventually, you find a way through. I had to remove everything that could distract them in order to get them to focus. That period 2 told me that their favorite part of the year was reading *The Count of Monte Cristo.* I thought it was interesting that their favorite novel was all about getting revenge. I should be wary about them seeking revenge on me.

Food Drive

I became a student council advisor sometime in my third or fourth year of teaching. I had watched from the sidelines, and it looked like fun. I had seen the student council advisor and her kids hold dances and run spirit days. I wholeheartedly participated in all of them and always took the time to chaperone each event.

When the advisor asked me to take over, I said yes immediately. We had a new principal who had downgraded the position from an early bird class, which is a prep buy out, to a club. That translated from a few thousand dollars down to six hundred dollars a semester. I jumped at the chance. I didn't know what I was getting myself into.

My first meeting with the kids, half of them didn't show up. The ones that did argued and wouldn't let me talk or talked over me. They were rude and showed no respect at all. The huge missing component was the president of the student body.

After the first meeting, my head was spinning. We planned to meet three times a week. At the second meeting, the president didn't show up again. The kids announced they wanted to vote her out. I asked them if they could do that. They said sure, of course they could, as long as they had a majority vote. So, I said okay.

Oh, my little naive self. I didn't know what I was doing. Like everything else, I learned by doing.

One of the things as student council advisor that I wanted to instill in my students was that helping others was something to strive for. Our food drive service project grew each year. Our motto was, "Kids helping kids."

Our food drive filled another school's food pantry. The other middle school was a low-income school. They had an over 90 percent free and reduced lunch rate. Most of the students used the food pantry. They received assistance to take home food on the weekend. Many of them did not have food at home if they did not get food from the school. The food from school not only fed the student attending the school but also fed siblings.

When I first started out with the food drive as a baby advisor, the food drive was about filling pickup trucks. We wanted to send at least five truckloads to the school. My friend Pat told me it was important. He had built the partnership with the other school through his friendship with the principal, Jorge.

In the beginning, it was just about the challenge of getting the trucks filled and making sure we met that goal so as not to disappoint Pat. Pat left my school, and I had to build my own relationship with Jorge. I wanted our partnership to continue. Through building that relationship, I learned about the adversity the school's children were actually facing. It broke my heart.

I began to dig in and really push my food drive. I talked to my students about how we could make changes to the drive and build it up.

Each year the drive got bigger and bigger.

One year, I told Jorge he was going to need a lot of trucks.

We had hallways full of food. He rented a small U-Haul truck and we filled it.

From then on, that's what we did. We rented a U-Haul truck, and we filled it.

Each year, Jorge told me he was renting a U-Haul, and each year I worried I was not going to fill it.

One year, my favorite year, I had a wonderful group of caring and kind kids. They really wanted a successful food drive. We talked about setting goals. They set a goal of 10,000 canned food items. How do we get more food?

They wanted to partner with our feeder schools to bring them into our drive. I reached out to the schools, and they all agreed to partner with us for the drive.

The students wanted to reach out to the grocery stores and see if we could stand out in front of the stores on certain days and ask for donations. The stores agreed. They filled the back of my van several times.

The students wanted the community to join in more, so they decided to walk door to door with a wagon and ask for canned food donations. We walked every weekend for a month with flyers asking for food donations throughout the neighborhood by the school. They received lots of donations and some cash donations.

Everything was off to a good start.

I, of course, was still worried that we were not going to make our goal.

One evening, after teaching yoga, I sat in silence and meditated and prayed on it. I just prayed to the cosmic universe to open up and help my students meet their goal. They were working so hard at helping others. Give them the energy to see things through. Heaven help us reach 10,000.

It was as if someone was standing right next to me. Someone whispered in my ear, "Twenty thousand is your goal."

I was alone in the studio. My mom was out front closing up. I opened my eyes. I was truly alone. Someone had spoken to me from the universe. Our new goal was 20,000.

My students knew I could be a bit crazy. I told them about my vision. They didn't think I was crazy. They just said they thought it was doable.

We continued with our efforts.

In the classrooms at schools, we had classroom competitions on who was bringing in the most food. We gave away prizes to students who brought in the most food. We had weekly giveaways and rewards.

I had certain teachers I knew I could count on. They could bring in thousands of canned food items in their classrooms just by themselves.

Teachers were stealing other teachers' food from other classrooms. Teachers were bribing kids to give them their food instead of giving it to other teachers.

I could always count on Myers and Badger. Myers could inspire her students to bring in close to three thousand canned food items. The front of her classroom would be full, and she couldn't use her board anymore. She couldn't reach it due to the amount of food that was there.

Badger bribed his kids with soda and snacks. One year, he gathered over five thousand canned food items in his classroom. Students who were not his students brought cans to his room. He doled out prizes to anyone who came into his room. I had to relieve his stash halfway through the drive so he could teach. His room was overflowing with food. It was pushed up against two walls.

I caught one teacher, who will remain nameless, breaking into another teacher's classroom before school. She was pilfering her canned food. She merely stated that the teacher she was stealing from didn't have enough cans in the class to matter, so she wanted it for her class. I turned a blind eye and kept walking.

I encouraged all the infighting if it meant we were getting donations.

This year, the principal and I decided we were going to take the student council kids with us on the pickups from the other school and the final delivery to the receiving middle school. This had not been done before. My students were very excited about this process.

The food was pouring in. The offices were packed with boxes. The hallways were packed. Classrooms were overflowing.

I called Jorge and told him I thought we might need two U-Haul trucks. He brought two trucks.

The day of collection, there was a buzz in the air. My students all wore matching shirts. They were excited. They began to collect the food from the classrooms and collect totals of food from the teachers. Teachers were also emailing me totals so I could get an electronic count.

There were also the one or two teachers who had NOT counted their food, and we had to stop everything and count four hundred cans of peas. It was frustrating but not the end of the world.

The kids hauled box after box to the front of the school. Two U-Haul trucks were backed up to the front of the school. We loaded box after box.

We filled one and a half of the U-Hauls. We still needed to go to three sister schools.

My students were loaded into some volunteer parent cars. My boss and I got into his vehicle. We followed the U-Hauls to the next school. We caravanned from school to school loading and packing, playing Tetris with boxes, and trying to get the back of the trucks to close.

We were very successful, but we still had one final stop.

We delivered our goods. The receiving school's student council came out to meet my student council. It was a cool moment, council to council. Kids meeting kids. Kids helping kids.

They all pitched in and got to work.

The food from the two U-Hauls filled an entire classroom. It was packed.

We started a tradition that day. We started taking the kids on the pickup and delivery, and we took them out to eat. Jorge paid for the kids to get lunch. We took them out to the buffet. They loved it.

At the end of the day, I added up the total. The total of all the donations from our school and our sister schools was over 25,000 canned food items. The kids' original goal and my whispered goal came to fruition.

Kids helping kids. The food drive went on to be successful the following year with around the same number of items.

This is one of my proudest moments as an advisor. The kids believed they could do something. They set it in motion and made it happen. Yes, I helped, but they believed in their project. They set a goal, did the work, and made the magic happen.

Losing the Best Job in the World

I became a student council advisor by default. I stayed on as the advisor because I fell in love with the job. It was my reason for teaching. Teaching leadership taught me to be a better special education teacher. It taught me to be a better person.

I loved my council kids. I started every day with them. I had an early bird class with them. It was like I got to be a kid again every morning. We would have games and plan, and then I would go about the rest of my day in the seriousness of the world as a regular teacher.

I was an advisor for ten years. I was nominated and won Advisor of Year for the state of Nevada. It was quite an honor. I was also recognized with a nomination for regional advisor of the year. There was a big mix-up. That was a strange turn of events. They accepted my application and mistakenly gave me an award and took it back. They called me to apologize. It hurt, but as everyone says, it was an honor to be recognized.

We changed the face of dances. Our most famous dance was an Alice in Wonderland dance. We spent three months working on it.

We created ten by-six-foot PVC stands to hold murals to be displayed in the cafeteria. We replicated scenes from the movie. We build three five-foot mushrooms out of papier-mâché. We even built a four-foot caterpillar to go on top of the mushroom. We built forty smaller mushrooms. We built a river filled with lights to wander through our wonderland.

We hung drapes from the ceiling in all colors to cover the rafters. Every inch of the place was covered. We transformed the cafeteria into Alice in Wonderland.

For games, the kids played croquet with flamingos. We had a candy bar for the sweet tooth with jars of candy lined up. We had punch and decorated water bottles. We had hot dogs. It was a dream.

To push our ticket sales, our principal and assistant principal had agreed if we reached a certain number of tickets, they would dress up as characters from the movie. We hit our number, and our principal came as Alice, and our assistant principal came as the Red Queen. It was wonderful.

The kids wanted to build excitement for the dance even further. They decorated the eighth-grade hallway. We stayed until midnight and covered the entire hallway from floor to ceiling with scenes from the movie. The hallway was transformed. We were in fire code violation, I was informed later, but the kids loved it. They bought tickets.

It was our highest-selling dance. We found our groove on how to do dances.

It was around this time I started to get sick with the bipolar.

It was starting to show.

It was harder and harder to be spunky with the kids in the morning.

I was often late. If you are late to the morning meeting, you are not reprimanded. You simply have to sing a song. Even I was breaking the rules and refused to play along.

I was depressed and could not get out of the funk. The kids began to notice my behavior. I thought I was hiding it. They were talking to each other about it. My kids who loved me were concerned about me. They thought I was mad at them. One of them asked me why I was upset with them.

It broke my heart.

My illness was affecting my interactions with the kids. I knew I couldn't do this to them. They deserved better. If I couldn't get a handle on my illness, I knew I wouldn't be a good advisor and friend to them.

I tried to explain to them what was going on. Some of the kids whom I had had for three years, I told the truth about my condition. I told them I was bipolar and having a tough time. My new kids, I just told I was sick. They all stood by me and supported me even though they didn't all understand it. They continued to do what I asked of them, even in my downtrodden condition.

The depression was really bad. There were constant minute-by-minute suicidal ideations. I wasn't showering or brushing my teeth. I wasn't eating but once a day. I was mostly living off of coffee and cigarettes.

I went to the principal and told him I couldn't continue like this with my kids. I would have to give up being the student council advisor. It wasn't fair to the kids. It wasn't healthy for them or me. I needed to get better.

It was a difficult decision. It was one of the toughest decisions I made, but I did it for my kids. They deserved someone who was well and able to smile. They thought I was mad at them. I couldn't emote anything but sadness to them.

At the end of the year, I stepped down as their advisor. That was the end of my career as a student council advisor.

The sad part is, over the summer, I got the right combination of meds. The following school year I felt wonderful. I would have been fine. I had a tough year; my meds weren't right. I gave up something I loved at the wrong time. I did it for the right reason, but I regretted it.

It has all worked out now. I have been in and out of being well and sick. Truth is, it was what was best for the kids. I wouldn't have wanted to let them down again. This illness limits me. I have to learn to accept that.

I had my fun, awards, and recognition. The best part is the love I shared with an amazing group of students who will always be my kids and the long-lasting friendships I have with some of them to this day.

He Always Chose Me

My brother Tom killed himself on May 10, 2010. He was 37 years old.

Darkness creeps in like smoke under a door. This darkness fills the cracks and crevices of my heart and soul. The day my brother took his life, he ended a part of mine. There was never a day I existed without him. He was always there.

There is such an emptiness left in the wake of his suicide. I see how others have coped with death and his death. I watched as Uncle Dave was consumed by cancer and slowly died in his home. I mourned and grieved but didn't feel this hollow nothingness that flows through me always.

My brother was smart, caring, generous, and funny. But for each of these wonderful traits, he had a darkness that matched them. Alcoholism, anger, depression, fear. I would say that most people suffer from these emotions, but my brother lived them in unison. He was in pain and laughed it off. He would drink and entertain. Each part of him lived simultaneously, in conjunction with each other. All of his emotions were tied to the negative. The heavy darkness would always win the battle.

The people who were closest to him would eventually see this darkness. Like a shadow that needs light to exist, this darkness sat in wait for Tom's light to shine. It was his shadow to everything.

My brother recently told me that he couldn't believe he hadn't confided in me about the anger he felt as a kid. We were discussing growing up as native kids, urban Indians in an all-white school. This was the root cause of a lot of his anger and a lot of his comedy. My brother was called Chief and made fun of a lot more than I was. I remember him telling my mom that he hated everything about himself. He hated the way he looked. He hated being an Indian. He hated was the bottom line.

This hatred started with himself and snowballed into other things in his life. Whatever he hated, he hated it with a passion. He threw everything he had into hating it. The last thing he said to me was he hated me. The anger and fierceness that he spoke to me told me that the darkness was ruling his mind and spirit. I knew he wasn't kidding or blowing steam as he had so many times in the past. He was going to kill himself if he could. He spoke with conviction.

I had to call so many people and tell them that my brother ended his life. The hardest call was to my father. I felt terrible having to tell him such news over the phone. I don't know the last time I had spoken to my dad on the phone. I didn't know the last time Tom had spoken to Dad. He was in disbelief. He didn't want to believe me. I waited on the phone for the truth to sink in that Tom was dead. I cried with my dad. He flew out immediately to be with me.

My aunties were just as grieved at this news. All who heard were shocked by this terrible event. I never was. Maybe it was my brother's voice echoing that he was going to kill himself, but I knew he had it in him to do.

While my dad was with me, we had long conversations over strong coffee. We held hands and cried. It seemed that all had been forgiven. I felt my dad's love. I knew he loved me. I had just been keeping him at a distance. My brother's death had shown me life was short, and I needed to keep my family close.

I needed my friends too. When Tom died, Myers was there for me like no one else could be. She also lost a brother to suicide. I knew her feelings of loss were like mine. I knew her condolences were not empty. She listened to me while I raved about my brother.

* * *

The darkness that marked Tom's soul marks mine as well. I know the feeling of falling victim to the abyss. Death sounds so much easier than fighting for life. Struggling daily to be happy. Wearing a smiling mask when all you want to do is die. My brother and I both bore the burden of these feelings. I often wonder if I was born to help him cope with his feelings.

I was quite often the outlet for my brother to feel better. As children, he insulted me to make himself feel more powerful. As a grown-up, he would call me and vent a plethora of profanity that would make him feel better. Not everyone saw this side of him. Even as a little kid, I knew he did these things to make himself feel better, so I would take one for the team.

He always called me to vent. He always called me to complain. He always called me when it mattered. He called me when he chose to end his life.

* * *

Mother's Day had just passed. It was a Monday. It was first or second period. I was in science, co-teaching with Myers. She was out sick that day or a doctor appointment for her pregnancy. I was standing in the back of the room on the black and white checkered floor. My Motorola flip phone vibrated in my bra. I discreetly pulled it out. Ten minutes before the bell was going to ring.

I saw it was my brother. We hadn't talked in over a week. A blow up over his daughter's baptism about his perception that our parents were being rude at the church by not accepting a welcome gift of a coffee mug. Then that argument turned into a discussion about how Tom wasn't spending time with my boys anymore. I told him that I thought his girlfriend was one of the best things that had happened to him. Then he said, "Oh, I get it. You hate my girlfriend." That was the end of the discussion. The last time I had heard from him. I didn't invite him over to Mother's Day breakfast. I figured it would blow over.

Now he was calling. He rarely called me at work unless it was important, so I answered. He blew up. "I fucking hate you! I'm going to kill myself and it is all your fault," he screamed at me.

"Tom, let's talk about this. What's going on? Where are you?"

"I just want you to know, I fucking hate you. It's all your fault. I fucking hate you. I'm going to kill myself," he screamed at me with pain and determination. Then hung up on me.

I knew he meant it. I knew he was sincere.

I was in the back of the class. The bell rang. I walked out of the class, down the hallway and into the quad. Classes resumed. I called my mom, told her what had happened. She called him. I called my cousin, Carrie, and she said maybe he was just venting. But I knew. He was speaking the truth. He wanted to die and was going to die. I felt it in my bones.

Time slowed.

My mom called back. She said she had spoken to Tom. She said he was disoriented. He said he was driving and running people off the road and that he hated me and was going to kill himself. Then he hung up. She would call me back.

I couldn't go back into the classroom. I went into the classroom of another teacher who didn't have any students. He was doing paperwork. I just asked him if I could hang out and wait on a phone call. He said sure and left the room to run copies.

A minute later, my mom called.

"Tom's dead." That's all she said. She hung up. What else could she say?

I was alone.

It started low and began to build. I thought it was a silent cry. But I began to wail. I was shouting and crying uncontrollably. A teacher from next door came in to see what the commotion was about, saw me and just held me. I could barely get out what was wrong. She called the office, I suppose. I don't recall what happened. I was passed from one person to the next.

From first conversation to last, it all took about fifteen minutes. I don't know how long he contemplated the suicide, but from when he first told me until he pulled the trigger, it took all of fifteen minutes.

All I wanted to do was to get in my car and drive to my mom's house up the street, but nobody would let me drive. They said I was unfit to drive. My boyfriend, Doug, came to pick me up. At first, they said that Tom was alive, and they were taking him to UMC trauma unit, but then we got the call he had passed in the ambulance and was being taken to Centennial Hills Hospital.

Together we gathered in a family room.

We learned that he had fallen asleep at work. They had to call his boss to get someone to unlock the doors at the bar. They were unsure whether he had been drinking. The relief bartender said that this was probably going to be the end for him there. He left in a rage. Called me. Said what he said. He spoke with my mom. A police officer, who had been on the job for a week, saw him swerving and flipped his lights to pull him over. Tom was very close to his house. He did not pull over but kept driving. He pulled in front of his house. The cop told him to get out of the car. Tom did not. Tom reached for the gun on the front seat. The gun he kept with him at the bar every night and shot himself in the head. At that moment, his girlfriend pulled into the driveway with their daughter.

While in the family room, my mom learned that Tom had been arrested and spent the weekend locked up for a DUI the previous summer. He had said he would never go back to jail again. My mom had no idea.

I remember just a feeling of shock and emptiness. I remember having to call my dad and tell him. I remember having to call everyone and tell them. I felt so hollow and empty.

When his birthday comes around and the anniversary of his death comes around, I relive these moments. I try to focus on the joyful events we shared, but this trauma triggers me. I try to think that in the worst moments of his life, even though he blamed me for his trouble, he still called me. In the end, it was just him and me. As it always was.

* * *

When my Tom died, Athena really became my big sister. She and Tom are the same age, a month apart. I don't know if I seemed wounded and needed to be looked after, but Athena, like Myers, looked after me. She stepped in and took care of me.

In my many bipolar episodes, Athena has been there for me. When I was hospitalized, she was one of the few people who came to check on me. I wasn't in there very long, but she showed up. She always shows up.

When I was sick most recently, she drove over and picked me up so I wouldn't be by myself and took me to her house just to keep an eye on me. When I'm out of sorts, she just kind of picks up on that and checks in with me. Checks in after I have sent her twenty texts about the same subject or offers to do something. She checks on my mania. If she doesn't hear from me and I'm in seclusion, she offers to get me out of the house. She's always trying to do what's best for my mental health.

I was short on cash for a school year due to not getting the extra money for a prep buy out and in debt on medical bills from a hospital stay. Athena helped me pay one of my bills. It helped me keep afloat.

I don't know what I did to deserve the blessings of a sister like Athena. Athena has always been there for me, more than just a friend. We are sisters of the heart. We are there for the good and the bad. We put up with each other's shit when everyone else bails. We are strong enough in ourselves to help each other pick up the pieces when all seems lost. We remind each other that we are intelligent, educated, amazing women with unending fortitude. No one else is strong enough to deal with us when we are falling apart.

She is my sister, and I am hers. I chose her and she agreed.

Spending Time with my Brother

Tom was an alcoholic. He became sober for about five years. We were all very proud of him. He lived a sober life. He went to AA and lived the life. He was productive and went to meetings. He worked at the bar, but that never tempted him. He was very involved in my life and my sons' lives.

Tom and I spent a lot of time together. During the summer, while Patrick was in year-round school, Jesse and I would go to the library. We would pick out books, music and movies. Tom lived around the corner from the library. We would wait until he got off work and then we would go over to his house.

Tom's girlfriend, Barb, would be there, usually cooking breakfast. We would put on the Elmo DVD for Jesse in the bedroom and sit at the tiny kitchen table in the apartment and eat breakfast.

Tom's apartment was immaculate. Tom had decorated his apartment with paintings he bought of flowers in vases. He had several of them. He had tea light candles and votive candles—light all around his house. They covered every surface. His house always smelled like roses. His place was always tidy. Nothing was ever out of place. There were house plants growing everywhere.

At the entrance to his apartment, he had planters with petunias and pansies. He loved those flowers. I don't know how he kept them alive in the Las Vegas heat. He had a green thumb.

For a month, Jesse and I spent time at my brother's apartment. If his girlfriend wasn't there, we would fix something for ourselves or we would go out to eat. We spent almost every day together.

On my brother's day off, he would often take my kids to the Shark Reef Aquarium. He loved to look at the jellyfish display. He would spend most of his time looking at them. He was mesmerized by them. Tom was a doting uncle.

We spent a lot of time at the movies together, sometimes with the kids, but most of the time just the two of us. We were movie buffs. The two of us collected DVDs and shared our collections. I still have movies marked with a sharpie "Tom T" inside the DVD case. I know there are movies of mine at his house with my initials in them.

Throughout childhood, once we had a television, we were obsessed with TV and movies. Tom loved *The Shawshank Redemption* and *Saving Private Ryan*. When *Saving Private Ryan* didn't win an academy award. Tom threw things and swore he'd never watch the Oscars again. He couldn't believe it lost to *Shakespeare in Love*. He said it was rigged. No way could it have lost to that piece-of-shit movie. I loved *Shakespeare in Love*. Tom and I not only shared a love of movies, but we shared a love of comic books. Tom was a collector of comic books as a kid. He constantly told me to stay out of his room, but when he left, I, of course, went into his room. In his closet was a treasure trove of comics, along with a stash of old, stinking, sour cereal bowls that he had not taken to the sink. It was gross.

I would steal his comics and read them. I read all his Spiderman, Wolverine and X-men comics. I read Batman and Ironman. Tom never knew. I kept it a secret. It wasn't until the first Spiderman movie came out and we were discussing the plot and how it related to the comics that Tom wondered how I knew about the comic books. I revealed to him that I had been reading all his stories throughout my childhood. He just laughed a huge belly laugh. Then told me when he died, all his comic books would be mine.

Tom and I shared so much. It's hard for me when I want to share something now that he's gone. He's the first person I want to share something with. Even though it's been nearly ten years, I still reach for the phone to call him. I have even picked up the phone to dial a number that has long been disconnected. I wish I could hear his voice one last time. Hear his deep, bellowing laugh like he laughed during the movie *Titanic* when the dude fell from the top of the ship and pinged off the propeller in the quiet movie theatre.

* * *

Tom's 46th Birthday Celebration 2019

Some years are tougher than others. Last week, I was a wreck in anticipation of this coming day, my brother's birthday. Today, I woke up early, cried, and posted some pics on Facebook. Then had a cup of coffee. My memory swam as I thought about all the things my brother has missed this year.

Every year, I type him a letter of things he would have liked and has missed since his death. When they happen, sometimes it stops me dead in my tracks, and I think, "Dang, Tom would have really liked that." I had a hard time pinpointing those thoughts this year. I even forgot to mention *Aquaman*! Although I'm sure I would have been more into it than him, I think he would have appreciated Jason Momoa.

I try to prepare for my triggers. Knowing your triggers and being able to proactively deal with them in a healthy way is a positive step in mental health. Everybody has triggers. People with bipolar have BIG triggers. Tom is my trigger. Twice a year he triggers me. His birthday and the day of his death. Sometimes it's weeks or days before the actual day and then the day of or just the day of. It's hard to predict.

The past nine years, I have tried to be active in remembering my brother. The first year I tried to gather his friends and our family at the Olive Garden for dinner. That didn't turn out too well. Then I tried to skip the next year, thinking I was over it. I didn't handle it very well. I have learned that I need to take the time to honor his memory. Each year I'm different, so I respond differently to the day.

As I said, last week I was a mess, but this week, I have been calm and felt ready to celebrate. I am wearing my "Aim to Misbehave!" Firefly t-shirt I bought for him this year. Several years ago, I started buying a t-shirt every year for him and wearing it the day of his birthday. We loved Firefly.

When my brother was alive, he would have me play hooky once in a while from school. I'd call in **cough cough** sick. I'd drop the boys off at school. Tom would pick me up. We would go have breakfast. Then go get a mani/pedi somewhere fancy. I was always amazed at how Tom loved to get the works when he went into those salons. Mud masks, sugar scrubs, didn't matter. He wanted it and made me get it too. He paid for everything. After being beautified, we would go to the movies. Depending on the time, sometimes we would movie hop and see another flick. Then we would pick up the boys and grab dinner. A full day with my brother. Just being treated like a princess. He always paid for everything. He knew I couldn't afford it.

So today, I took the day off. Not a sick day. I've evolved into having actual personal leave. I went to a fantastic breakfast place with Athena and her daughter. She paid for breakfast. Much like my brother, she always takes care of me. I felt loved. I enjoyed a great breakfast in honor of my brother's birthday. Something we would have done together.

Later, I went to the nail salon. I got my toes done. It's been about ten months since that has happened. But, if Tom was here, it would have been something we would have done today. He would have said it needed to be done. By now, we would be going to this nail salon. I would have convinced him that my little Asian nail parlor is better than the costly high-priced nail salon he was used to going to and just as good. We would have been regulars. We would have been getting the pedicures with the hot rocks and sugar scrubs, just like I got today. Except he would have made me get a manicure, and I wasn't into that today. But if he was there, we would have done it together.

I felt like he was with me today. I cried on and off as I listened to some Johnny Cash and Bare Naked Ladies. Some of the last music we listened to together. I don't feel dread. I don't feel overwhelming sadness like I have in past years. I feel a lightness as I remember him. I don't know if that is because I am taking the steps to honor his memory and actively doing these things or if it is time that has gently lifted that stone from my heart of grief.

Later tonight we will finish our celebration with diner with my folks. We regularly shared meals together. It was one of our favorite things to do as grown-ups. Tonight, we will eat Thai food. Tom liked Thai food. He really liked Pinkow. The first time I tried Thai food was with him at that restaurant. He will appreciate our gathering.

I've cried on and off as I've written this. I miss my brother. My heart is still broken. But maybe not quite as shattered.

* * *

After my dad went home after Tom's funeral, I tried to stay in contact, but we went back to our old ways. We just stopped talking to each other. It's just what we knew.

In the past year, my dad was back at the reservation and my aunt asked me to come visit while he was there. I almost didn't go. I wasn't sure he would want to see me, but I went.

When I walked in the door of my aunt's home, my dad greeted me with warm hugs and whispers of love in Navajo and English. He wouldn't stop hugging and kissing me. I was overcome with love for my dad. It had been a while since I had seen him. He had aged. His long salt and pepper hair was shorter and whiter. He had more wrinkles around his brown eyes.

We just sat on the couch across from each other, smiling.

He told me he had not been well. I instantly felt terrible. We had not been in communication. I didn't know. He hadn't told me. I had not asked. He said he only told close friends and family. That hurt, too.

We had a very nice visit, but I was determined to know

more about my dad. I wanted to end this stagnation of our communication.

Since that visit, I have started texting my dad monthly. Some of the times he responds. I check on his health and overall just say hi and I love him. I've called him and we've talked on the phone.

Most of time, we communicate through Facebook. Just when I think he doesn't see me or isn't paying attention—I will have sent him three text messages on his phone that he hasn't responded to—he will respond to a post on Facebook with, "I love you, Bah."

I recently did a Christmas drive for families at our school and with the help of our staff provided presents and food for six families. I posted pictures on Facebook. My dad posted to me how proud he was of me and what a difference I was making. It made my heart warm and happy.

We may not have the best father-daughter relationship. We are working on it. After years of thinking my dad did not love me or even like me, I don't think that anymore. I know my dad loves me. I love my dad. We just have a different relationship and that is okay.

Brawl Buster Bartender

Tom was a bartender. He worked at little dive bars mostly. Almost always he worked the graveyard shift from 12 am to 8 am. On days he was without a vehicle, I would get up and drive him to work. Tom fell asleep driving and wrecked his car when he drove into a house. He was without a car for some time. I would stay and have a drink and some food. I would go home and sleep. Then, I'd get up, grab the kids, and go pick him up. We would usually all go out for breakfast.

On nights I didn't have to drive him, I would still go visit him anyway. I just wanted to visit my brother. My brother was never more than twenty minutes away. Traffic at midnight in Vegas is pretty slow. You really can get anywhere in Vegas in twenty minutes, at the right speed, if you are close to a freeway and your destination is close to a freeway.

For years, I treasured the time I would go and hang out with my brother. My kids would be asleep. My husband would be asleep. My parents would be asleep. The whole world would be asleep, except me and the drunks who visited the bar. This was the time for me to watch my brother in action.

He worked at a couple of bars. One of the bars he worked at was next to a strip club. You can't drink alcohol in a strip club, so the patrons would come over to the bar and get liquored up before heading in to see some tits and ass. They would then come back over after seeing all the boobs and butts. There were a fair number of strippers who frequented the bar as well.

The bar was in a seedy part of town. It was mostly industrial, by the strip club. Inside the bar, it was dark. The bar was longer than it was wide. When you walked in, there was a small area to the right with a few high-top tables. If you continued to walk, you'd run into the bar. The bar itself was wooden with a lip to keep drinks from falling off. There were a few more seats, and to the right was how you made your way around the back of the bar.

To the left, the bar was like a peninsula. It jutted out with high chairs tucked in every few feet in front of a poker machine. If you followed the peninsula, it rounded the tip and made a long line down to the back of the bar where the bathrooms were. I usually sat on this side of the bar.

Tom had a steady clientele of strippers, hookers, pimps and playboys. It was an eclectic mix. I loved watching it all. I just sat back with my vodka and soda. Sometimes, I would gamble, if Tom gave me twenty bucks. A lot of the time, Tom would introduce me to these late-night people, "This is my little sister."

I would have shots bought for me. Conversations ensued. These people were crazy fun and just all around crazy.

Some nights were rowdy. Pimps and hookers shouting about money. Tom didn't stand for it. He told them to take it outside. They respected him and always did.

When lowlifes were trying to pick up the strippers after a long shift of stripping, he interceded and had them move along. Those girls just wanted to drink in peace.

Tom was a good bartender. He knew when to fill a drink, dump an ashtray or order you some food. He was almost a mind reader. He memorized people's drink orders. He was a very social person and people loved him. He could talk about anything and hold a conversation with anyone.

One of my favorite things that happened at the bar with the strippers was a fight.

There were three women, not sure if they were hookers or not, but a guy approached them and started getting into their business. The ladies got pissed and told him to fuck off. The guy didn't get the message. He kept pestering them. Tom interceded. He bought the guy a drink and led him to one side of the bar and bought the girls a drink and took them to the other side of the bar. Problem solved.

About an hour or so later, the groups met back in the middle by the jukebox. A clash ensued. The guy said something to one of the girls. She smacked him and threw her drink, glass and all, in his face. He turned around and backhanded her.

The two other girls jumped on the dude and wrestled him to the ground. They were all a blur.

Next thing I saw was Super Tom leap over the bar with a baseball bat in one hand. He was throwing bitches right and left. He called me over to keep the girls off the guy. He had separated them, but the guy was still on the ground. Tom had the guy's arm wrenched behind his back. Tom was kneeling on him telling him to calm down.

Tom had me usher the girls to the other side of the bar and call the police. When I went behind the bar to get the phone, one of the girls started grabbing glasses and throwing them at the dude on the ground. It wouldn't have been a problem, but my brother was down there, too. I had the police on the phone in one hand and I karate-chopped the arm of the chick holding a glass with my other hand. I warned her to stop or I would be hitting her in the face next glass she threw at my brother. She stopped.

The police came and arrested one of the girls for having a warrant and the guy for assaulting the girl.

I went home after writing up my statement. It was getting to be light outside, and I needed to be home for breakfast with the kids. I drove home, amazed at my brother in action. He was like a superhero. He flew over that bar in one single leap.

I would go on to spend many nights with my brother at all his bars. This was the most memorable.

I would go in late. He would make me a drink. Sometimes, I would just stare at my brother while he worked. I was taller than him by an inch or so. He was very handsome. Short dark hair, black. Perfectly groomed. He had a goatee. His weight fluctuated, like mine. Athena always called us the incredible growing and shrinking twins. His eyes were dark, almost black. He had great eyebrows, full but not bushy. His hands were perfect. Nails were always cut and clean. In high school, he smelled like Drakkar Noir, but now he had a new smell. Something nice and fragrant but not overpowering.

I would sit and wait while he served his customers, then he would come over and we would just talk. We would talk about everything. We would catch up on what was happening for the week, what was happening in each other's lives, how the kids were doing. We would plan what movies we were going to see. We would plan to go have breakfast.

These late-night excursions are some of the things I miss most about my brother being gone. It was time I had alone with just me and him. It was our time.

White Lens

For a long time, I didn't know what it meant to be Native. I was just brown. I honestly thought I was white, even though I was clearly brown. My mom was white. I saw the world through a white lens and only when it was pointed out to me that I wasn't white was I aware that I wasn't white. The world did a good job reminding me that I was brown.

I usually was made aware of this during Thanksgiving when I was the only "Indian" at the feast of Pilgrims. I was still made to dress up with paper feathers and a paper vest with Indian symbols on it. But I was also asked to speak on behalf of ALL Indians of all tribes everywhere. I didn't know anything, so I just went with what was told to be by my white teachers. "In 1492, Columbus sailed the ocean blue."

I knew I was Navajo. I knew that Navajo lived on reservations. I knew that my family sold jewelry roadside. I knew that Navajos lived in hogans, not teepees. That was about the extent of my knowledge.

In third grade, my principal found out I was Navajo, and he started greeting me with "Yat-ta- hay." I was confused. He told me that it meant hello in Navajo. It was my first word, or so I thought. I was excited to learn something.

The next summer I tried to use that word with my family,

and they laughed and said I sounded like a white man. Well, considering that's exactly where I learned it from, that's what I should sound like. They taught me how to say it right, and I learned. After being laughed at, of course. Always being laughed at.

My brother and I spent many summers with our Navajo family. There were conversations that happened in Navajo but never any explanations in English.

My grandmother, Shinálí, which of course was my first Navajo word, did not speak English. That never stopped us from communicating. But all conversations were in Navajo. I only caught words and remembered words from my childhood and translated them as an adult.

My family never talked about what it meant to be a Native American. Never talked about any social justice or injustice, strife or consequences of brown skin. I never heard about the struggles of our people from my family. I never heard anything. I just watched and listened to them speak in Navajo and laugh and enjoy each other's company. We kids played and had our own fun.

I grew up ignorant of my culture, clan, and struggles. I did not know my origin story, our name in Navajo and what it meant; I didn't even know what my name really meant. I also didn't ask. I didn't know that I didn't know. I was ignorant.

In sixth grade, in our reading book, there was a Navajo poem about the months of the year. It was in Navajo. The teacher asked me if I could read it. I said I couldn't, but I would ask my dad. When I called my dad, he said it was inaccurate because Navajos didn't have names for those things. So that's what I told my teacher. A lesson for both of us.

On one of the trips back to the reservation when I was a

teenager, my auntie taught me how to make fry bread. I worked and worked at it and practiced. I used to make it for my friends all the time. It was the one Native thing that I could do besides making jewelry.

Throughout high school, the first thing I would do is look in the back of my history book and look up the information that was listed under American Indian. I would read and see what information was listed. There was always the information on the Navajo Code Talkers. The same picture of the man on the radio and the brief description of how the Navajo language was the unbreakable code. I was always called upon to bring light to this subject and never could answer anything more than what was written in the book.

When I started college at the University of Nevada, Las Vegas (UNLV), I joined the Native American Student Association (NASA). I was introduced to different tribal cultures. I learned a bit about Navajos, but I also learned a lot about Plains tribes. I went to my first powwow. It was a learning experience.

The next year, I took Native American Literature with Dr. Hafen. I was still learning about myself. Taking Dr. Hafen's class was a crash course in discovery. We learned all about everyone's tribe and background and origin stories. She encouraged me to discover my family roots and ask questions.

I spent long nights on the internet searching tribal history and learning about the long walk, boarding schools, and Luci Tapahanso, a Navajo author. It was one of the best, informative semesters of my life. I went on to work more and more with NASA.

Eventually, I became the president of NASA. I held that position for a few years. I helped promote events at UNLV and celebrate Native American Heritage Month on campus through the diversity office that I was also a part of. We organized all kinds of events on campus.

Throughout my time at UNLV, I learned more about my tribe and my culture through the people I was around and from my family.

* * *

Tom and I took two trips back to the reservation together. One time was in college in his VW Bus another time was when I was working as a teacher, we took my car.

The first trip, we took Patrick. He was little. I'm not sure why we went on the trip. We were driving late at night. We were snorting NoDoz tablets to stay awake and have a buzz. We were just driving along, talking and listening to music.

Red and blue lights flashed behind us. Tom pulled over. He had been speeding. There is a spot on Highway 89, Grey Mountain, where the speed limit drops to 45 or 35 miles per hour. He blew right through it. He was pissed. He got a ticket.

When the cop approached, I had the binder with the NoDoz on my lap. I slowly let it slide to the floorboards. The cop was not nice. He just saw us as a bunch of Indians. He gave Tom his ticket.

We went to the reservation and visited. We saw Aunt Tillie and Aunt Margaret. We only stayed a night, then turned around and came home.

On our way back, we slowed down through Grey Mountain and were cautious, no ticket.

Tom refused to pay that speeding ticket. He never paid it. When Tom died, I laughed that he never paid that ticket. I smile when I slow down through Grey Mountain and think of him.

We went back to the reservation another time when I was teaching. We drove my Toyota Camry. I was recently divorced. Tom and I spent a lot of time together. We took Jesse and Patrick with us. We just decided to drive to the rez for a weekend trip. We stayed the night at Aunt Tillie's and visited.

It was a quick trip. We went to the Grand Canyon. We paid to get in. Only later did someone tell us that we didn't need to pay; we just needed to tell them that we were Navajo and they'd let us in for free. We were suckers.

We had a good time. We took lots of pictures. It was a very windy day. I have a picture on the fridge one of the boys took of my brother and me. Tom and I are both in jackets. Tom is wearing a tan jacket. He has dark sunglasses on. I have on a blue-green plaid jacket. I'm wearing old wire-framed glasses. I'm smiling. He's smiling. My hair is in a ponytail. The wind is blowing so hard that my ponytail is blowing behind Tom's head. We are captured this way. Smiling at the camera together with our arms around each other. Standing at the rim of the Grand Canyon.

While we were there, Aunt Tillie drove us around the reservation. We drove up the main street. Tuba City has two stoplights. One on the highway and the main street and another at the main street by the trading post and the McDonald's. We drove past the trading post. She pointed out abandoned buildings that used to be used for official business. The drive took all of twenty minutes. We didn't drive very far.

We stopped at the flea market located in a red sandy area behind some buildings. The flea market is a collection of traders selling their wares. There are people selling handmade jewelry, beadwork, turquoise, and native herbs. There are also foods you can buy, such as fry bread, mutton, blue corn mush, and stews. Just like any other flea market, you have people selling junk, clothes and trinkets. We once found a Nintendo controller backpack there for five dollars. Jesse loved it.

We bought some fry bread with some powdered sugar and walked around looking at the stalls. My aunt bought the boys some necklaces. She bought Tom and me some corn pollen to take with us. She told us to sprinkle some out the window as we crossed the Colorado River on our way over the Hoover Dam on our way back to Vegas as an offering. The corn pollen came in tiny Ziploc baggies, about the size of my thumb. The corn pollen is a mustard yellow color, and it is powdery and fine.

You bless yourself with corn pollen by sprinkling it on the top of your head, the whirl of your head, and then your tongue. You should always give an offering to the water.

We left the market and took Aunt Tillie back to her house. We gathered our overnight bags and packed the car. We decided to stop over and see Aunt Margaret on the way out. It was a short visit, so we didn't tell her we were coming. We drove over; it was just a few houses down.

Aunt Margaret owns a bead shop and trades with people. She sells a lot to tourists. Her shop is on her property next to her home. She gets lots of strangers coming up to her house.

Tom and I walked up to her house and rang the bell. A child answered the door and asked us what we wanted. We asked to see Margaret. The little girl shouted, "Grandma, there's some white people at the door for you."

We laughed. It had been some time since we had seen each other. It took her a moment to recognize us. Aunt Margaret was happy to see us. It was a brief visit. Just a quick hello and goodbye. Short hugs and kisses.

Just outside of Tuba City off the highway, on the turn off to Moenave, there are dinosaur tracks. There are Navajos who serve as tour guides and will show you where the tracks are. Many of them are good guides. Aunt Tillie took my boys and me one time to look at the tracks, and a guide showed us where the tracks were. I thought I would just show Tom where the tracks were.

We got out of the car. There were jewelry stands in front of the parking area. Immediately we were swarmed by men who wanted to be our guides. I told them we didn't need a guide. We walked around the stands and started walking to the site. We were surrounded by red earth. The ground was hard as cement.

We began walking toward the first track, and a Navajo man stepped in front of me and said, "You have no business here."

I said, "This is Navajo land. It's open to everyone. We are Navajo."

"You have to pay me to visit here. This is my family's land," he said.

"I do not have to pay you. I know where the tracks are at. We will guide ourselves." I was getting pissed off.

We tried to walk off. He stepped in front of me again. He said, "Are you really Navajo? Your car says Nevada. If you were a real Navajo, you would live here. This is my backyard. You don't see me coming into your backyard walking around. You're not a real Indian. You're probably just some half-breed. Get the fuck out of here!" He yelled at us.

I was scared. There were more of them than there were of us. We walked back to the car and got in and drove away.

The car was silent. I cried all the way into Flagstaff up

Highway 89. That man calling me a half-breed. Telling me that I didn't belong. It hurt. That's what I felt sometimes. I wasn't white; I wasn't Navajo. I was in between, mixed. I know he was probably drunk and was an asshole, but it still hurt.

Tom and I looked at each other as we pulled into the gas station and said at the same time, "We should have knocked over their sign!"

Dang! Every time I drive by their sign, I want to knock it over or paint it. I've heard that the boozy tour guides have moved on or died due to drinking. It's been cleaned up and is friendlier. I haven't been back to the dinosaur tracks. It just left me feeling so bad, I've never wanted to go back.

* * *

Since Tom's death, I've taken several trips back to the reservation and asked questions. My aunties were very forthcoming. I learned about my clan and how to say the name in Navajo. I learned about different foods. At a certain point I didn't know what to ask anymore. I was ignorant all over. I was just an observer again. Waiting to see what I didn't know.

As events come, I am an observer, and I learn. When I do not know something, I ask. If something is said in Navajo, I ask what is being said. I don't know if I have an answer to what being indigenous is, but I would know better how to answer my teachers if they asked me to speak about my tribe or other tribes.

I have more confidence as a Native American woman. I identify as a Native woman. Gone are the paper feathers. I have earned my eagle feathers through my degrees.

Walking Many Roads of Religion

I did not grow up in a religious household. I was baptized Catholic, but that's where my religious education ended. I asked my mom to take me to church once, and I remember holding hands, saying prayers and wishing peace to everyone. I liked it. I didn't know why we never went back.

My neighbors were super religious nuts. They were born again Christians and super judgy. That kind of turned me off from religion.

Other than my neighbors, I didn't have any religious influences. My best friend was not religious. I was always curious about religion.

I was never quite sure about God. I never believed that there was an omnipotent guy in the sky making judgments on people. That didn't seem right either.

As a teenager, I found my way into believing in the occult. I found a connection into believing in nature and magic, spells and witchcraft. I bought and read tarot cards.

As I learned more about being a Navajo, I learned to pray with corn pollen and cedar. I believed in that. I prayed with that to the Creator.

When I was pregnant with Patrick, I found my way back to the Catholic Church. Patrick's father was also Catholic. It was a good fit. I was curious about the faith I had been christened in. I began to take classes to understand what it was to be Catholic. I did my first communion and confirmation. I went to church regularly for a year or so.

Once I had started college and had moved to across campus, I no longer went to church. There wasn't a church close to me, so I just stopped going.

At the university, I grew closer to having an understanding of my native beliefs. I rarely prayed the rosary or to the Christian god. I didn't deny Him. I just didn't pray to Him anymore. Maybe I had lost some faith.

I took a class at UNLV called Native American Literature. In that class, I learned about Black Elk, a Lakota Indian. He was a medicine man. He was also a Catholic. He had found a way to combine his faiths without compromising either one. He found a balance between the two roads. It was the first time I saw that there could be more than one way of seeing the world. Not just one religion or nothing, but your heart could belong to two things, and it would be okay.

Black Elk is now being looked at for sainthood by the Catholic Church. We are just waiting on the miracles.

I went back to the Catholic Church with my soon-to-be husband, Charles. He didn't approve. He very much disliked it. We went for a month and never went back. So again, I strayed from the Church.

While I was married, I started going to a Baptist church with my friend. I loved the energy. It was a predominately African American church. I loved the choir. It was fascinating. So fascinating that I got baptized again. I figured a second helping of holy water wouldn't do any harm. I went to that church for about a year before something turned me off about it.

The one thing about Christianity that had always stuck hard in the craw was the views about gay people and abortion. I disagreed with them on all fronts. I believed in equal marriage rights, even if my parents didn't want to get married. I believe there is nothing wrong with being gay. I also believed in a woman's right to choose even if I would never have another abortion. Can you be a part of something that at its core has these beliefs?

But like all the things with the faiths I had been a part of, I picked what I liked and threw out the rest.

Jesse's dad wanted to start going to church. We started going to one of those mega-churches. A huge coliseum of a church. I really like the pastor. He had a good message. The kids liked the kids' program. Jesse's dad surprised us all on Easter when he just up and decided to get baptized.

They dunked him in the holy water and all his sins were forgiven but given all the sins he would commit in the future; he should have waited longer for his divine dip.

We continued to go to this church every Sunday. Pretty soon it was just the kids and me going. Charles started sleeping in or wasn't even home yet on Sunday morning from his drunken nights out. I was religiously going. I still enjoyed the service.

At my last service there, the regular pastor was not presenting. Someone else was giving the message. He started off by talking about how women should be submissive to their husbands and then went on to how being gay is a sin. I'm sure if I had stayed, he would have worked in abortion.

I walked out. I couldn't take it. The only reason I was going was that my husband had wanted to go to church, and now he was too drunk to go and didn't care. I stopped going.

After the divorce, I moved in with my moms. My parents began getting into a Korean yoga that involved mind, body and spirit. They went in full force. I went to a couple of classes and really liked it. They talked about cosmic energy and forces in the universe. I began to believe in what they were selling.

When my brother died, my mom had a ceremony led by the yoga people. We all gathered at a place in Sedona. There was bowing and chanting. The yoga master called my brother's spirit to come talk to us. My mom sat in front of us. We sat in lines behind her.

My mom talked openly to my brother. She said all the things that she had not had a chance to say to him before he passed. She cried.

I was emotional and pissed off. My mom had said to dress nicely, so I wore a skirt. Everyone else was in yoga pants. I was trying to get over my emotions. I was also emotional at seeing my mom crying.

The yoga master said my brother's spirit was in the room. Now was the time to say what you had to say before he leaves.

With my eyes closed, I said silently, "I love you, Tom. I miss you."

A hand brushed my hair.

My eyes popped open. I thought maybe my boyfriend Doug had gotten up from his mat and come over to check on me. I looked over and he was sitting two people down from me with his eyes closed.

My brother had reached out from beyond and touched me.

I believed in the energy of the cosmic universe.

For the next few years, I became a yoga practitioner. I studied, I read books, and I became an instructor. I used these techniques in my teachings at school. I used them in my life. I truly believed in mind, body and spirit.

Through yoga, I found peace inside myself. I learned I could be by myself and be okay. I learned I was a good person.. I didn't need to please people in order to make me feel better about myself. Through meditation, I connected with the universe and found peace in my spirit. I found power in my soul. I was a strong person. I was always a strong person; I just never saw it or believed in myself. I could do anything. In meditation, I'd say, "I'm sorry, please forgive me, thank you, I love you." These words healed me.

During all this, it was easy to still believe in my native beliefs. I would regularly burn cedar and pray with corn pollen. They went hand in hand. The yoga was very nature-oriented.

When the bipolar came back, when I got sick, I lost faith in everything. I didn't believe there was anything out there. There was no magic, no nature, no energy, no gods, or God. I felt alone. I was sick, and nothing had prevented it. No belief system had helped me not be sick.

It took some time, but one day, I woke up and wanted to pray. I pulled cedar out of my pouch and burned it on the stove. I smudged myself. I prayed for guidance. I prayed for help. I prayed for healing. I prayed for my family. I just prayed.

Last year, I had a manic episode during winter break. The buzzing in my head was very loud. It made it hard to concentrate. I couldn't read or watch TV. I couldn't do much of anything. I found my way to the Catholic Church across the street from my house.

I always knew it was there, but I never went.

A lot had changed in the twenty years I had been away, but the format was still the same. The priest was wonderful. He was very welcoming and genuine. The choir director was another welcome sight. He used to be my boss. It was just a great welcoming feeling.

After going to church, the buzzing in my head lessened. I had a bit more focus. I don't know if it was the Holy Spirit or just the energy of all the people in the church or my focus on the prayers, but I felt better. I went to church every day for the two weeks we were out of school. I didn't miss a day.

Once school had started, I was still manic. I went to church three times a week and listened to mass on YouTube. It helped quite a bit to calm the mania.

I have heard that a lot of people find religion while they are manic. I don't know if it is because of the same reasons that I went. Going back to the Church has provided me a sense of peace that I haven't had in a long time.

Since I have gone back to the Church, I have gone regularly. I don't go three times a week anymore. During the summer, if I'm up, I do go to weekly mass. If I'm home on the weekend, I go to mass.

Church is a regular part of my life. Praying with cedar and corn pollen is a part of my life. Centering myself and asking the universe and cosmic energy to open my mind for healing and calm is a part of my life. Through all these roads, I have a balance. I walk all these roads. These cords of different religions braid my inner being. I feel peace and harmony.

Those That Walked On

Uncle Dave was a man's man. He was my mom's sister's husband. He was a large, strong, rough and tough, cigar-smoking, Clint Eastwood lovin', motorcycle-riding man. He was also someone who loved animals. All types. He had a pet goose that used to wait for him by the sliding glass doors every morning. He would pick him up and that goose would wind its neck around him and nuzzle him. Everyone loved Uncle Dave. The world loved him. When the wind went out of his sails, our boat was moored for a long time.

Aunt Cindy and Uncle Dave lived in an area of Las Vegas that was considered rural in the early 1980s. Now, it is smack dab in the middle of town. They owned a pig, chickens, horses and goats. We used to sing, "Old Aunt Cindy had a farm!" And so on. We milked goats, rode horses and collected eggs.

They had two horses. One horse named Chief was a bit rough. He didn't like people. Didn't like Dave. He kept bucking him off. Finally, after weeks of being patient and being nipped and bit. The horse thought he had won. My uncle had been thrown again. He got up, walked over to the horse and punched him. It was like watching the scene out of *Blazing Saddles*, except the horse didn't dramatically fall over. But the horse did look like it got the sense knocked out of it. After that, Dave was the only one who could ride Chief. Nobody could get near that horse.

Animals flocked to my uncle. Dogs loved him. The goose loved him. The peacocks loved him. That goose ONLY loved my uncle. The goose terrorized everyone else who walked on the property biting and hissing, with its head low to the ground and wings spread out. More than once, I fell victim to being chased up on top of a car crying for my uncle to rescue me while that goose surrounded me hissing his terrible hiss. When you came onto the property, there was a line of sticks to fend off the goose attacks. A range of sticks, depending on your size. You picked your stick and readied for battle—to run from the road to the front door of the house.

One time, a friend thought it was a joke and pick up a twig. She didn't think it was funny when she was chased into the pine trees that filled the front yard of my aunt's home. But my uncle loved that goose. The dog, Tara, did not love that goose. She did not like the competition, I think, between her and the goose or that the goose would hiss at the dog too. One day, the dog attacked the goose and broke its neck. My uncle shamed the dog by hanging that goose around the dog's neck for a few days. The dog never attacked another bird. My uncle never got another goose.

My uncle had an old 1929 Model A with a rumble seat in the back. He was always tinkering with it. It needed some work. The paint was rusted in spots. The upholstery was faded and torn. But when he pulled it out, we all knew it meant a ride around town and a trip to get some ice cream. All us kids would pile in the back of the rumble seat with the wind flapping in our hair. It was fun to be a part of a vehicle but be independent of the adults. We could talk about whatever kids talk about and not worry about the adults. It was just fun and thrilling riding around in this old vehicle. Our trip would always end up with us getting ice cream, which was a real treat for me since I was allergic and wasn't supposed to have any. I'd eat it anyway and hope I didn't have any reactions. Uncle Dave just let me have want I wanted. We would have our cones and be jostled around in the back, waving at people. It was great.

My uncle was a motorcycle enthusiast. As a younger man, he raced motorcycles and was quite good. He taught his sons. As a father and uncle, he would take us for rides when we were young on his bike or scooter, as he sometimes called his motorcycle. However, he made these contraptions for us to wear on the bikes. He had harnesses and straps. Some made from straps or bungee cords. We were either lashed to the bike or to his back, sometimes front. We didn't go for a far ride, just around the corner in a circle again and again. It was thrilling. But it was always about the safety. Thinking back, I don't know how safe those things were, but they made me feel safe.

My uncle always greeted me with singing "Ave Maria" or "How Do You Solve a Problem like Maria?" from the *Sound of Music*. He loved musicals. He was always finding ways to bring them into a way of singing them. Also when he greeted me, he would grab me and rub his rusty beard on my soft cheeks. It would turn my face red and rash them up a bit, but it would make me laugh. He did it every time, even as an adult, up until his beard wasn't so red anymore.

Uncle Dave filled that role of father for me. He was always there for me. We had a bond. He treated me special. He was like my dad and he told me, in the end, that I was like a daughter to him.

When he got sick, it all happened pretty fast. He was diagnosed with throat cancer. A small bit of tonsil that didn't get removed when he was little had turned cancerous and had now infected a part of his throat and a mass was growing. I went to the hospital where they were doing the surgery to remove it.

The surgeon had placed a little tiny "x" on his neck where they were going to cut the tumor out. Unfortunately, they left us with the marker and that had us drawing all over my uncle like a treasure map with, "X marks the spot," "treasure buried here," "do not dig here!"

MAN! The surgeon was fucking pissed when he saw what we had done. They had to wash my uncle's neck and remark his neck with the simple "x" and took our marker away.

The surgery lasted some time. I stayed for the entirety. I made arrangements for my kids to be taken care of. I needed to be there for Uncle Dave. Someone should be there for him when he woke up. Nobody should have to stay in a hospital at night by themselves. I was ready with a notebook, ready to take notes, list vitals, and whatever else the doctor had to say.

They removed the mass and the jugular vein on one side of his neck. He was not going to be able to speak for a while. He was also going to have to aspirate himself. Which I thought was insane, more reason to stay in the hospital with him. I camped out. His sons, my cousins, came and went throughout the night. I crocheted a green scarf.

I stayed all night, making sure he didn't choke on his spit. I slept a little but crocheted more. I left in the morning once Aunt Cindy had come to relieve me. I went home to be with my family.

That's how it went while he was sick. I would go out and visit. Slowly he was getting worse. He was trying all these different treatments. Food mostly. Oils. Cannabis. Hypobaric chambers. He just kept getting weaker. The cancer was spreading. The chemo and radiation weren't working. His rusty hair turned white. His hearing completely left him.

The last hospitalization was the worst. There was nothing more they could do for him. My aunt had to make a decision for him. Stay in the hospital or go home and have end-of-life care. Where did he want to be? She knew. We all knew. He wanted to be home.

I packed up the kids and my life for a week and moved in with my aunt. I took care of my uncle. I monitored him. I gave him his medicine. I emptied his urine bag. I made sure he had fluids. I made sure he was getting his oxygen. I made sure he was getting plenty of laughs.

He was the center of it all. We always gathered around my uncle and at their house. One year for his birthday, we threw him a musical birthday party. People took turns singing songs from musicals. People dressed up. A friend of the family had painted back drops for each scene. I was in a mood and did not perform. My mom performed "If I Were a Rich Man" from *Fiddler on the Roof*. She had a beard and a stuffed belly. I don't recall what part I had, but I didn't perform. I regret not being a part of it. He loved every minute of it.

I stayed up real late one night with him, just holding his hand. Kissed him and went to bed. It was really late. I only slept a few hours. I got up as the sun was rising. I went out on the porch and saw a coyote walking the dirt road. It was strange. He wasn't walking through the desert but walking the road like a white man. I heard the oxygen machine going.

I thought my uncle was still breathing.

I walked over and could tell he wasn't. I touched his face. He was still slightly warm, but there was no breath.

I turned the oxygen machine off. The noise in the room dropped to silence. Tears filled my eyes. I took my silent turn to mourn my uncle, my dad. I kissed his cheek and hand, then went to wake my aunt up.

She wailed. She crawled into bed with him and just cried. The love of her life was gone. The gentle giant, lover of animals, was gone.

The dad who gave me motorcycle rides was gone. The dad who built us zip lines in the trees was gone. The dad who taught me to love westerns was gone. The dad who showed me a softer side of men who loved musicals was gone. The man who bought me ice cream when I shouldn't have it was gone. The dad who loved me was gone.

It took all day, but they came and took his body away. We tried to make some semblance of the living room livable again. It was empty without my uncle's presence. We threw away a ton of morphine and Ativan.

A few weeks later, after the memorial service, we scattered his ashes. We borrowed someone's houseboat and went out on Lake Mead, where he spent a lot of time with his family. On the way to the lake, we caravanned out there. My cousin Brian was the lead on his motorcycle. He was speeding and had been pulled over. We all pulled over. Brian had Dave's ashes in his backpack. Instead of giving him a ticket, the police officers gave us a police escort to the turnoff, lights and sirens as a sendoff. My uncle would have loved that. It was great.

There were several of us, family and friends, gathered together. Some went into the water. Some just watched. As the sun lowered in the sky, two clouds formed around the sun like hands reaching around holding the orb. We released some of his ashes to the lake. My aunt saved some for herself, to keep close to her.

I was happy to see my uncle at rest in the lake, where he loved to spend so much time sailing his ship *Blow Me*.

* * *

Even in the end, Aunt Tillie, Dad's sister, was elegant. Her nails naturally long and manicured. Painted the color of the desert, shimmering like the red Arizona sand.

I drove five hours from Vegas to Phoenix. No stops. Straight to the hospital. I walked into the room, said my hellos to my family, and turned to say my goodbyes to my aunt.

She was so small. Swallowed in the bed by blankets and machines. I enclosed her tiny hand in both my hands and leaned in close.

"Hi, Auntie. It's Bah. I drove all the way from Las Vegas this morning to be with you. I love you. If Tom were still here, he'd be with me. We both loved you very much. You always took very good care of us. We know you loved us very much. Thank you for everything you have done for me."

I bowed my head and wept. I touched her hand to my cheek and cried. I moved my glasses to the top of my head. I just stayed there, crying and giving her my love. Hoping she felt it, knowing I was there.

I let go and sat down, looking at her. Watching the machines breathe for her.

A short while later the nurse came in and began to disconnect the tubes. The family gathered around her. We cried. Wailed.

Prayed. Aunt Tillie breathed on her own for about an hour until she passed. We played Elvis music in the background to ease her passing. We all held on. Taking turns comforting one another. Taking turns crying or in stunned silence watching others grieve.

The nurse came in and checked her vitals one last time and pronounced she had passed.

Things I should have said. Thank you for having a Navajo dress made for me for graduation. Thank you for coming to graduation. Thank you for loaning me jewelry for graduation. Thank you for slipping me $50 when I was poor. Thank you for taking me out to dinner when you were in town on business. Thank you for always making time for me. Thank you for giving me earrings on my wedding day. Thank you for coming to my wedding. Thank you for having a sense of humor about seeing *The 40-Year-Old Virgin*. Thank you for taking the bus to see me. Thank you for comforting me when my brother died. Thank you for the books. Thank you for taking me to the reservation. Thank you for teaching me to say *chidí*.

* * *

The same week Aunt Tillie died, a student I knew at school died by suicide. Both deaths were hard to process. They triggered with suicidal ideation and wanting to self-harm. But I did not really want to kill myself. I've seen what suicide does to people. Firsthand, I had seen what my brother's death had done to my family and myself. I was seeing what this student's death was doing to the students and staff. I had seen enough of death. I did not want to kill myself.

My bouts with suicidal ideations are a part of my bipolar. I suffer with thoughts of death in the back of my mind. I think terrible things. Sometimes I feel it is unsafe for me to even drive when I'm in those states. I think of ways I could crash my truck. I count the streetlight poles and think which one would be the best to crash in to. But even though I am feeling at my worst, I don't really want to die. I am in terrible pain, but I don't want to die by suicide. I don't want to do that to my friends and family.

Endless One Night Stand

Doug was the one-night stand that never ended. I met him because his son was in my student council class. There had been a mix-up with his mom trying to get a refund on the Disneyland trip that Doug had paid for. I had helped solve this problem for Doug. As a favor, he offered to bug-spray my house for free.

Doug was very handsome. He had dark blond hair that he kept buzzed very short. He was shorter than me, a bit stocky. His eyes were blue like the desert sky on a clear day. He was very strong and extremely funny. He turned everything into a joke. He had a great laugh and laughed often. He would sometimes laugh for fun like Salacious Crumb from *Return of the Jedi*. He was a smoker and a drinker.

He came over one night, sprayed for bugs, and we started drinking. We drank, talked, laughed, and ended up in bed. He later told me he couldn't remember where he was, he had so much to drink. I had a lot to drink but not that much. Doug turned out to be an alcoholic and a gambler. Boy, did I have a type.

It took me a little bit of time to figure it out, but I did. One night, Doug was supposed to be at my house to drop off a suitcase for me to go New York the next day. I kept calling him.

He kept saying he was on his way. An hour would go by and I would call again; each time he would say he was coming by. I gave up. I went to the bar and had a few drinks. He still had not called.

I went home and went to sleep. Something woke me up. I still needed the suitcase. I decided to go to the bar to look for him. It was close to three in the morning. I walked into the bar near my house.

At the far end of the bar, tucked in the corner, was Doug.

I heard, "Uh-oh. I'm in trouble."

I walked over and said, "Well, were you ever going to show up? Do you have the suitcase?"

"I was just having a drink. I was hanging out with some friends catching up. Did some gambling and hit a royal. We celebrated and now I'm here. I was having one more drink before I went to see you."

I wanted to grab him by the ear and drag him out of there. I just stared at him.

I said, "Come on, let's go."

He downed his drink and stumbled after me. He was so drunk he could barely walk. We got back to my house, and I was seething mad. He had not brought the suitcase. I went outside on the patio to smoke a cigarette. He mumbled something about taking a shower.

I fumed as I smoked my cigarette. One cigarette turned into two. I thought, "I hope he drowns in there." Then I realized, "Oh my god, he's probably drowning in there."

I went into the bedroom. The bathroom was directly to the left. When I stepped on the carpet, it squished. Water was everywhere. I could see into the bathroom; there was water all over the floor, leaking into the carpet.

Doug was probably drowning.

I ran over to the shower, splashing water with each step.

Now, the shower was just a shower; there was no tub. And Doug was close to drowning. His naked body had covered the drain. Water had filled the bottom of the shower and was spilling over into the bathroom and bedroom. Doug's nose and mouth were barely above water.

I panicked. I turned off the water and hauled him out of the shower. I put him in bed. Now, I was even angrier. I used his clothes to clean up the water on the floor and threw them into the shower with some towels. I opened the patio doors to get some air flowing to dry the carpet.

I was so angry my vision was blurred. I looked over and Doug was fast asleep. Peaceful. Motherfucker. I went back into the bathroom and saw Doug's belt on the counter. I picked it up. I calmly walked back into the bedroom to the bed.

I wrapped the buckle around my hand and let loose the rest of the belt. I whipped Doug's ass with the belt. The first strike didn't move him. He was so drunk it didn't startle him. I hit him again and he jumped up and screamed, "Why?"

"You don't get to sleep peacefully after you fucked everything up!" I yelled at him, hitting him again. I had lost my shit. I hit him in the ass about four times and dropped the belt. I had never done anything like that before.

Doug whimpered and rolled over and went to sleep.

I went out and smoked a cigarette. I was terrified of my violence.

I apologized the next day, and Doug accepted. We never really discussed it again except jokingly. Our relationship moved along quickly, and Doug moved in shortly after.

The weekend he moved in, we were to start our teacher

bowling league. It was not a serious league. It was mostly drinking and tossing a ball down a lane. It was during the cosmic bowling with the neon lights and loud music. My team consisted of Doug, his stepdad, and his sister.

The bowling was starting, and Doug was nowhere to be found. He was supposed to meet us there after work. We started without him. He staggered in about thirty minutes later.

He was completely shitfaced. I don't know how he drove to the bowling alley at the casino. He hardly bowled. He walked around to my co-workers and would grab their pitchers of beer and guzzle them before anyone could stop him. He started throwing twenty-dollar bills at them, saying, "Don't hate Ahiddibah because of me. Here, have some money. I won big tonight."

I was so embarrassed I just wanted the night to end. When the bowling ended, Doug had disappeared. Doug's family had left. Doug's shoes were left behind. I changed my shoes and grabbed my bowling bag.

I had no idea where he was. I figured he had left. I was glad he was gone. I sat down and was finishing a drink with some friends when one of them pointed a finger and said, "Hey, isn't that your boyfriend being escorted out by security?"

"Oh shit! I gotta go."

I chased down the security and Doug. They were standing in front of an ATM. Doug was trying to get money out without success. They had told him that he needed to call a cab and he had given away all his money. The security officer was calm but clearly upset. She kept telling him he had to leave but could not drive.

The security officer then noticed he had on the bowling

shoes and told him he had to give her the shoes. He started to argue. I gave him his shoes and he calmed down.

Apparently, there had been some sort of scene in the men's bathroom caused by Doug throwing shit and security was called. He was being escorted out. Security asked if I was taking him home, I could have him.

Doug and I walked to my car. During the walk, he seemed to sober up. He stopped slurring his words. He focused. He was calm. We got into my car and he tossed a half-drunk soda into the back seat of my car to make room for his water. I shouted at him.

I was losing my patience. He just wanted his truck. He told me he could drive home. I told him I didn't think it was a good idea. We argued over it for a good ten minutes. Finally, I just acquiesced and said fine.

We drove around looking for his truck. He kept telling me it was on the top floor. We circled the top floor over and over again. The truck was nowhere to be found. Then he remembered it was in the other parking lot.

I had had my fill. I was done. I drove him to the other parking lot. We found his truck. I told him I would follow him home to make sure he was okay.

He got into his truck. He revved up the engine and proceeded to do donuts in the parking lot. He whirled around like the Tasmanian Devil. He skidded out of the garage and down the ramp. I followed him. We turned to the road going home. He gunned it. He turned off his lights and vanished into the desert night. I couldn't see him.

I thought, "Fuck it. I'm done."

I turned around and went to my brother's bar. He wasn't on shift yet, but I went to have a drink.

While I was there, I got a phone call from Doug. He said he had crashed his truck and needed me to bring home some ice. He was banged up from the crash. He just left his truck at the scene.

I told him I'd be home after I finished my drink or after I had another one. He begged me to come home. I didn't care.

I finally paid my tab. The bartender gave me two bags of ice.

On my way home, I drove by the truck. It had been crashed into a streetlight pole. The airbags had gone off. The door was open. The cops were there. I drove past and went home. There was a boot on the ground. While running from the scene, Doug had run out of his boot and made it home with one shoe on.

Doug was in bed. Bruises were forming on his chest from the seatbelt and airbag. He fell asleep with the ice on his chest.

The next morning, I told him he had a serious problem. It wasn't just the police; it was the drinking. He made a decision to go to the cops and turn himself in.

We went to the police station to report the incident. They did not arrest him. I don't recall what they told him, but he walked out of the station and got back into the car with me. My sister, Athena, would help him with the legal issues of that situation.

That was also the beginning of his sobriety.

Unlike my ex-husband, Doug turned things around. Doug is a good man. We had a wonderful relationship for eight years. We raised five kids together. His three kids and my two boys. We were a big family. I tried to be a good mom to his kids. I wasn't always the best stepmom, but I tried. Doug was a good dad to my boys.

Doug said I won him over after I cooked for him. I cooked my brother's recipe of chicken cutlets and my bow tie pasta with Alfredo sauce. He caveman-ate the whole thing.

One of the first things we did together as a family was go camping. We drove to Cave Lake outside of Ely, Nevada. We had never been there, but Doug's brother and his family often camped there.

Doug packed everything but the kitchen sink. I have never seen so much crap packed for two days of camping. Doug and I had never camped together before. He said he wanted to set everything up. He wanted to get the fire going. He wanted to take care of everything. I agreed and set up my chair and watched the kids play.

Doug did okay with the tents. He really struggled with fire. After a few goes, I finally interceded and got the fire going. I took over the cooking and had our meal started. He looked at me and said, "I didn't know you knew how to do any of that."

I just smiled and said, "You didn't ask."

I further surprised him with catching a fish and gutting it without pause. That's when I really sold him on how much he loved me.

Doug and I loved similar things. We went to the movies often. We watched a lot of TV shows together. Even after we broke up, we continued to watch *Game of Thrones* together for a time. Some bonds are never broken.

While Doug and I were together, Charles came around less and less and eventually not at all.. The last time he was supposed to pick Jesse up for a weekend visit, he left him sitting on the front step with his bag packed for hours. With a broken heart, Jesse came inside and said, "I guess he's done with me." He unpacked his bag and didn't see his dad until after my brother died. Even then, it was sporadic, and eventually, he dropped out again all together. I don't know where he lives or what his phone number is.

I loved Doug's family. They accepted my boys and me, unlike Charles' family. We had large gatherings for dinners. Doug's stepdad, Bill, who was no longer married to his mom, was still involved with the family. We spent a lot of time with Bill. We watched the Cowboys football games every Sunday at Bill's house. We had pizza dinners with Bill. Once Doug and I broke up, Bill and I continued to see each other for breakfast every couple of months.

We traveled with Bill a couple of times on dive trips. We went to Bonaire and Belize. My first open water dive since I was twelve was with Doug in Bonaire. We stayed at a little hole in the wall place on the water with a dive shack. You could leave your room, suit up, grab your tank, and be in the water in fifteen minutes. We were there for several days. There was a coral reef shelf when you went into the water. The whole island is a dive site. We dove the Hilma Hooker, which is a shipwreck dive. It was a little scary. I didn't go all the way inside the ship. Doug was excited to explore it. I was a chicken and stayed outside.

We went to Belize after Doug's affair. Things were a little tense between us, and it was supposed to get us back on track. It was good for us. We dove The Blue Hole. I got yelled at underwater by the dive master for going under the group in the hole. We were supposed to stay at 130 feet. I was at 136 feet. I was fascinated with the stalactites in the water. Bill was unable to make the dive in the hole due to an ear issue. We made a few dives on that trip. We did a float dive and saw turtles, lobsters, rays, barracudas, and all kinds of fish. It was beautiful.

On one of our last days on the mainland, we zip-lined

through the trees and floated down a river on tubes through some mystic caves. To me, it seemed wrong to be in the caves. The native guide said that the indigenous people used to hold rituals there. I felt like a trespasser. Doug loved it. As we exited the dark cave, there was some fallen rock. Out of the fallen rock was growing an enormous tree with huge fan leaves at an angle, reaching for the light.

We traveled well together. We never fought on trips. We hardly fought while we were together except about yard work. I detested yard work and he acted bullish when it came to doing it. I refused to be dictated to and would just leave and go see a movie. I only did it once or twice. But I didn't want the conflict, so I just left. When we argued, it was about the kids or yard work.

Doug said I was never right after my brother died. He said the light went out of me. He said he lost me after my brother died.

We went through some very dark times. The loss of my brother, the loss of some pets, the custodial loss of his daughters, an emotional affair on my part, and a sexual affair on his part while he was out of town. The affairs we could get past. The lapse in sobriety I could not.

* * *

Doug's wavering in his sobriety is what ended our relationship ultimately. It did not just end. The night we ended it, he fucked this skank and then called and told me about it because he felt guilty. This started our on-and-off-again thing.

We did this for months. When Doug left me at Christmas, he

packed his suitcase and took only his belongings. He moved in with skankasauras. He left me with a house filled with his daughters' toys and clothes. Rooms full of memories. Doug took what he wanted. He left me and all the shit behind.

I wanted to burn it all. Athena and her soon to be husband, Adam, came over and helped me pack up the unwanted belongings nicely. I was stuffing things and crumbling up Doug's leftover clothes. Athena told me to stop doing that and fold them. I was out of my mind, but I listened to her.

Years of our lives were down to a few boxes. I was a mess. We were planning a wedding months before this break-up. I had been trying on wedding dresses. We had put down a deposit on a wedding venue. Things seemed to be coming together, then Doug started drinking again. It was like he was sabotaging it.

Doug was the ultimate love of my life. He was my best friend. My true love. It broke me when he left. A chasm opened in my heart and mind.

My future was uncertain. I went from a two-family income to a single-family income, from being a mom of five to a mom of two again. I had a boyfriend and his family, then I didn't. Doug's family were still friendly with me, but I was the ex now. I felt lost and alone.

Doug was dating and living with skankasaurus but sleeping with me on the side. I was the other woman. He was drinking heavily.

I was in the bar one night, and Doug came in with skankasaurus. The bar was full. I was playing one of the poker machines and drinking. They sat a few chairs down from me.

She saw me and started talking shit. She started talking loudly about having her man by her side all the time. She started calling me lonely and pathetic.

I said, "Well, I was neither lonely nor pathetic when I fucked your man last Wednesday."

She tried to jump at me across the bar, but Doug held her back.

I didn't even look in her direction. I just pushed the play button on the poker game and took a sip from my drink with an evil, knowing smile.

I got too drunk to drive home that night, and Myers came and picked me up. Patrick took me to get my van the next morning, and the tire was flat. That bitch did get the last word. She had slashed my tire. She admitted it to Doug's brother a month later.

Later that year, April Fool's Day, I got a call from Doug. He was in an urgent care, in trouble. He didn't remember where the car was, and he was injured. I went to pick him up. We got him sorted out and got him to a meeting. We sorted out a living situation and got him away from the crazy lady. Doug rented my mom's condo. We started dating again.

Things were good again. We traveled, we fished, we did things together.

I realized that Doug still needed to work on himself. He was jumping from relationship to relationship. I knew who I was. I knew I would be okay by myself. I wanted Doug in my life, but he always needed a partner in his. He had never been without a girlfriend or a wife. I told him he still needed to figure himself out. Things got weird between us. I told him he needed to spend more time by himself. He stopped sleeping over. He got quiet. We still hung out, but we grew apart.

I held a big Thanksgiving Day dinner. Doug's family and my family had attended. I had recently started treating the bipolar.

At the dinner, I had asked Doug if he would help me pay for the flooring in the living room. In a mad moment, Doug had ripped up all the carpet in the living room one day and never replaced it. We were left with concrete. I simply asked him if he would help me with the expense of the tile. He said he'd get back to me.

I woke up the next morning with a text message from the skank saying to stay away from her man and the flooring was my problem. I had a manic episode. The Batman gardener episode. Skankasaurus had been living with him at my mom's condo. I lost my shit. I went over to the condo, which I had a key to, and surprised her. I took all my belongings and left. Not before I dumped all of Doug's shit in his parking spot. I proceeded to lose my shit for the next thirty-six hours.

Doug became a trigger for me. I had to cut him out of my life completely. I loved him so deeply that any mention of him would send me spiraling into a deep depression. I couldn't function if I thought about him.

It took a long time for that hurt to burn away, but it did.

Not too long ago, Doug called and asked to speak to me. We sat in the garage, and he made amends with me. He told me all the terrible shit he did to me while we were together. Most of it, I was unaware of. Some of it, I was made to believe was my fault and only now learned it was not my fault. Doug told me that he would make it right.

I guess I asked him, "Oh yeah, when's that gonna happen?" What an asshole thing to say to someone who just apologized. But I was reminded recently that I said it.

Since Doug has left me, anytime something around the house has broken or I can't find the right switch, he has come over to fix it. He has never told me to figure it out, I'm on my own. He has either done it himself or sent someone to do it.

The spring on my garage door broke on Mother's Day weekend this year. He sent a guy to fix it. The guy came to look at it and said, don't worry, it's been taken care of. Doug paid for it.

Doug has been paying it forward. The best thing he has done is the refinancing of the house. When the garage door broke, he told me he wanted to look at my finances. He told me to send him my bills and credit scores, so I did. It took a few weeks, but he got back to me.

In a day, we were on the phone with a mortgage company working on a new loan. I needed to get an appraisal done. He paid for the appraisal. He came over and helped fix some of the things that needed fixing. He helped clean the pool and acid wash it. He has gone above and beyond to help me.

I stopped him at the door after he had fixed a broken sprinkler and asked, "Why are you doing all this for me? You don't owe me anything. I'm just your ex."

He sincerely replied, "Remember when you asked when you would get your amends? Here is it is. I left you in a shitty way. What I did to you was bad. I left you in a bad way. I need to make up for that. Hopefully, what I'm doing is going to make that better." Then he left.

Those words filled my heart with joy and my eyes with tears.

Dating Post Doug

It's been about five years since Doug and I broke up. He was able to move on and eventually got married. He is married to a lovely woman. They have a lot in common and met through their secret society.

I, on the other hand, have a hard time meeting people. I do not frequent bars. I do not work with single men. I do not belong to any clubs. I do not have friends who have single friends. I do not have single friends that I would date. I do not belong to a church group. I do not have a way of meeting eligible single men.

My niece suggested I try online dating. I figured what the heck. I'll give it a whirl. I downloaded the app. Swiping right and left was fun. Reading bios of likes and dislikes was interesting. It filled a lot of time. I usually spent time with the app in the mornings, drinking coffee, smoking cigarettes and sending greetings to strangers.

One guy got real belligerent with me and cussed me out because he sent me five "Hi's" and I didn't acknowledge him. Then he called me a bitch and a cunt. I blocked him. But if you want something to do, you can engage in conversations with these guys and see where it goes.

After years of using this online dating app, I've been on five dates. I mostly use the app as entertainment. I don't go on it much. In the summer, I'm more active because I have more time and am usually bored. The last date was something that must be shared as a warning to all.

I've been off the dating site since December 2018 since being stood up. I've had a couple hits and texts with people, but no big fishes.

I met Hank. He was a teacher. We did not have a lot in common, but our first couple of messages on the app were friendly. I suggested we exchange numbers.

We started texting. I should have stopped immediately. All of his text messages were single word answers. Yes. No. Karaoke. Golf. Beer. Hi. Hey. 1. There were very few actual sentences. We did sometimes have a conversation, but I always had to prompt the conversation. I knew better, but I thought *this guy has a master's degree, maybe he's just a bad texter.*

We texted for a couple of weeks and decided to meet up. I went with my Starbucks. I only meet guys at Starbucks. It's a quick out if things are bad. He agreed but then asked if we could go for a beer instead. I said I didn't mind but that I didn't drink. I didn't mind if he drinks. We agreed to go to the sports bar at the casino near our houses.

He got there first. He was sitting at the bar in front of a keno machine. There was money in the machine. He was drinking a beer. He had not paid for the beer. The keno had paid for the beer. There was a dollar in the tip cup.

When I walked over, he stood up and shook hands with me. We sat down. He did not offer me a drink. The bartender came over and asked if I wanted something and I asked for a Diet Coke.

He did not prompt a conversation. I asked how he was doing.

He said fine. Then he asked, "What's your name again?"

I was dismayed. I told him my name.

He talked about teaching, mostly bitching about kids and how he hated sharing his space with another teacher. He said he couldn't wait to retire.

He didn't ask anything about me or what my plans were for the summer. I prompted him with questions about his kids, golf, teaching, and Arizona. During his responses, he played keno, drank his free beer, and watched a sporting event on one of the many TVs in the sports bar.

At some point we talked about how much time was left of the summer, and I mentioned how we report back August 7th. He repeated the date back to me. I repeated it back to him.

He ran his fingers through his sandy, blond hair in dismay. He was distraught by the thought. He argued with me that we had more time before we went back.

He said, "Hold on, I got to call my wife. I mean, my ex-wife."

He proceeded to call her, then text her. They texted for a few minutes. Then he went on about how half his summer was gone and he was pissed.

He finished his beer, stood up and proclaimed he was going to the gym.

I stood up and said I needed to pick up my son. Which was a lie.

He shook my hand and walked away.

I didn't even have time for my emergency phone call to happen. I had Myers on standby to call me thirty minutes in to save me in case it was going bad. The date ended in under thirty minutes.

An hour later he texted me, "It was nice to me you."

That was date five.

I shared this story at work with my bosses and a coworker when school started. They knew the guy. They also said he was still married. I said he told me was recently divorced. My coworker said, "No, they just got married a few months ago."

I'm pretty sure I'm done with dating. Sure, it's entertaining to talk to people, but I don't think I'm really invested in getting to know anyone. I'm perfectly content being single. I don't need a man in my life. It would just complicate my life. I have friends to fill the void of companionship. I'm not really all that interested in sex. Once you've gone without it, it doesn't seem to matter. Whoever said, "There are plenty of fish in the sea," was not talking about modern-day society. There may be lots of fish, but they are nasty fish. They are like those crazy-looking fish, the Anglerfish, with their crazy lights at the bottom of the ocean. That's what's left of the fish in the sea.

My History with Bipolar

For close to fifteen years, I went without medication. I had bouts of depression and suicidal ideations but nothing severe. When I went to the doctor, I never noted anything about being bipolar. It was as if I just forgot about it. I had few symptoms.

I had some hormonal swings with my monthly cycle, but when I had a full hysterectomy that stopped for the most part. I did some hormone replacement, but that made things worse, so I stopped that and just put up with the hot flashes and night sweats.

I tried to eat well. I was a yoga instructor at my mom's studio. I had a holistic idea of medicine and believed I could treat my mind with my energy. It was a balance I was able to achieve for a time.

I started to have trouble with my thyroid. I started to get irritable and had mood swings. I would rage at everything and everyone. I yelled at the kids. I had an argument with Doug at work. I was so angry, I took my phone and beat it on my desk. I broke the receiver. It only recently has been replaced.

I put all these mood swings up to hormones, not bipolar. My hormones were out of balance. That had to be the cause.

Once again, I got a chest cold and went to quick care. They

gave me a course of steroids. It had been so long I had forgotten what they did to me.

Within two days of taking them, I was in a full manic swing. I had left a suicide note and disappeared for hours. Doug found me drinking at the bar where the skankasaurus worked. She had called him about my erratic behavior. I had gambled about eight hundred dollars and was drinking like a fish. I don't remember any of it.

I remember being in the garage, upset with Doug, writing in a journal in my pajamas. Next, I was at the bar in a dress with full make-up and hair done. There was a complete blackout. I don't know how I got there or how much time was lost. I don't remember.

Later that night, or early that morning, it was 2 am and the entire house was clean. I was scrubbing floorboards with a toothbrush. I had gone grocery shopping and bought items to make an extravagant breakfast that could feed an army. I woke everyone up at 6 am to eat it. I was buzzing.

I realized it was the steroids. I just quit taking them. As soon as I did, I dropped. I dropped low. I was suicidal. I wanted to die. I called Doug and wanted him to take me to the hospital. I knew I was in trouble. He didn't want to take me. We had had a fight over me disappearing during the manic episode. I hadn't had any big episodes of bipolar and had not treated the bipolar while Doug and I had dated. Doug and I were in the on again and off again part of our relationship. I'm not sure we were even living together at this time. He thought I was being dramatic.

I crawled onto the floor in the corner of my room in the fetal position and hid in a blanket. I just cried. I hid away from the world. After he got off work, Doug came to pick me up. He was mad at me. He wasn't taking me seriously. He thought I was being dramatic to bring attention to myself.

On the way to the hospital, I remember unbuckling my seatbelt. I was going to throw myself out of the car while we were driving. Something stopped me. I don't know what. I had my hand on the door handle.

At the emergency room, they took my blood pressure. It was through the roof. That was the first time Doug took me seriously. He saw I wasn't faking. I was in crisis. They were admitting me. He called my boss and told him I wouldn't be in the next day.

I spent the part of the night in the hospital in the hallway and part of the night in the psych ward in a room under a light with a camera on me. I was waiting to be assessed.

Doug later told me he spent the night in the waiting room.

By the time they came to assess me, I had calmed down. I was at zero. I didn't feel suicidal. I was fine. I just wanted out of there. It was the snake pit effect. I just wanted to be in my own bed, in my own clothes and not wearing fishnet underwear.

The assessor asked me if I had other episodes. I told him I had an allergic reaction to the steroids. I told him to look it up if he didn't believe me. I again denied being bipolar. I didn't want to check into a facility. They released me. I took the rest of the week off work.

I didn't have any other episodes that year. I felt down at times but not super down and suicidal. How bad could it really be if you're not suicidal?

The next school year started, and I was depressed. I couldn't shake it. I was super depressed and couldn't stop crying. I confided in a friend about how I was feeling and that I was bipolar. She told me it was an easy fix. She was bipolar too. All I needed was meds. She told me what she was taking. Told me to get to a doctor and all would be well.

I went to my doctor and asked to take what was working for my friend. The doctor gave me the script.

For the next couple of months, I took a low dose of Lexapro and Lamictal. My mood changed; I felt great. I was no longer depressed. I felt like I could take on the world. I upped my Lexapro to the clinical dose. I didn't notice right away, but my mood began to climb.

This led to the Batman dragon gardener episode. The antidepressant had caused the manic episode.

I finally went to see a psychiatrist. Sort of. They got me in to see a nurse who specialized in mental health. They reclassified me as a bipolar type I.

She put me on Seroquel, a med that made me angry. This is what led me to calling people cunts and dumbasses. I tried it for a month and gave up. I researched my own cocktail and went back to her with a plan. She gave me what I chose.

I took that cocktail for almost four years until I trialed out of that med, too. I had a bad mixed episode that sent me into the hospital and kept me out of work for two weeks.

Now, I'm on a new cocktail mix that seems to be working.

When I first started out with this illness, I trialed out of so many combinations of drugs. None of them worked. It could be because they were treating me as a bipolar type II.

In the early stages of this illness, I did not have many manic episodes. I had hypomanic episodes. That's why they thought I was a bipolar type II.

As I have gotten older, the depression has become less intense and less frequent, but when it's bad, it's bad. Full swings of suicidal ideation. Depression that makes me just want to die. The mania is more powerful. Full energy that spins all day long, creating alternate realities, almost parallel universes that are so convincing it's hard to tell reality from fantasy.

As I get older, this illness get is getting harder to manage. The swings are getting tougher. They are getting longer. They are getting more creative. It's like they are finding ways to trick my brain that I haven't seen before, so I don't know what's happening.

I will keep fighting it. I don't want to be sick. I have bouts of wellness and remission of symptoms. I have been well for months at a time without any symptoms. I can only pray that I get the right concoction of cocktails that work well for a time. Bipolar is a bitch, and she isn't going to win.

* * *

When I was first diagnosed as being bipolar, my parents did not want to believe it. My mom sent me to her doctor, wanting a second opinion. Her doctor confirmed that it was most likely bipolar disorder and wrote me a script for Wellbutrin.

I'm not sure why my mom was so adamant that it wasn't bipolar. Mental illness seemed to run in our family, undiagnosed, maybe hidden by the alcoholism that is also prevalent on both sides of my family. My brother suffered from depression and anxiety issues. On my dad's side of the family, there are depression and anxiety issues. There could be other mental health issues that I am unaware of. For whatever reason, she was very sure that I wasn't bipolar.

My mom and Sara did not accept my diagnosis initially; it was something I just did not discuss with them. I did not want to be lectured about how I was trying to take care of myself.

When I was finally diagnosed in college, it was the first thing that had made sense about my mood for the first time in many years. It explained the feelings of extreme depression and suicidal ideation. It explained the jump into hyper cleaning modes and need for less sleep. A bipolar diagnosis fit. Maybe I had hidden so much from them over the years that they just did not see it. Maybe, they just saw me as a sensitive, moody kid.

After all, they were unaware of my suicide attempts. They were unaware of how depressed I was. They were not aware of my insomnia. I didn't share these things with them as a kid because I didn't want to worry them. I don't know why. Maybe it went back to my grandmother and her treatment of me with the sexual assault. I have no idea.

My mom was a kind and generous soul. She never gave me a reason not to trust her. Sara also cared for me and gave me no reason not to trust her. But I felt justified in not having shared these thoughts with my parents when they didn't believe me that I was bipolar.

After I went off my meds, it was something we didn't discuss, because even I was in denial of being bipolar again.

When I could no longer deny the bipolar and started taking medicine, I spoke openly about taking medicine. The drugs I took caused sedation and I had a strict regimen. I didn't hide the fact that I had bipolar and I openly talked about it with everyone. The more people that knew, the better. I needed people to monitor me, to tell me if I seemed off.

When I spoke about this with my parents, their concern was

the medication. They didn't like the fact that I was having to take drugs. I think they had come to terms with the diagnosis, though we never discussed it.

I still kept them in the dark about my day-to-day illness. They don't know a whole lot about the Batman gardener episode. They are unaware of my buzzing highs and suicidal lows. I kept it hidden from them.

I remember having dinner one night, and my stepmom was talking about the evils of the pharmaceutical companies. She spoke about how she didn't want to rely on medication. I told her that I needed medication to function so I did not commit suicide. It was one of the first times we had an open conversation. It didn't last long, but it was a start.

My parents have seen me on my meds, the bad ones. The ones that made me doped up and sedated. That was difficult. They didn't lecture me about it. They just accepted it. I was very grateful.

I had an episode in the summer, 2018, before school started. My stepmom took me to the psychiatrist. She came in with me to the appointment. She had asked the doctor whether I should seek outside counseling for issues I had not dealt with.

He told her counseling is always good for people, but I loved what he said next.

"You do realize your daughter has a medical condition that requires medication to treat? It's a very treatable illness," he said to her.

My stepmom didn't respond, but it seemed like for the first time, maybe she took it to heart.

Recently my mom and I chatted over breakfast. We were in the kitchen seated at the bar that connected the blue marbled countered to the kitchen. Sitting on high topped chairs, we ate our breakfast of scrambled eggs and fresh fruit.

We started talking about my book and if it had been therapeutic to write. I told her I had recently written something that I had some questions about.

I asked her, "How come, when I was first diagnosed, you refused to believe I was bipolar?"

She responded, "I was in denial. I didn't want that kind of future for you. I knew it would be tough. I didn't want you to go through that."

I went on to tell her that I felt if I had been honest with her about my emotions and my suicide attempts, she would have maybe believed me. I kept it all hidden from her, so maybe the diagnosis was hard to believe. I revealed to my mom all my suicide attempts from the age of eight or nine, after the sexual abuse, until after I had Jesse.

My mom just listened.

She started to cry. She said, "I just thought you were going through regular things all teenagers went through. I didn't realize you were in such pain. I wish I had known."

"I know, Mom. I don't blame you. I didn't tell you. I don't know why I didn't tell you. I just didn't. I felt like I needed to keep it a secret," I told her through tears.

We held hands and cried together.

The dog was lying on the floor behind us and started snoring loudly and then farted. It made us both laugh and lightened the mood. I got up from my seat and hugged my mom.

I have noticed that my parents do seem to take notice of my mood and inquire about it. When I am acting out of sorts, too high or low, they notice and ask about my meds. It's nice to finally be open with them about it.

The light in my eyes has come back with the new meds I

have been taking. My parents have noticed and commented on it. I feel like another part of my life has finally opened up to share with my parents and I've been accepted.

BIPOLAR DIARY

Nicotine No More

March 17, 2019

It's been a month since I've had a cigarette. A week and a half since I've had some nicotine. I have gained five pounds. My diet has gone to shit. I have craved nothing but sweets and fried food and have given in to most of those cravings.

I have tried to balance that out a bit. I eat really well in the morning and for lunch. Then for dinner, all bets are off. I can't help myself. I have no control. There's nobody here to monitor me. I have nobody to check my impulses. I feel guilty, but I do it anyway.

It's spring break. I've made a bargain with myself. Once I'm back on my school schedule, next week, I'll be back on my diet schedule. It makes more sense. I do much better with a schedule. Sleep-wise, eating-wise, everything-wise. I need structure. Once that structure is gone, I fall flat on my face.

I was doing great on my diet when I had the schedule to follow. Once I had to fill in the blanks and follow my own schedule, I started getting lazy. I cut in too many free days. I started eating out more and more.

The biggest adjustment was the cigarettes. The first two weeks without the smokes weren't bad, but I was on the patch. In fact, my gym participation increased a lot, and I was feeling good. It was when I decreased the nicotine and then went off the nicotine completely that the diet failed me, and I lost all hope.

I read that nicotine is just as addictive as heroin. The receptors in the brain that cause the pleasure of being on heroin are the same for nicotine. In a PET scan, the same receptors light up.

I've always been a smoker, just not a heavy smoker. I've smoked on and off since high school. Some throughout college. Some while being a teacher. There were long stretches when I didn't smoke at all. But in the last four to five years, I started smoking pretty heavily. When I got sick, I started smoking heavily, half a pack to a pack a day.

It became my crutch. Something to pass the time. Something to get me through the next hour of the pain that was my life. As little bit of comfort in the hell I was going through.

It also gave me routine. Something I desperately needed. Cigarettes were a part of my daily routine.

I would get up. Make coffee. I would have a cup of coffee and smoke a couple of cigarettes with each cup of coffee. I would have a few cups of coffee each morning, depending on what time I got up.

I would have a cigarette once I hit Decatur Boulevard in the truck. That would last me until I got to Rancho Drive and Lone Mountain Road. I'd go to Starbucks, get my coffee. Light up another one on my way to school out of the drive-through.

During first period, I had a break at school. I would drive

around the school and smoke a cigarette. Then at lunch, before I ate, if I ate, I would smoke another. Then at the end of the day, another cigarette.

That would be my day at work.

I would drop Athena's daughter off and light up another one on the way home.

Once home, I would sit in my spot in the garage and have a cigarette before going into the house to make dinner. While dinner was cooking, I'd go back out to the garage and smoke again.

Then, of course, the after-dinner smoke. I'd have one or two. Depending on what was going on. Sometimes, one of my boys would also be smoking, so we would be sitting around and socializing, all smoking. One cig led to two after an hour or so.

Right as I started to get sleepy, I would go out to the garage and have a final puff. Sometimes it would be a whole cigarette, sometimes just a puff or even a half.

During the night, if I couldn't sleep, I would go out and smoke a cigarette. I'd finish the one I'd started or start a whole new one. I'd go back to bed like nothing had happened. Keeping a steady stream of nicotine in my system.

I'd wake up and start the day over all over again.

Removing the cigarette routine has been a challenge this month. I miss my garage time. I don't play games on my phone like I used to. That was also what I would do in the garage whilst I smoked and drank my coffee for hours on end. I have found other ways to fill the gaps in my morning. I listen to Daily TV Mass in the mornings now. That keeps me occupied.

I go for walks at work. I find busy work for me to do. I plan and plan. It's March, and I have lesson plans for the next school year done through Christmas 2019.

I know the weight will come off with a little bit of exercise, and now that I have stopped smoking, I might even be able to start running again. That was one of my goals in stopping smoking. I don't know that I want to run another half marathon, but I'd like to be able to run three miles and not die. I'd like to be able to enjoy my runs. I'd like to do it in a timely manner, too.

All these things will happen in time. In one month, I have stopped smoking. That is one transformation. In another month, there will be another transformation. I cannot wait to see what that will be.

* * *

Putting Away Sharp Objects

March 18, 2019

I'm feeling the tug of an old, hidden secret I buried over twenty-five years ago. It resurfaced this August. It is most common in young teens but prevalent in adults as well. According to Crissestext.org, "People who hurt themselves most often start as teens or young adults, with adolescent rates of nonsuicidal self-injury being tracked at rates from 15% to 40% depending on the study."

I started around the age of twelve, when I attempted suicide. I found out how much release from pain can come at the sharp end of the razor blade and the appearance of the droplets of blood. The pain—emotional, then physical as the razor bit—would peak with the action of cutting, then fade quickly. The rush of calm and serenity from the blood flow was like taking an Ativan. It took the heavy feeling away and brought me peace. This reaction is a big part of why people cut. After I cut myself, I was able to handle whatever calamity I was facing.

I have been bipolar symptom-free for the past four weeks. A little hiccup here and there. A day of feeling down. A day of feeling up. But no recognizable pattern to indicate a swing in emotion. Yet I have felt a buildup of tension. Something I don't have on my graph to gauge. The need to purge a backup of some sort of emotion to stay even. To keep my mood level.

I solved that by running a razor blade up my left arm. Just a quick small cut. It hasn't been a big deal as the weather has been cold, and everyone has been wearing jackets. It has only become a big deal today when the weather warmed up and I had three equal-sized, two-inch cuts up the inside fleshy part of my left arm at varied stages of healing.

I felt ashamed. I knew I shouldn't do it. I was, am, worried what others will make of it. Will I be sent home? Will they make me be evaluated? Will I be fit to work? Am I sick? It was a decision I made to ease my pain. A temporary solution. A trick that would have stayed hidden from the world.

My arm is my preferred area to harm. It always has been. As a seventh-grader, I wore long sleeves and lots of bangle bracelets. That covered everything up. Bangles are not in style at the moment, plus the cuts are fairly high up my entire arm as if I'm marking them in stages.

I have thought of clever things to say. "I was gardening, and I got my arm stuck in some chicken wire." "I caught my arm in some old student council mess left over from a dance in a long-lost box." "A desk caught me. It was sharp underneath.

I don't know what it was." Since the marks are equally spaced, in the same direction, all these answers make sense. Except the cuts are at different stages in healing.

I covered them in bandages today. Nobody noticed, or if they did, they didn't say anything. I tried to leave my jacket on for as long as I could.

I don't plan for this to be my out. I know I need to stop. I am working on my coping skills. Writing. Calling or texting a friend. Holding a piece of ice. All these things have worked in the past. Drawing. Walking. On top off all this, I have given up smoking. Normally, I would just go have a smoke, but that is also off the table. I know I should have taken this one at a time, but it just couldn't wait.

I need to take things seriously, and this is serious. I will work on this day by day. Starting with getting rid of the sharp objects. That's where to start. Lord, give me the strength to deal with the pain without this.

* * *

Facing Fears of Past Episodes

June 18, 2019

It's strange being back at the cabin. Coming back to a place where I lost my shit last summer. The last time I was here, I was in a mixed episode. I wanted to really hurt myself. I wanted to grab a sharp knife and slit my wrists open. The urge was so overpowering that I held the knife in my hand and put it to my skin. I pushed it into my flesh, but I didn't make the cut.

I put it down and packed everything up. I cried the entire time. Mind was buzzing. Thoughts were racing. I tried to be aware of what I was doing. I needed to make sure the cabin was safely buttoned up, but I needed to get the fuck out of there and back to the city before I hurt myself.

Now that I'm here a year later, I almost don't know how to act. There is a lot on my mind. There's a lot to get done. We are prepping to do the floors this season. The entire contents of the main floor need to be moved to the loft. However, it needs to be made into a livable situation because I will still be up here, living in it. So, I busy myself with these things.

This is my third time up here this season. The first time I came up with my sister, Athena. I busied myself with papering the cabinets.

The next time I came up was with my son, Patrick. I busied myself with putting the kitchen together and taking down the temporary kitchen.

Now, most of what I can do is done. I'm struggling with how to relax and focus. I want to read my book, but I can't.

Reading is my escape from life, the go-to fun thing I love to do. I have read one book so far this summer. I just lose focus. My eyes wander, my brain wanders. I can't maintain what's happening.

I guess I just feel kinda mixed up. I feel strange being up here still. Like I'm waiting to be sick.

I see the doctor next week, and I need to figure out what to tell him. I don't feel depressed or manic, but I don't feel well exactly. I feel off. I don't feel right. I feel unfocused. Maybe it is a bit of mania in a strange way. I don't know. It doesn't register on my chart as anything. Maybe he will be able to shed some light on it.

I feel so much more clear-headed versus the meds I was on before. I feel like I am starting to be me again. I feel some inkling of who I used to be and a new person starting to form. I feel like I have been asleep for a long time.

When you sleep for a long time, things begin to atrophy. Things in my brain atrophied. I lost my drawing ability. I am working on bringing that back. I feel like I have lost a huge part of my creativity. It really sucks to lose a part of who you think you are. I am trying to work on that a little each day.

The writing is another form of creativity that is coming back from the dead. It is something that has blossomed since the ending of the old meds. I am able to see and form words again. Not only can I use written words, I can speak the words again. For so long, my speech was hindered by the meds. They caused me to have a heavy tongue and a speech impediment. Some people thought I was drugged or drunk due, or that something was wrong with me. My boss was constantly asking if I was okay.

I feel robbed of the last four years of my life. I feel like I was in a dream, watching my life go by. My life was scheduled around my medication. I had to take it by five in the evening for it to wear off by seven in the morning. Even then, it was not always completely worn off.

My life ended at five in the evening. I could not go to after-school functions, parties, dinners, dates. Everything had to be scheduled during the day or afternoons.

I also had to schedule my meds around food. I had to eat a minimum of 200 calories with the meds or they would not work effectively, and the side effects would be worse. If I took them without food, I would feel drugged. I couldn't talk. My speech would be slurred. I couldn't walk and would run into walls.

With all these hindrances, I still thought the benefits of the medication outweighed the bad. My mood, for the most part, was stable, except when I needed a med adjustment. I did well with the medication. I didn't gain too much weight. I actually lost some weight initially.

At one point, while the meds were not balanced, I suffered a bad depression, but once the dosage was right, I felt great. But I gained weight immediately. My mood was stable, so I didn't think too much about that.

I continued with this medication for four years, upping dosages when needed until I was at the maximum dosage. I worried once I hit that dosage what would happen when I needed to up again. I feared what would happen, but I never expressed that fear to my doctor. In hindsight, I should have.

What I didn't realize was I wasn't really living. I was surviving. I was scared. I was scared of having another episode and ending up in the hospital. I was scared of killing myself. I was scared of living with suicidal ideation.

It all came to a head last July. I just started to feel off. I didn't know what was off exactly. I had a week of depression. I burned myself with a lighter. Immediately, mania set in, but it was a strange mania. I was unfocused. I just wanted to sit still. I was afraid if I didn't sit still, I would float away.

I just sat on the porch at the cabin and watched the birds. I didn't read. I was here with Pat. We did some work. I went home. Was buzzy but not terrible. Went back to the cabin with my cousin and auntie.

We had a good morning. Went to the point. I took a picture. All smiles. They left. Minutes later, the urge to hurt myself took over.

When I got back to Vegas, I took another selfie. A vision of what it looks like to have a manic episode. I recently looked at the contrast between those two pictures. Night and day. Bipolar. The two poles of this illness.

Since I'm back at the cabin, I am going to take a new selfie. Mark a new day. Pray the rosary. Meditate. Try to calm the restlessness that has taken over my mind and try to read my book.

* * *

Medication Noncompliance

July 14, 2019

For the most part, I have accepted that I will have to take medicine for the rest of my life.

There are days when I have absolutely no issue with this. I eat my dinner and take my pills, then settle in for the evening.

Then, there are the other nights. I have a silent fight with myself. I don't want to take my pills. I will walk over with a bottle of water and just glare at the five bottles and walk away. I refuse to take them. I will go watch another episode of *Deadwood* and put it off.

There is no reason behind this silent fight. I know I'll give in and eventually take my pills, but the fight and resistance are there.

I am not one of those bipolars, now, who think they are cured and stop taking their meds. I am strictly compliant when it comes to my meds, which is why this behavior is strange.

I become resentful that I have to take them. It's a silent

protest, even if it is just a few hours.

Mind you, that few hours of not being compliant can fuck up my whole next day.

Sometimes, it alters my mood or makes me sleep in.

It is important to try to take your meds around the same time of day each day. That allows your brain to receive the chemicals and stay as balanced as possible. If you start messing with that, you make yourself prone to swings.

You can set your clock to my med regimen. Everyone knows that.

Last night, I thought about not taking my meds. I must have looked at the bottles for five minutes. I thought what it would be like to not have to be anchored by medication.

How would life be different?

I would be able to go to the movies or a show in the evening and not worry about getting home to take my meds.

I could go out on a date in the evening and not worry about having to go back home and take my meds.

I wouldn't have to worry about having a meal before taking my meds.

There are then the side effects of taking the medications.

The weight gain has been the worst. The previous meds did not have such a bad side effect, but new meds have packed a punch of almost eighty pounds. This weight gain caused my blood sugar to increase to where I am now a diabetic.

There are other side effects: tremors. These have started to go away but have left a strange lingering influence on how I hold my left arm. The tremors started with the old medication and started up again with the new. They have subsided, but when I walk, I hold my left arm as if it were injured and sometimes point my fingers in an odd way. My arm is rigid.

I am unaware that I am doing it. Sometimes, I catch myself, and I feel self-aware and relax my arm to a normal position. I wonder how long I had been walking around like that. I wonder who saw me walking like a spaz.

Memory loss is another side effect. The meds I take now do not seem to lead to as much memory loss as the old one. The older medication put me in a four-year haze. I don't remember a lot of that time. I put in a whole drip line system for watering in my backyard, but I don't remember doing it. I don't know how to work it.

The new meds have me a bit off too. In January, I went to get my toes done with my sister. She said I was very quiet. I don't remember anything about the entire encounter. I don't remember the day. I remember her birthday, but I don't remember us doing anything. That was on the new meds, but only a few months into a med change. That could be the issue.

There are a lot of reasons for not taking medication. There are many reasons to take the medication.

By taking the medication, I am more often symptom-free. I have been in remission of symptoms for a few months. I have had no big swings for four months. Three months completely symptom-free.

Taking medication helps alleviate the possibility of me ending up a suicide. If I wasn't being treated, I would likely be suicidal. Not just prone to suicidal ideations but actually suicidal. When the meds are off, having suicidal ideation is tough, but being suicidal is deadly. You want to be dead; everything is telling you that you are better off dead. It makes total sense. Medication makes this better.

Medication makes mania manageable. I always thought the depression would kill me, but my mania has gotten worse as

I have gotten older. The older I get, the tougher it hits me, and the harder I spin, the longer the spells get, the louder the buzzing persists.

Even with medication, I get highs and lows, but they are more manageable. Sometimes I need a bump up or down in the meds; usually, it's an up. Without the medication, the swings would be intolerable. They would swing so great and wide my mind would crack like the Grand Canyon.

Taking the meds also allows me to come out of the swing easily and not get too manic or too depressed so quickly.

Now, a lot of the time, I go from manic to normal and never hit depressed. I do this all with a little med bump. The doctor gave me Ativan to treat the highs as needed to bring me out of the mania.

The problem is when I'm in a high, I don't recognize that I need to take the med to bring me down. I just assume I'm fine until someone says something to me, or I realize I just texted twenty people to see what they are up to. Then I know I need a pill.

With all these reasons why and why not to take meds, I'm still an advocate of medication. It has saved my life. It allows me to work, be stable, for the most part, and have a life.

I will fight with myself again about taking my meds. It is just a fact. It may not be today or tomorrow, but it will be again in the coming months. I will feel sorry for myself that I'm bipolar and not want to rely on medication. I will fight it. In the end, I will be compliant because I want to be healthy.

I know for sure I do not want to be in a psych ward with net underwear or no underwear. I'll take the meds.

* * *

Death, Batman, Kayaks, Running and Writing

July 15, 2019

I have always suffered from low mood swings, some sort of emotional swings. Even as a young child, I would obsess over things to the point of making myself cry.

One time, around the age of seven, I was at a sleepover. I became severely sad. I began to think about the fact I had never met my paternal grandfather. He had died long before I was born. The thought that he was dead struck me deep and saddened me to the point of tears.

The sleepover was a birthday party for a friend. While the other girls were downstairs having fun, I was sitting at the top of the stairs crying. The girl's older sister came to see why I was not down with the others.

I was full-on crying. Snot was running out of my nose. I was heaving giant sobs. I was hysterically crying. In full grief, I cried. The sister sat down beside me, not knowing what was wrong. She asked me. I told her my grandfather was dead. She asked me if he died recently. I said no. I never knew him. I remember her being puzzled.

My grief was real and so strong. I was so sad. She asked me if I wanted to go home. I wasn't sure what I wanted to do. She sat with me for a while.

I finally stopped crying. She patted my back. I wiped my tears. I felt better and went down to the party.

I don't remember the rest of the party, or if I ever talked about it with my mom, but I remember feeling so sad I couldn't take it. It was one of the first times I felt that way. It wouldn't be the last.

Bipolar people obsess over things. Sometimes they are

good things; sometimes they are bad things. Sometimes the obsessions help you get through the bad parts of swings. Sometimes, they are what drives the swings.

I can name four things I have been obsessive over: Batman, owning a kayak, running, and writing this book. None of these things are harmful, but they were obsessive.

For whatever reason, when the bipolar kicked back up, Batman became my savior. I was obsessed with all things Batman. I bought t-shirts, onesies, socks, hats, sweatshirts, pants, slippers, posters. I'm sure there are other things. I threw a Batman-themed fortieth birthday party. I loved Batman. People knew I loved Batman, and they bought me Batman things. I still love Batman, but I'm not obsessed. I have always liked Batman, but I wasn't obsessed. I read Batman comics as a kid and know Batman lore. I just went Batman loco for a while.

For an entire year, I was convinced I needed a kayak. I kept going to the sporting goods shop and looking at them. I told everyone I was buying one. I was planning on using it at Lake Mead and up at the cabin on Navajo Lake in Utah. I was looking into kayak clubs. My students bought me gift cards to the sporting goods store to go toward my kayak. My parents pitched in toward my kayak. At some point, I realized I was not going to go kayaking, so I bought a fishing pole, which I use.

Running was a healthy obsession. I would run a hundred miles a month. It was a contest. I ran in the morning before work and after work. I was only running three miles a day when I decided to run a half marathon. I just signed up for it. I trained for three months. Then just did it. Once I had done it, I quit running. I barely made thirty miles a month. Then no miles a month. Now, I'm overweight and can't run at all.

Writing each day, several times a day is the newest obsession. I can't stop. I feel a need, a compulsion to share what's on my mind with everyone. I feel that the world needs to hear what I have to say. It's important that what I say is known. Now, I doubt that. This is just another obsessive thought.

Around my brother's birthday and the the anniversary of his death, I replay the conversations we had the day he died. Sometimes it's what he said to me; sometimes, it just a loop of other things. Whatever it is, it is obsessive. I can't let it go. Usually, it triggers me into a bad mood swing.

I have to work hard at not falling for my obsessive behaviors. I have to be vigilant in finding my behaviors. If they aren't hurting me or anyone, then there may not be anything to worry about. It may also be a symptom of a manic episode, and I may need help.

As a bipolar, there is a constant need to police my behavior. I have to be my own traffic cop. I've been running the red lights, and nobody has pulled me over. I need to write myself a ticket.

* * *

Hard Hit

July 16, 2019

I have never felt more bipolar than in the last couple of days. I have truly felt the swing from manic to depression. One day everything was bright and sunny. I thought I was going to write the next best thing in literature. I thought it was going to be great.

Then, I slept for thirteen hours and woke up in a haze. I

found myself kinda down, but not super down, maybe a little air let out of the tires. I did some writing. I found a little focus. Felt a little sorry for myself. I tried to steer my mood back on track.

Today, I spiraled out of control into hysterics. I sobbed and sobbed the snot-sob of all sobs. I texted my friends, asking forgiveness for having put my "book" in front of them. I felt inauthentic. I felt a fraud. I felt stupid and embarrassed.

I just cried uncontrollably for hours. I wasn't necessarily depressed, but I was sad. I was upset that I didn't see that I was manic for most of the summer. I registered two days of mania on my chart. That's all that I noticed around the Fourth of July. I was buzzing then but didn't look at the rest of my behavior too closely.

I did mention to my doctor when I saw him the month before that something was off. I couldn't place my finger on it. I knew my mood was off, but I didn't know what it was. I was sleeping a good amount, at least six to eight hours a night.

It didn't seem like hypomania was on the rise. The obsession of the book should have been the key. All I did was eat, sleep, breathe and talk about my book and writings. I haven't done anything else all summer. My summer is gone, and I have done nothing but write. I spent all my time in front of this computer. It was mania.

I feel deflated. I was a helium balloon a few days ago, full and floating. Now I'm what's left over after the party has been done for a few days. I'm shrunken up and fallen to the floor, no longer flying high. I'm on the ground with the dirt and the bugs. I feel low and dirty.

My mood hit me hard and fast late in the morning. It hit me how stupid it was to invest all this time into this "book." It might be okay for a blog, but who would want to read the diary of a manic madwoman? I just cried heaving sobs.

I sent out mass apology texts to everyone. I was so embarrassed by the thought of what I had done. Most sent back not to worry about it. It doesn't stop the utter shame of what I've done. The embarrassment that I feel. The lack of self-control I had while in my delusional state of mind that I'm a great writer. Some sent some encouragement to keep writing, but it's hard to hear that when you feel so bad for being sick.

A few days ago, life was great. Summer had been wonderful. The house refi went well. The house got cleaned and redone. The cabin work went smoothly. The relaxing at the cabin has been relaxing. Writing has been going well. All of this made me think it was the perfect summer, only to find out that it was tinted rosy by mania.

It was so great because everything is great when you're manic. Everything is more beautiful when you're manic. The music is louder. The colors are brighter. The smells are stronger. Beauty is more beautiful.

All of this was taken away by that thirteen-hour sleeping episode. I woke up and a dullness edged the frame of my vision. The shiny halo of the sun dimmed. The real darkness of feeling the effect didn't hit until this morning. The reality check that I had wasted my time and the time of others this summer by making them read sixty-plus stories about me and the antics of my childhood.

The dream of being a writer crushed by the reality of today. Yesterday, it was so real that I could be a writer. Today, the reality is it's just a blog. It's nothing special. There is no magic. There are rainbows because of the rain and sun, not because of the little people. The shine has worn off and the harshness is cold.

There will be more writing, but I don't know what it will look like under the guise of "normal." Will the creative brain be able to handle "normal"? Will my upped meds even allow me to form sentences that make sense?

I have one dream. I dream that I can stay healthy and stable without mood swings. I dream that I can feel emotions without feeling them so deep that it makes me want to drown or soar. I dream that I can do a project and not spiral out of control with it; that I can put it away when it's done. Small dreams for some. Impossible dreams for me.

* * *

Medication Management

July 27, 2019

In the wake of having a manic episode and coming out of a manic episode, I saw the psychiatrist. Keeping tabs on my behavior and communicating this to my doctor is key in keeping healthy. This summer, manic episodes seems to be a cycle.

I had an episode last summer and for the past few winters I have had manic episodes. Armed with this information, I went to the doctor.

I told him about the mild manic episode, which I felt was mild due to the Ativan I was taking. The Ativan made it mild like it was supposed to. I had been sleeping fairly well, but in retrospect, I had telltale signs of manic behavior.

I had written almost 80,000 words in five weeks. I had written two curricula for two colleagues. I had completed my folders for the following school year for my consulting job in google docs. I had refinanced my house. I had renovated both my front yard and back yard. I acid washed my pool and spa. I cleaned the garage. I cleaned the fridge. I scrubbed the tile and grout. I dusted. I cleaned the blinds. I washed the walls, doors and frames. I cleaned the baseboards with a toothbrush.

Some of those things I had to do for the appraisal for my home. I think some of those things kick-started the mania. It's a chicken and egg thing. One thing happened and then another, I'm just not sure when the mania came into play.

I told the doctor about all of this and my descent into hysterics after my thirteen-hour sleep. I told him it was a rough swing. I didn't recall having a swing that rough before or that sudden. I also don't recall coming out of it so suddenly either. It only lasted a day and it was done.

I spoke with him about my concerns about starting the new school year. I am not typically concerned with starting the school year. A schedule is usually the best thing for me. I thrive on a set schedule. I have anxiety about my new responsibilities. I don't want to mess it up and have manic episodes. The mania is getting worse and more unpredictable. I wasn't even aware I was manic until I was out of it and spiraling down.

We carefully discussed which medication to adjust. I take three medications. I take an antipsychotic and two anti-seizure medications as mood stabilizers. We decided on one of the mood stabilizers to be increased as it has the least number of side effects.

You have to increase these medications in steps. You cannot jump from 100 milligrams to 200 milligrams. You have to go up in small doses. Sometimes, it can take a month to get you to the right dosage.

Right now, I am riding the escalator up, slowly increasing my dosage week by week until I'm at the right level.

With all medications, there are side effects. For me, the side effects affect my creative brain. I can already feel the cloudiness of thought at the slight increase in the dosage. It scrambles my brain. It causes me to have trouble recalling words when speaking. It's like always searching for the right word and never being able to say it. It makes me subdued and lethargic.

Another side effect of this medication is a tingling sensation in the tips of the fingers, nose and cheeks. It feels like they have gone to sleep, or you have snorted a line of cocaine. I'm constantly rubbing my nose like I did a line of something or I've got a booger. It's just tingling, and I'm rubbing it to get some life back into it. My fingers don't bother me so much. Once in a while I feel it in my cheeks, but it passes quickly. The nose tingle happens all the time.

I'm writing this now, under the haze of the new dose. I worry I won't be creative enough to finish what I've started.

* * *

Depression Dive

September 2, 2019

I had another swing recently. I think it was due to the med increase. This time it was a depressive episode with self-harm. It was a short episode, but it was intense.

I had upped the Topamax to 200mg. I had been slowly increasing the dosage. When I first bumped the dosage, I felt a slight down but nothing too significant. I just felt a little down.

I barely even registered it. The sun just didn't seem so bright.

The day I upped to the 200mg dose I didn't immediately feel anything. The next day, however, I felt it. I felt sluggish and low. I was tired. I felt heavy and drained. I felt foggy. I didn't brush my teeth. I wanted to cry.

It was the last day of our back to school staff development days. I was surrounded by my coworkers. I do not have a poker face. Whatever mood I am in is reflected in my face. I was asked by several people if I was feeling okay. I just played it off as I was tired and explained that I had been adjusting my meds. They accepted that explanation. I accepted that explanation.

We did an activity where we all ended up walking around the room. For some reason, we all ended up on one side of the room. I was squished into a large group of people. I got claustrophobic. I began to have a panic attack. I quickly got to the bathroom. I closed myself in a stall and began to cry.

I cried silent tears and hoped nobody heard me. I wanted to cut myself and release some of my tension. I took an Ativan and tried to calm down. I counted my breaths. I opened and closed my hands. I wiped away my tears, washed my face, and returned to the staff development.

We moved on to the next activity. I participated. I was foggy and don't recall much of what was going on. I just went through the motions.

Pretty soon lunch was called. I went out and had a cigarette. When I came back, all the people from my table had gone elsewhere to eat. I was all alone. I sat and ate by myself. I felt abandoned. I looked around, but it seemed like all the tables were filled. I'm sure I could have found a table to sit at, but in my depression, it seemed impossible.

I went to check in with my friend who is my emotional

barometer. As soon as she saw me, she asked what was wrong. I burst into tears trying to explain that I was just a little down.

She said I was more than a little down and could not go back to the training. I needed to go home. She asked why I was holding back my tears. Why didn't I just cry and let them out?

I didn't know why. I just didn't want to cry. She told me I was like a pimple that needed to be popped. She sent me home.

All the way home, I just cried. I could not be consoled.

I got home and the first thing I did was cut myself. It released some of the pain. Seeing the blood made me feel better. The tears stopped, and the heaviness in my chest lifted for a moment. It didn't last.

Unfortunately, I had to go out. I had dinner plans with Sedlak, who was visiting from out of state and whom I had not seen in a long time. We went to dinner, and I cried on and off throughout the meal. She just talked to me like a normal person and didn't flinch at my tears. It's great having friends who accept me.

I went home and continued to cry. Pimple popped and oozing. I couldn't really focus on anything. I just watching mindless TV. I had tons of *America's Got Talent* to get caught up on. That just made me cry even more. I cried myself to sleep.

I dreamed weird dreams. I dreamed about my brother. I dreamed sad things. I dreamed about being lost. I woke up crying.

I got a message from my friend Andrea about our lunch plans, asking if I could change them to breakfast plans. I warned her I was in despair and might not be good company. She said to come anyway.

I cried on and off throughout breakfast, just as I had through dinner the night before.

I realized I needed to be in bed and do nothing. Before going to bed, I cut myself again. It released a bit more tension. I felt a little bit better. I knew it was not a solution, but I felt better. Something in my brain wanted me to hurt myself.

I stayed in bed and did just that, nothing. I didn't eat anything but a snack for dinner and took my meds and went to bed.

I woke up very late the next morning. I had slept for fourteen hours. I woke up, and the sun was shining. I think the birds were chirping. I felt great. All glimmers of sadness and thoughts of self-harm were gone. The depressive episode had vanished completely. I made it through with only a couple of scabs from the self-harm.

I'm seeing clearly now a few weeks out of this episode. We upped this med to be proactive against the mania that has been plaguing me. I haven't had any depressive episodes in a long time, and none like this, so intense with crying and self-harm.

I don't know what the pattern is, but the episodes are coming on quickly and leaving quickly. I'm not cycling into another one. There is a respite in between cycles. The episodes hit hard, fast and mean. There does not seem to be a trigger, other than the meds this time, possibly.

I'm puzzled by these new events and concerned. I avoid stress and my triggers to keep episodes at bay. If episodes just start to appear at random, then my whole system is shot. This has me on edge. I am waiting in anticipation for another episode. It's unsettling to live in the unknown.

Shadow People

With bipolar, you can have psychotic episodes, such as Pandora the Magic Dragon. She was fun and talked too much. There was also the creepy man who was standing on my table. These are psychotic episodes. The unreal that the mind makes up. There's also an unknown that lies beyond the mind—religious or spiritual experiences. When you meditate, you can easily find yourself in a different spiritual world with cosmic energy. You see things and hear things in meditations. In meditations, I've heard my dead brother's voice call to me from beyond this world. I heard his booming laugh and him telling me he loved me. I was not psychotic at the time but in a meditative state. The forces for cosmic energy at work. It's hard to truly know where the mind is tricking you when you've experienced both a spiritual event *and* a psychotic episode. You must rely on your gut instinct. You learn to know the difference between the worlds of the beyond and the now and the crazy. You can also consider whether other people are seeing the same thing you are seeing. As a child, I saw the supernatural before I became ill. I saw it again when I became ill. I will see it again. It is not a psychotic episode like Pandora but a glimpse into the realm of the beyond into the supernatural world of spirits.

* * *

As a child, I used to see glimmers of things beyond this world. I didn't know what they were. They looked like the dark shadow of a person. If I stared too long, they wouldn't be there. They would walk by and disappear. It was as if they just wanted me to know they were there. I never knew when they would pop up. It only happened when I was alone. Sometimes, the drawer on my dresser would be open in the morning when I know it was closed at night.

When I became a teenager, I stopped seeing them. I forgot about them. I dismissed it as a figment of my imagination, a childlike fantasy. I never told anyone about them.

By the time I moved into my own apartment as an adult in college with Patrick, I had long forgotten the shadow people.

One night, I was studying at my table in the kitchen. I looked up, and a shadow person walked through my kitchen. My stomach lurched. I was uneasy. I thought I was hallucinating. Was I drinking too much coffee? Had I been up too long studying? Maybe I was just seeing things? Were they the same things I saw as a child?

I went to bed shortly after with an uneasy mind.

Life went on. I forgot about that night. Then I was watching TV with Patrick. From my bedroom, a shadow person walked toward the kitchen and disappeared. Patrick didn't notice.

I burned some cedar that night and said a silent prayer for good things.

As the weeks went on, every so often, a shadow person would just float in and out. Times were hard for me. I was a single parent. I was struggling with school. Patrick was a handful. Now, I was seeing the shadow people. They would just walk across the room and disappear.

I realized they didn't mean any harm; they were just there. They were not malevolent. They did not bring cold energy with them, but they didn't bring any happiness with them either. I didn't know why they were there.

Sometimes, we would go to bed and wake up to the cabinets in the kitchen open. The first time it happened, it freaked me out. I realized it was the shadow people trying to tell me something; I just didn't know what. Maybe they wanted me to clean up my house. I stuck spatulas in the door handles so they couldn't do it again. That seemed to do the trick.

Every now again, lights would come on after they had been shut off. I would wake up to lights that had been shut off at night on in the morning. There was no fix for that except to unplug the lamps or unscrew the lightbulbs, and that was one step too far.

Other than those two things, they didn't really bother me.

Then one day, they just stopped being there. Again, as in childhood, I thought maybe I had just made up the whole thing. Maybe I really hadn't seen all those things. Maybe I was hallucinating.

As the years wore on, I forgot about the shadow people. I lived my life. I got married, had another child. I was divorced and in another relationship. My brother had recently died.

My son Jesse turned eleven years old. He started having trouble focusing. I watched as he would gaze at things in the room. He would watch something that wasn't there move from one side of the room to the other.

I finally asked him what he was looking at. Begrudgingly, he told me he was seeing ghost-like beings. They were whispering to him. They were walking by him. They were not being mean or anything, but they were distracting him, bothering him. They were following him around.

I realized the shadow people were back. I couldn't see them, but I believed Jesse. He described them just as I had remembered. They never whispered to me, but I'm sure they had the ability to do so.

I spoke with Aunt Margaret about it, and we made arrangements for Jesse to see a medicine man on the reservation. My auntie didn't tell me what she thought it was, just that we should have a ceremony for him. We held a ceremony for him to help him get some relief. We weren't sure if the shadow people had anything to do with the recent passing of my brother. Maybe there was some connection to the spirit world.

After the ceremony, Jesse said the shadow people were gone. A few months later, he said they had come back, but they weren't as intrusive. Eventually, they left him like they left me. Soon, they left altogether.

It had been years since anyone had seen the shadow people. I had recently been sick with a bipolar episode. I was sitting on the couch watching TV in the living room. The dogs started barking and growling at an empty corner of the living room.

At that moment, two shadow people walked across my field of vision in the living room and disappeared. The dogs stopped barking. I wasn't sure if I saw what I saw. It was the first time in almost twenty years that I had seen the shadow people. I wasn't sure why they were back now.

Since the bipolar has come back with a vengeance, the shadow people have visited every now and again. They just pop up and leave. Sometimes they leave a light on. Jesse and I sometimes see them at the same time. Sometimes we just hear the dogs bark at emptiness and know that they are approaching.

The last time I saw a shadow person, I was at work. It freaked me out. I had never seen one outside my home. I was sitting at my desk. I had been typing at my computer. I looked up from my monitor. From the right side of my desk, a shadow person walked in front of my desk toward the door and disappeared.

They had never intruded in my workspace before. They were confined to my home. The hair on my neck and arms stood up. I got up from my desk and walked out of my classroom. I went to the staff lounge and joined one of the custodians who was waiting to clock in.

He asked me if I was okay. I hesitated to tell him why I was edgy, but I did tell him. He didn't make fun of me. He listened and told me that he believed in paranormal activity. He just told me he wasn't going to be the one cleaning my room that night.

I went back to my classroom. Nobody or nothing was there. I packed up my things and went home.

The shadow people have not been back.

I don't know why Jesse and I are the only ones who see them. Maybe it has something to do with our Navajo blood. I don't know. They seem to come around when times are tough. They seem to want to say something. They just want us to know they are there.

I don't know how to tell them, WE KNOW.

Bugging Out

My boys are grown. Patrick doesn't live at home but comes over for dinner. Jesse lives at home but is busy with his job and friends. We are all busy with our schedules. In all this craziness, we make time in our busy lives to have dinner once a week together. I am still their mother. They need me.

For example, Jesse has always had ear issues. We figured this out early on. As a baby, he struggled with ear infections and buildup of ear wax in the canal. The infection would be behind the wax. They would have to clear the wax to even see if he had an infection.

One time when he was about four, we had to take him to an urgent care. He was doubled over with pain in his ear. I looked in his ear but couldn't see anything. They irrigated his ear and flushed it with something that looked like a power tool that pulsed water.

Eventually, after working the water hose and using a tool, they pried a piece of wax the size of the tip of my pinkie out of his ear. Immediately, he sighed and said, "Mommy, I can hear again."

From then on, I checked his ears regularly.

My mom always used to check our ears. My brother and I

loved it. I loved the feeling of my mom cleaning out my ears. She would use a bobby pin to pull any ear wax out. We would lie on her bed. Our heads in her lap on a pillow. She had a lamp that would extend over our ear. It would be warm on our heads. She would then proceed to gently pull the wax from our ears.

After she was done, we would then all stare at the collection of wax that had been gathered and oh and ah at who had more wax, my brother or me.

I cleaned Patrick's ears every now and again, but he didn't require a regular cleaning. He didn't get a major buildup. He also did not enjoy me touching his ears as much. It was just wasn't something I did, so I didn't really consider it with Jesse until he started having issues.

Unlike my mom, I didn't have a good setup. I didn't have a nice pullover lamp attached to my bed to look deep into an ear canal. Instead, I have a tiny flashlight that I click on and hold between my teeth. Holding this flashlight causes me to drool. It's quite the sight.

I go in armed with my bobby pin.

Jesse needs his ears cleaned out at least once a month. For whatever reason, it's something he has never really been able to figure out how to do well by himself. He does use a Q-Tip, but that only gets the water out of his ear. He needs a good bobby pin to really pull the wax from his ears and for that, he still needs his momma.

Late, the other night, around 2 am, I felt someone nudging my foot. It was Jesse. Everyone knows my sleep is precious and rarely disturbs me.

Jesse says, "Mom, my ear really hurts. It feels like there is water trapped inside. Can you look at it? I can't get it out."

I wake up immediately. I bring him into my bathroom. I

forgo the flashlight. I figure if its water, I can just flush it with some peroxide.

He sits on the toilet and turns his sore ear up toward me. I pour peroxide in his ear. I tell him to plug his nose and blow, to equalize the pressure in his ears. He blows.

And this is where it gets weird.

As soon as he does, this bug came furiously scrambling out of his ear—an earwig, to be precise.

I didn't freak out. I just quickly grabbed it and threw it in the sink. It just crawled around, confused.

I calmly tell him, "There was a bug in your ear."

"OH MY GOD! GET THE TWEEZERS!" he screamed.

I tell him it's already out. He still had his head turned. I don't think he realized I had grabbed it whole and threw it in the sink.

I told him, "I got it! It's in the sink."

He stood up. Looked in the sink and turned on the water, flushing it down the drain.

"I thought it was water in my ear. I kept digging and digging in it, and I couldn't get it to stop."

I told him it was gone now. I also told him I would call Grandpa Bill to come spray for bugs.

He went back to bed and went back to sleep. I don't know how he was able to go back to bed. I would have had to strip down my bed, wash my sheets and blankets, vacuum my room, sweep the corners, and then burn everything.

He was so calm but later said he had been doing *A Night at the Roxbury* head bob dance to get the "water" out of his ear. I thought maybe it was because he had been at a party earlier and had been drinking. Maybe he was still a little drunk. Who knows? But he handled it like a champ. I would have freaked the fuck out.

*

I love my boys. I love spending time with them.

Patrick has long, dishwater blond hair and beautiful green eyes. He has a beard that he keeps neat for work, with red flecks throughout. He works at a grocery store in produce. He loves to wear tie-dyed shirts. He has a pair of tie-dyed shoes that are worn and bruised and need to be thrown away, but he never does. He always gives the best hugs and always smells faintly of weed. He's my best friend.

Jesse is tall at six feet. His hair is as long as mine and down to his waist, dark brown but wavy, like his dad's. He has brown eyes and a pointy chin. He has scruff that tries to pass for a beard, but it hasn't really grown in yet. He is super skinny. Thin like my mom. Most of the time, he wears his hair up in a man bun. He works a lot as a cook. He's still my baby.

My boys and I share a love of TV and movies. That love of TV for me started with the *Wizard of Oz* on that black and white TV. It endures with me as I watch *Big Bang Theory* every night to go to bed. Patrick and I love movies more than Jesse. Jesse loves anime and other strange TV shows. He turns me on to all kinds of TV I normally would not watch. *Parks and Rec*, *American Horror Story*, *Rick and Morty*, *South Park.*

I turned my kids onto the classics. *Star Wars, Indiana Jones, Lord of the Rings,* and anything by Kevin Smith.

My kids grew up with a love of Jay and Silent Bob. It's no wonder they ended up being stoners and having a love of the green. They both look the part of stoners.

Kevin Smith's new movie, *Jay and Silent Bob Reboot*, came out in a limited release. We got tickets for the one night showing. It was the first time in a theatre I was able to watch my kids watch the antics of Jay and Silent Bob on the big screen. It was a treasured moment.

We used to have dinner every Sunday night. For a while, this was focused around *Game of Thrones*. We would cook dinner and sit around as a family to watch the show. Jesse hung out mostly for the food. Patrick and I were highly invested in the show.

When *Game of Thrones* ended, we continued with our Sunday night dinners. Jesse has turned into an amazing cook. I have been surpassed in the kitchen. His new career as a cook shines through. He adds flavors to meals I would never think of.

I love watching my boys in the kitchen. The two of them heating up pans, chopping vegetables, searing meat. They are a whirl of boys in the open kitchen at the island in the center. Jesse gets very bossy in the kitchen. He knows what he's talking about. Even I don't question him.

Patrick and I started watching *Watchmen*. Jesse now works nights, and we have no one to cook for us. I no longer have the desire to cook for just the two of us. Patrick and I have made a treat of ordering Thai food and settling in to watch our new show.

I am mostly by myself, but my boys are only a text away. Jesse is home in the day while I'm at work. He does the grocery shopping. Patrick comes over on the weekends and sometimes during the week for dinner. I love the relationship I have with my kids. They are amazing. I am proud of them. They are good men, strong, smart, kind, handsome, and generous. I couldn't ask for a better legacy.

Loving Me

Most of my life, I have been chasing the dragon of love, to be loved by others. I always felt the need to seek out people's attention. As a kid, that was in the form of returning to the boys who abused me and going back to my brother after his teasing and verbal assaults. As a teen, it was being promiscuous and having sex with boys to get attention. As an adult, it was getting into relationships with men who were addicts and needed me so I could be a victim.

I have been in and out of relationships since I was twelve years old, all in the name of love. Dancing from one boy's enticing unrequited words of love to another. I was a hopeless romantic.

Now I know that much of that low self-esteem, people-pleasing and seeking attention is part of the self-coping mechanism of fawning to deal with the abuse I suffered as a child. Some of these traits of being a romantic and generous person are my true traits but it difficult to separate what is my personality and trauma identity.

I had a teacher once tell me, "Boys use love to get sex. Girls use sex to get love." At the time, I didn't know what he was talking about, but now it makes sense. I did use sex to get love, and it failed all the time. Once the sex was given, the love I thought I was about to receive was taken away.

I always believed they loved me. I always believed there was more to it than just sex. I was naïve, and my trust misplaced. I always thought it was love that I was seeking, but truly I wanted to appease people in my life. I wanted to be loved and assured that I was good enough to be loved. I wanted the attention, so I felt worthy and not worthless.

Through self-discovery, I have found my worth. I am worthy of true love and it starts with me, not a boy or a man. My uncle did not rob me of my self-worth, I only perceived that as happening and let that carry on in my life for a long time. I developed habits of not believing in myself when I am a miracle. I am a survivor, not only of sexual abuse but of my suicide attempts and my brother's suicide. I am strong. My will to live is strong. I am a fighter. Each day I fight off the demons in my mind and find a balance to be normal. I take medication to survive.

Now, at forty-three, I have no attachments to any lover. I don't know why I even seek any out on the worthless dating website. I truly have no desire for someone else's companionship. I'm not that interested in sex.

It's been two years since I've had sex. This could be a side effect of my medication for the bipolar, but I don't think so. I think I have just come into a time of my own.

I am okay on my own. I am my best friend before anyone else. I am the best company I can keep. I amuse myself.

I am at a time in my life where I only must look after my own needs. My children are grown. I don't have to worry about the needs of a companion. I don't have to worry about another person's feelings or share in their joy or misery. I can get that on Facebook with any one of my hundred friends, and I don't have to leave my bed. Just gives a thumbs up or a heart and move on.

I have companionship. I have friends. If I want to go to the movies, I go with Rick. We even have a rating system in place and a document to rate our movies. We score them by dogs. One dog if the movie is great. Five dogs if the movie was terrible. We came up with the dog system after watching *Widows*. One of the actresses carried around a white dog throughout the whole terrible movie. It got five dogs. If I want to see a movie, I go with Rick.

When I want to go out for breakfast, I can go with any number of people. If I want to go have lunch, I call others. If I want to have a spa day, I call Athena. There are different people in my life that fulfill my different needs. In the end, I don't need any of these people to make me whole, but I want them in my life because I love them. I don't need a lover to meet those needs, and I don't have to share my blanket at night with him either.

I don't have to worry that I will get shoved out of bed, as I was with Doug. I don't have to worry that the room is too cold. I don't have to worry that the TV is too loud at night. I can sleep three different ways on the bed if I want to. My dogs are the only ones that are allowed to take up space.

I enjoy being by myself. Everyone keeps asking me when I am going to find myself a nice guy. When am I going to find the next boyfriend? The truth is I don't want one. I'm not interested. I have my dogs.

I've had a lot of dogs in my life, but now I have three. Eddie and Bella (named after the *Twilight* characters) are little: Bella is a Yorkie Eddie a Maltese. Kitty is a black lab that is frightened of everything but is sweet and friendly once she stops barking and running away from you. She's supposed to be Jesse's dog and takes turns sleeping on my bed, Jesse's bed and the couch.

Now that Doug is gone, Patrick is gone, Jesse works a lot and is hardly home, it's just me and the dogs. They sleep with me most nights. They are my cuddle buddies. They know when I'm upset or in despair. They relieve my anxiety. They take up half the bed. Eddie sleeps at the top of the bed by my head, licking a hole in the pillow with his nasty breath. Bella curls up next to me, making me hot. Kitty is at the end of the bed. Sometimes she flops down on top of my feet. They are my company. There's no room for a man in my bed.

I used to need to be around people. I had to be the center of attention. I had to be doing things all the time. I was always busy doing something. I also had young kids. If they weren't my kids, they were someone else's kids. I don't have that anymore. I have only me and my concerns. I used to believe in putting everyone's needs in front of my own. I thought it was selfish of me to take time for myself. I put everyone and everything before me. I lived to be in the service of others.

Now, I see that I am important. I deserve to give myself attention. I deserve the spa day. I deserve to buy myself something nice if I can afford it. I deserve to be happy, and if that's by myself, then that's okay.

My mental health and physical health are my main concern. My sleep hygiene and taking my meds are my number one priority. Those drive all other things in my life. Then I allow other things to fill my world. Romantic love is no longer one of my priorities. It just doesn't seem important.

Who knows? Maybe I will meet a guy, and he will knock my socks off! But as it stands now, I am content living my life with my dogs, family and the people who fill my world with joy. The people who accept me as being a bit quirky and moody. I don't have to justify why I need to be home by six or in bed by eight. They just know and accept that.

This book was a dive into self-discovery. Multiple times I was asked if this book was cathartic. I found this book to be a guide into my past and give me a lens to look at my relationships with my family and myself. In writing about my abuse and self-harm, I did find it healing. I am a flawed person. I'd like to think that I'm healed and ready to move forward. It's going to take a lot of medication, but I'm on the right path.

I will happily be the sexless, crazy dog lady who takes her meds and goes to bed early. I'm happy; I'm working on my health. What's not to love? I love me. Shouldn't that be enough?

If you feel suicidal or have thoughts of self-harm, reach out to one of the hotlines. There are people who care. They will talk to you.

If you are a victim and survivor of sexual abuse and need support, contact RAINN. They have resources.

With all the above, please seek out professional help to guide you. In your darkest hours, there is always hope.

National Suicide Prevention Lifeline
1-800-273-8255
https://suicidepreventionlifeline.org

Self-Injury Foundation's 24-hour national crisis line
1-800-344-HELP
www.crisistextline.org

RAINN (Rape, Abuse & Incest, National Network)
1-800-656-HOPE (4673)
www.rainn.org

About the Author

Ahiddibah Tsinnie is a Navajo author born and raised in Las Vegas, Nevada. She continues to live and teach in the Vegas Valley. Every Sunday, she watches *Real Time with Bill Maher* with her mom in the afternoon. Sunday evenings are spent watching an HBO show with her boys and eating take out Thai food. Every night she watches *The Big Bang Theory* to go to sleep. In her free time, she is learning to speak and write Navajo.

Made in the USA
Coppell, TX
17 May 2020

25440148R00196